M000308394

PSYCHOLOGY

for Cambridge International AS & A Level

Craig Roberts

OXFORD
UNIVERSITY PRESS

OXFORD
UNIVERSITY PRESS

Great Clarendon Street, Oxford, OX2 6DP, United Kingdom

Oxford University Press is a department of the University of Oxford.It furthers the University's objective of excellence in research, scholarship, and education by publishing worldwide. Oxford is a registered trade mark of Oxford University Press in the UK and in certain other countries

British Library Cataloguing in Publication Data
Data available

978-0-19-830706-8

10 9 8 7 6 5 4 3

Paper used in the production of this book is a natural, recyclable product made from wood grown in sustainable forests. The manufacturing process conforms to the environmental regulations of the country of origin.

Printed in China by Golden Cup

Acknowledgements

The questions, example answers, marks awarded and/or comments that appear in this book and CD were written by the authors. In examination, the way marks would be awarded to answers like these may be different.

The publishers would like to thank the following for permissions to use their photographs:

Cover image: James Daniels/Shutterstock; **p22:** lekcej/Shutterstock; **p73:** James Holmes/Science Photo Library; **p99:** Sally Wheelwright/Science Direct; **p191:** Anita Westervelt/FEMA; **p192:** Lloyd Cluff/CORBIS; **p193:** Heinz Ducklau/AP; **p198:** Anne Kitzman/Shutterstock; **p205:** He Yi/ChinaFotoPress; **p206:** Steve Vidler / Alamy; **p249:** Van D Bucher/Getty Images; **p243:** Associated Press

Artwork by Six Red Marbles

The author and publisher are grateful to the following for permission to reprint copyright material:

American Psychological Association (APA) for extract from the Hassles/Uplifts Scale Questionnaire in the Appendix to 'The Impact of Daily Stress on Health and Mood: Psychological and Social Resources as Mediators' by Anita DeLongis, Susan Folkman & Richard S Lazarus, Journal of Personality and Social Psychology Vol. 54:3 (1988), pp 486-495.

Bowling Green State University, Psychology Department for extract from the Job Descriptive Index from The Measurement of Satisfaction in Work and Retirement: a Strategy for the Study of

Attitudes by P C Smith, L M Kendall, & C L Hullin (Rand McNally, 1969).

Elsevier for the SRRS questionnaire from 'The Social Readjustment Rating Scale' by T H Holmes & R H Rahe, Journal of Pyschosomatic Research , Vol 11: 2 (1967), pp 213-218, copyright © 1967.

International Association for the Study of Pain (IASP) for the MPQ in 'The McGill Pain Questionnaire: Major properties and scoring methods' by Ronald Melzack, Journal of Pain, Vol 1 (1975), pp 277-299.

IOS Press BV for figure 2: 'Randomization of participants to one of two test conditions', from Yi-Nuo Shih, Rong-Hwa Huang & Hsing-Yu Chiang: 'Background Music: Effects on attention performance', work 42 (2012), pp 573-578.

PARS International Corp for '37 who saw murder didn't call the police: Apathy at stabbing of Queen's woman shocks Inspector' by Martin Gansberg, The New York Times, 27 March 1964, copyright © The New York Times 1964. All Rights reserved. Used by permission and protected by the Copyright Laws of the United States. The printing, copying, redistribution, or retransmission of this Content without express permission is prohibited.

David J Weiss for extract from the Minnesota Satisfaction Questionnaire in Vocational Psychology Research by D J Weiss, G W England, & L H Lofquist, University of Minnesota, copyright © 1977.

Although we have made every effort to trace and contact all copyright holders before publication this has not been possible in all cases. If notified, the publisher will rectify any errors or omissions at the earliest opportunity.

Any third party use of this material outside of this publication is prohibited. Interested parties should apply to the copyright holders indicated in each case.

INTRODUCTION

This book has been written as a companion to support you throughout your Psychology International AS and A Level course.

The book is divided into two parts: one for the AS Level and one for the A Level. The AS part will guide you through all 20 Core Studies and the A Level part will guide you through the two options you have chosen to study (from the five available). There are a range of activities throughout the book to get you thinking psychologically which is ideal preparation for the examinations. There are also sample examination questions for you to answer.

Chapter 1 introduces the reader to the different research methods that psychologists commonly use and Chapter 2 introduces the reader to a range of issues and debates that happen within psychological research. These form a 'toolkit' that students can use to help them evaluate studies and concepts in the entire course.

The book uses 'speech bubbles' throughout to highlight to students when these important ideas feature in a Core Study. They are also used in the A Level section of the book to help students evaluate the topic area in preparation for the examination.

In the AS Level section of the book, the 'speech bubbles' appear throughout each study to highlight where examples can be found within that study. In the A Level section of the book, the Evaluation Boxes at the end of each topic highlight a range of 'speech bubbles' which point the student towards the main evaluation points that could be made in an examination answer.

There is an accompanying Revision Guide which will cover marked student examples so you can practise answering exam-style questions to the best of your abilities. This will be a separate book.

CD contents

The CD has a range of material that can be used for revision purposes:

The **A Level checklists** allow students to track which issues and debates are relevant to the sections of each option they have chosen to study.

The **A Level options** allow students to track that they have covered all of the content necessary for the examination and can evaluate each of these.

The **AS Psychology** section allows students to track that they have covered all of the main components of every core study and that they can evaluate each one effectively.

The **Ethics** section introduces students to the British Psychological Guidelines for the use of humans in research.

The **Example Question** section has a bank of sample examination questions for Papers 1, 2 and 3.

Author

Craig is a freelance tutor and author of psychology textbooks. He has been teaching for over 20 years and is an experienced examiner with a number of National and International examination boards.

Acknowledgements

I simply have to thank everyone who has made an impact on my life and who support me through every venture I take on. This includes my family, closest friends and cat! I could and would not be doing this without any of you. A special thank you has to go to all the teachers I trained in Florida in February 2014 for making my first training event brilliant.

I would also like to thank Matt Jarvis for his kind permission to use his material from OCR AS Psychology.

Dedication

To Mum & Dad. Always love you.

CONTENTS

Approaches and perspectives in psychology v

1 How psychologists research 1

2 Issues and debates within psychological research 7

3 Cognitive psychology 13

4 Social psychology 29

5 Developmental psychology 47

6 Physiological psychology 65

7 The psychology of individual differences 87

AS-Level Exam Centre 107

8 Psychology and education 111

9 Psychology and health 147

10 Psychology and environment 177

11 Psychology and models of abnormality 207

12 Psychology and organisations 239

A-Level Exam Centre 275

APPROACHES AND PERSPECTIVES IN PSYCHOLOGY

There are many different ways in which psychologists try to explain human and animal behaviour. These approaches and perspectives in psychology form the whole discipline of "psychology". However, they are all very different and this chapter will cover how these different types of psychologist try to explain behaviour. There are five approaches and two perspectives that CIE expect you to know about. We will look at each in turn highlighting their general assumptions, the main research methodology they use and which studies from AS-level fit into each one.

Cognitive psychology

Cognitive psychologists are interested in how we process information. They look into how we input information, then how we process that information and finally how we retrieve and/or use that information. Some cognitive psychologists believe that the brain works like a computer following the procedure of input-process/storage-output. Areas of interest include memory and forgetting, perception, language and attention.

The AS-level studies listed in the Cambridge syllabus under this section are:

1. Mann, Vrij & Bull (2002)

2. Loftus & Pickrell (1995)

3. Baron-Cohen *et al* (2001)

4. Held & Hein (1963).

The main research method used in this approach is laboratory experiments.

Strengths	Weaknesses
Many findings are based on research conducted in a laboratory. As variables are controlled it means that findings are more likely to be reliable. Therefore, it can be seen as being a scientific approach.	As cognitive psychologists are investigating processed information that cannot be seen directly, there is still an element of guesswork and inferences.

The approach is useful in terms of being able to help improve everyday life in humans by, for example, improving memory or improving eyewitness testimony.	Comparing the human information processing system to that of a computer is reductionist. It ignores the role of emotional and social factors on how we process information.

Social psychology

Social psychologists are interested in how we "work" in the social world. They look at how individuals interact with each other and how we interact in "groups". Therefore, they look at the individual as an individual but also as a group member and see how this affects behaviour. They also examine how the role of culture and society affects our behaviour. Areas of interest include prejudice, obedience and conformity.

The AS-level studies listed in the Cambridge syllabus under this section are:

1. Milgram (1963)

2. Haney, Banks & Zimbardo (1973)

3. Piliavin, Rodin & Piliavin (1969)

4. Tajfel (1970).

The main research methods used in this approach are questionnaires and interviews.

Strengths	Weaknesses
The approach does tend to look at the individual "as a whole" to try to explain behaviour across situations. Therefore, it is more holistic rather than reductionist.	A lot of evidence from this approach is from studies that have used questionnaires and interviews. Therefore, the validity may be reduced as what people say they will do and what they actually do can be very different.
The approach is useful in terms of being able to help improve everyday life in humans by, for example, reducing prejudice or explaining atrocities.	It can be very difficult sometimes to distinguish between what is influenced by the individual and what is influenced by the situation people find themselves in. This can make designing studies difficult and then drawing the correct conclusion may be difficult.

Development psychology

Development psychologists are interested in how we "develop" as a person from birth to death. Many development psychologists focus on "child development" and what sorts of things affect how a child develops psychologically and socially. They also look at how physical development might affect psychological development. However, there are other psychologists who will examine development over a lifespan. Therefore, they may examine development from adolescence through early adulthood into late adulthood. Areas of interest include moral development, cognitive development and social development.

The AS-level studies listed in the Cambridge syllabus under this section are:

1. Bandura, Ross & Ross (1961)
2. Freud (1909)
3. Langlois *et al* (1991)
4. Nelson (1980).

The main research methods used in this approach are observations and longitudinal studies.

Strengths	Weaknesses
Longitudinal studies are an excellent way to assess development over time with participant variables being controlled for. This makes findings from these types of study more valid as the same people are being followed over a period of time.

Also, as we are following the same people over time, we can examine what is down to nature and what is down to nurture in terms of how these influence people's developmental pathways as humans. | Longitudinal studies can be very time consuming and costly and participants will drop out (participant attrition can be high). As a result, findings may be difficult to generalise to outside of the participants who are left as there may only be a few and they could be unique.

There may be ethical issues with studying children over time. This is because before they are 16 years old their parents have to give informed consent. Therefore, the children are not giving their own informed consent and may never want to take part in tests and studies. |

Physiological psychology

Physiological psychologists are interested in how our biology affects our psychology. They look at the role of things like genetics, brain function, hormones and neurotransmitters have on our behaviour. Many physiological psychologists believe that our behaviour can be explained via biological mechanisms more so than psychological mechanisms. However, others believe that it may be an interaction between the two. Areas of interest include origins of mental disorders, treatments of mental disorders, sleep, circadian rhythms and localisation of brain function (which parts of the brain are responsible for different behaviours).

The AS-level studies listed in the Cambridge syllabus under this section are:

1. Schachter & Singer (1962)
2. Dement & Kleitman (1957)
3. Maguire, Frackowiak & Frith (1997)
4. Demattè, Österbauer & Spence (2007).

The main research method used in this approach is laboratory experiments.

Strengths	Weaknesses
The approach is very scientific as it uses methods such as laboratory experiments, blood tests, brain scanning, etc. These are highly controlled methods that can easily be tested for reliability. We can draw cause–effect conclusions more easily as a result. As we are dealing with biological mechanisms, it is an excellent way to assess which of our behaviours are due to nature and which are due to nurture.	The approach can be seen as being reductionist as it ignores the roles of social and emotional factors in our development. As many studies take place under controlled laboratory conditions, many studies lack ecological validity and mundane realism. Therefore, some biological reactions may be triggered because of being in a controlled environment and may not necessarily be the same in a real-world setting.

The psychology of individual differences

This approach looks at how, as individuals, we differ from one another. Instead of looking for explanations that could explain how lots of people may behave, psychologists who research into this area look at what makes the individual unique. Therefore, there are differences between people that may be part of the same group. Rather than looking for general laws, psychologists who research into this area may focus more on what makes the individual different from the others around him or her.

The AS-level studies listed in the Cambridge syllabus under this section are:

1. Rosenhan (1973)

2. Thigpen & Cleckley (1954)

3. Billington, Baron-Cohen & Wheelwright (2007)

4. Veale & Riley (2001)

Strengths	Weaknesses
This approach can be useful in explaining differences between individuals in the cause of behaviours. These can be useful during, for example, therapy so the treatment can be tailored to the individual rather than following general laws of behaviour.	Findings from studies may have limited generalisability as they are focusing on the individual rather than a group of people. The people being studied may be unique in some way and therefore findings have limited use. This approach can be seen as being reductionist as it ignores the way we behave in groups and follow group laws of behaviour.

The behaviourist perspective

Behaviourist psychologists are interested in ways in which both humans and animals learn. They look into general laws that can apply to all species and how the experiences we have mould our behaviour over time. There are three main areas within this perspective:

▶ learning by the consequences of our behaviour (operant conditioning)

▶ learning through association (classical conditioning)

▶ learning through observation, imitation and modelling (social learning).

Strict behaviourism follows the idea that we should "observe the observable" and not examine mental processes as they cannot be directly seen. Behaviours can be directly seen so we have objective measures of behaviour. Areas of interest include behaviour modification, therapies for mental health disorders or for prisoners, etc. and development of behaviours such as aggression.

There are no named studies for this perspective but Bandura, Ross & Ross (1961) can be used as an example of social learning. The main research methods used in this perspective are laboratory experiments and observations.

Strengths	Weaknesses
The perspective is very objective as it "observes the observable" – this means that data is scientific and quantitative and likely not to be biased. This makes findings from studies reliable.	Parts of this perspective ignore the role of social, cognitive and emotional aspects of behaviour. Therefore it can be seen as being reductionist in just focusing on observable aspects and ignoring internal mechanisms such as biology too.
The approach is useful in terms of being able to help improve everyday life in humans by, for example, reducing phobias or modifying a child's behaviour for the better.	Some psychologists disagree that there are general laws that govern animal and human behaviour – humans are more complex than rats, pigeons, dogs and cats so generalising findings from animal research to humans may not be valid.

The psychodynamic perspective

Psychodynamic psychologists are interested in how our early lives and our unconscious mind affect our behaviour. They look at the role of early childhood development and how traumas that occur at various stages may affect adult personality. They also look at how our unconscious mind (the part of the mind that we are unaware of) affects our everyday behaviour. We have structures of personality such as the id (driven by pleasure), the ego (driven by reality) and the superego (driven by morality). All of these have an influence on our behaviour. Areas of interest include development of mental health disorders (e.g. phobias), dreaming and the treatment of mental health disorders.

There are no named studies for this perspective but Freud (1909) is a psychodynamic case study. The main research methods used in this perspective are case studies and interviews.

Strengths	Weaknesses
The approach is useful in terms of being able to help improve every day life in humans such as helping to understand why we have a mental health disorder and then helping to overcome it.	Ideas such as those relating to the unconscious mind cannot be directly tested and are therefore unscientific. How can you assess something that cannot be directly seen or manipulated? It is an abstract concept that might not even exist.
Supporting evidence tends to come from case studies which are very detailed collecting qualitative data. This should improve the validity of findings as the whole person is examined rather than just one aspect of them.	Many findings from this perspective are based on case studies. These findings may be difficult to generalise to a larger group of people as the case studies may be unique in some way.

1 HOW PSYCHOLOGISTS RESEARCH

There are many different ways in which psychologists can collect information for their study. These are called research methods and it is up to psychologists to choose the one they think is the most appropriate for their study. The main ones are:

▶ experiments (laboratory and field)

▶ self-reports (questionnaires and interviews)

▶ case studies

▶ observations (naturalistic, controlled, participant).

As well as choosing the most appropriate research method, psychologists have to decide:

▶ who the participants are (the sample) and how they are going to recruit (the sampling technique)

▶ if they are using an experiment, which design of study to use (e.g. repeated measures, independent groups or matched pairs)

▶ what the procedure of the study will be for participants including what apparatus is needed

▶ the type of data they want to collect (e.g. quantitative or qualitative).

RESEARCH METHODS

Laboratory experiments

These take place in a situation or environment that is artificial to participants in the study. There are two main types of variable that need to be considered when running any experiment:

▶ *Independent variable (IV)* – the variable that psychologists choose to manipulate or change. This represents the different conditions that are being compared in any study. So, for example, if a psychologist wants to investigate memory in school children, then the variable that requires "changing" is age. Therefore, age is the IV. However, the IV requires some form of operationalisation. To do this, the psychologist must clearly define what the different conditions are. For the example of memory in school children the operationalised IV could be: level 1 = 5–6 years old and level 2 = 7–8 years old.

▶ *Dependent variable (DV)* – the variable that psychologists choose to measure. It is always hoped that the IV is directly affecting the DV in an experiment. Also, the DV needs some form of operationalisation. To do this, psychologists must clearly define how they will measure. For the example of memory in school children the operationalised DV could be the amount of items that a child remembers from a tray of objects (maximum 25).

The psychologist will attempt to *control* as many other variables as possible to try to ensure that it is the IV directly affecting the DV. There are different types of variable that can affect the DV that have to be controlled if possible. One of these is called *participant variables*. These are the traits and behaviours that participants bring to the study that may affect the DV (e.g. level of intelligence, prejudices or any previous experiences).

Lab

1

Strengths of laboratory experiments	Weaknesses of laboratory experiments
Laboratory experiments have high levels of control and so can be replicated to test for reliability. As laboratory experiments have high levels of control, researchers can be more confident it is the IV directly affecting the DV.	As laboratory experiments take place in an artificial setting, it is said that they can lack ecological validity. Many laboratory experiments can make participants take part in tasks that are nothing like real-life ones so they lack what is known as "mundane realism".

FIELD EXPERIMENTS

These are experiments that take place in participants' own natural environment rather than in an artificial laboratory. The researcher still tries to manipulate or change an IV while measuring the DV in an attempt to see how the IV affects the DV. There is an attempt to control other variables that could affect the DV. One of these is called *situational variables*.

Field

These are variables from the setting that might affect the DV, such as the weather or time of day.

Strengths of field experiments	Weaknesses of field experiments
As field experiments take place in a realistic setting, it is said that they have ecological validity. As the participants will not know they are taking part in a study, there will be few or no demand characteristics so behaviour is more likely to be natural and valid.	Situational variables can be difficult to control so sometimes it is difficult to know if it is the IV affecting the DV. It could be an uncontrolled variable causing the DV to change. As the participants will not know they are taking part in a study, there are issues with breaking ethical guidelines including informed consent and deception.

QUESTIONNAIRES

When a study uses a questionnaire, it is asking participants to answer a series of questions in the written form. There are various types of question that a psychologist can use in a questionnaire-based study:

Quest

▶ Likert scales: these are statements that participants read and then state whether they strongly agree, disagree, etc. For example, the statement might be "Owning a pet is good for your psychological health".

▶ Rating scales: these are questions or statements where participants give an answer in the form of a number. For example: "On a scale of 0–10, how happy are you today?"

▶ Open-ended: these are questions that allow participants to develop an answer and write it in their own words. They write sentences to answer the question. For example: "Can you tell me about a happy childhood memory?"

▶ Closed: these are questions where there are a set amount of answers and participants choose which answer best fits how they want to respond. For example: "Pick the emotion that best describes how you feel today: happy, sad, cheerful, moody".

Strengths of questionnaires	Weaknesses of questionnaires
Participants may be more likely to reveal truthful answers in a questionnaire as it does not involve talking face to face with someone. A large sample of participants can answer the questionnaire in a short time. This should increase the representativeness and generalisability of the findings.	Participants may give socially desirable answers as they want to look good rather than giving truthful answers. This lowers the validity of findings. If the questionnaire has a lot of closed questions then participants might be forced into choosing an answer that does not reflect their true opinion.

2 ISSUES AND DEBATES WITHIN PSYCHOLOGICAL RESEARCH

This chapter will outline the different issues and debates that you need to know for the exam. The icons by each issue will turn up, when relevant, in the 20 core studies for the AS qualification. You can then apply the relevant issues and debates to the study as required in some exam questions.

THE APPLICATION OF PSYCHOLOGY TO EVERYDAY LIFE (ITS USEFULNESS)

Some people argue that if studies and ideas from psychology cannot be used in everyday life then they are not useful. All psychologists have to consider this before they complete a study. Once a study has been published, other psychologists may evaluate its usefulness. This can be positive or negative. A study may only have been conducted on one sex so it may not be useful in explaining the behaviour of the opposite sex. The *extent* to which something is useful is debating *how* the findings can be used (or not used) in everyday life.

Useful

ECOLOGICAL VALIDITY

This refers to the extent that the setting a study has been conducted in can be relevant to everyday life. A study conducted in a laboratory using human participants may be low in ecological validity as it is not a setting that humans are used to. Sometimes the task given to participants might also not be something that happens in everyday life – the term "mundane realism" describes this. If a task involves something that could happen in everyday life then we say it has high mundane realism.

ETHICS

The British Psychological Society has strict guidelines on what can and cannot be done to human participants in the name of psychological research. Some of the main guidelines are listed below:

Ethics

1. Informed consent. This is when participants are fully aware of what the study is about and they then give their permission to be used in the study. Psychologists may not give the full aims of a study

Strength of conducting useful research	Problems of conducting useful research
The main advantage is that it is can be used to improve human behaviour in some way. For example, if we find a better way to treat a mental illness then it is useful to society as a whole.	Studies might be unethical to gain more valid results.
	Studies need to be high in ecological validity to be of more use to society but this can be quite difficult if they are conducted in a laboratory, for instance.

in order to reduce demand characteristics. This is when features of a study hint to participants what the aims are so they behave or answer relating to the hint rather than how they would truly behave or answer.

2. Deception. Participants should not be deceived about aspects of a study unless the study would otherwise be useless due to demand characteristics.

3. Debriefing. Psychologists must explain the full aim of the study (especially if they had to deceive participants) at the end of the study. They should answer any questions participants have and check that participants are still happy to have their data used. Some psychologists follow up participants at a later date to check again that everything is all right.

4. Right to withdraw. Participants should know that they can leave the study at any time and that their data will not be used in the published study.

5. Confidentiality. Psychologists must tell participants that their responses will not be identifiable as their own and that all data will be pooled when analysed (except when it is a case study).

6. Protection. Psychologists must ensure that participants leave the study in the same physical and psychological state in which they entered it.

7. Observations. These can only take place where any member of the public can see the behaviour.

ETHNOCENTRIC BIAS

This is when psychologists view the results, behaviours or responses of a study that used participants *not from their own ethnic group* through the eyes of their own ethnic experiences. As a result, the psychologists may feel that their own ethnic group is superior to the one(s) they are studying and may misinterpret behaviours and draw the wrong conclusions about the behaviour being studied.

Ethno

RELIABILITY AND VALIDITY

Reliability refers to whether researchers can test something again to see if they gain similar results. Laboratory experiments, with all of their controls, are said to be reliable as they can be replicated quite easily to see if similar results are obtained.

Reliable

Validity refers to how accurate the findings are from a study (e.g. see ecological validity above).

EcoV

INDIVIDUAL VERSUS SITUATIONAL EXPLANATIONS

Individual explanations account for behaviours using factors from within the person (called dispositional factors, such as personality). Situational explanations account for behaviours using factors from the external environment (situations that people find themselves in).

Ind vs sit

Strengths of this debate	Problems with this debate
The findings can be very useful to society as a whole. If we find out which behaviours are down to individuals and which are down to the situations we find ourselves in, then we can help explain human behaviour more clearly. If psychologists find that there is an interaction between both sides of the debate then this is useful too.	It is not always easy to separate out individual and situational factors. Studies might be unethical to gain more valid results. Studies need high ecological validity to be of more use to this debate but this can be difficult if they take place in a laboratory, for instance.

NATURE AND NURTURE

Nature refers to behaviours that are thought to be hard-wired into people pre-birth (innate or genetic). Nurture refers to behaviours that are thought to develop through the lifetime of the person. Therefore, nature tends to be based on biological factors whereas nurture tends to be based on social and psychological factors.

Strengths of this debate	Problems with this debate
The findings can be very useful to society as a whole. If we find out which behaviours come from nature and which from nurture, we can help to explain behaviour more clearly. If there is an interaction between both sides of the debate this is useful too.	It is not always easy to separate out what is nature and what is nurture. If behaviour is seen to be purely down to nature (genetics) this can be very socially sensitive. Sections of society could use this to undertake a "eugenic" movement to get rid of people with "inferior genes". This is clearly unacceptable. Studies might be unethical in order to gain more valid results.

PSYCHOMETRICS

These are usually paper-and-pen tasks that literally mean "measurement of the mind". Examples are an intelligence quotient (IQ) test, an aptitude test or a test to help with educational needs. They are standardised, so people's results can be compared to a "norm" to see how intelligent they are or how much of a certain personality they have.

Psychom

Strengths of psychometrics	Problems with using psychometrics
As they are standardised on a large sample of	There may be issues with validity. Is the test actually measuring the

people, they can be seen as being more objective and scientific.

Comparisons can be *useful* as people's results are compared on the same, standardised scale.

As they are standardised, they are reliable measures – we can use them again and again to see if we get similar results.

behaviour it is supposed to measure? (e.g. Some psychologists believe that an IQ test does *not* measure intelligence, but instead measures someone's ability to complete an IQ test).

If tests measure specific cultural knowledge rather than the behaviour they are supposed to measure, they will be seen as ethnocentric.

QUANTITATIVE AND QUALITATIVE DATA

Anything in the form of a number is quantitative data. You can analyse this data statistically. Qualitative data take the form of descriptions in words, sentences and paragraphs. They are rich in detail and allow participants to explain their answers to questions.

Quant

Strengths of quantitative data	Problems with quantitative data
As the data are numerical, this allows easier comparison and statistical analysis (e.g. the average score of two different groups of participants can easily be compared). Numerical data are objective and scientific – there is only minimal chance of miscalculating the data and drawing invalid conclusions.	As the data are numerical, they miss out on valuable information. If the answer is simply yes/no or on a rating scale we do not know *why* participants chose the answers they did. It can be seen as reductionist as complex ideas and behaviours are simply reduced to a number or percentage.

Strengths of qualitative data	Problems with qualitative data
The data collected are rich and in-depth responses, in the words of participants, so they represent what participants believe. Therefore, it can be argued that they are not reductionist. As the data come directly from participants we can understand *why* participants think, feel and act in a certain way.	Interpretation of the data could be subjective – a psychologist could misinterpret what a participant meant to say or be biased against some of the person's views. There may be researcher bias. Psychologists might only select data that fits their hypothesis or aim of the study. This cannot be done with quantitative data.

GENERALISATIONS

This term refers to how much the findings from a study can be applied to/is representative of people who never directly took part in the study (those from the target population – TP – but *not* the sample studied). This is not always directly linked to sample size (e.g. a small sample size does not automatically mean we cannot generalise). If behaviour is biological in nature (e.g. sleep and daily rhythms) and all humans have the same biological mechanisms then finding something out using less than ten participants may be generalisable to a lot of other humans. When assessing studies in terms of generalisations, consider what the findings of the study are and then decide whether we can or cannot generalise the findings to the TP.

SNAPSHOT AND LONGITUDINAL DATA

Both of these terms refer to the time frame in which a study takes place:

▶ Snapshot: this is when data are collected at one point in time using a group of participants performing a task, being interviewed, etc.

▶ Longitudinal: this is when the same set of participants is followed over a longer period of time to examine things such as developmental changes. They may repeat similar tasks once per year, for example.

> **Snap**

Strengths of snapshot studies	Problems with snapshot studies
These can be a time-efficient way of collecting a lot of data. A study might only take a few weeks to complete and for results to be analysed. These can be useful for conducting "pilot research" to see whether a study is feasible (before you run a large-scale study and find it does not work).	These studies do not follow people over a period of time, so they are not useful in tracking how behaviour develops or the long-term effects of something. They only represent participants showing a behaviour or opinion at one point in time. Generalisation may therefore be limited.

Strengths of longitudinal studies	Problems with longitudinal studies
These studies allow analysis of how behaviour develops over time (e.g. throughout childhood) and long-term effects (e.g. of life events on development). Individual differences between people in the study are controlled as the same people are tracked over a set amount of time. Therefore, findings are more likely to be valid.	Not all participants will want to be followed for the length of the study and will **Long** drop out (called "participant attrition"). This can reduce the sample size and then the generalisability and/ or validity of the study as time progresses. Psychologists could become attached to participants and be subjective in their analysis of the data.

THE USE OF CHILDREN IN PSYCHOLOGICAL RESEARCH

We have already covered ethics above but there are extra rules about using children in psychological research:

▶ Children aged under 16 cannot give their own informed consent to take part in a study.

▶ Children aged under 16 must get parental permission to participate in studies or *loco parentis* permission (e.g. someone who looks after them in a nursery or school).

Child

THE USE OF ANIMALS IN PSYCHOLOGICAL RESEARCH

Animal There are ethical guidelines and rules for using animals in psychological research. The main ones are as follows:

▶ The law – psychologists must work within the law about protecting animals.

▶ Number of animals – this should be a kept to the minimum amount to make statistical analysis meaningful.

▶ Social environment – social species should be kept together and non-social species kept apart.

▶ Caging – housing in cages should not lead to overcrowding and increased stress levels.

Strength	Weakness
We can conduct research on animals that we cannot do on humans for ethical reasons.	Due to the differences in physiological and psychological 'make-ups' of animals and humans it can be difficult to generalise from animal studies to human behaviour.

REDUCTIONISM

This is when a psychologist believes that a complex behaviour can be explained by reducing it to one single cause or a series of component parts. For example, a researcher might state that some aspect of personality is caused only by biological mechanism. This could easily overlook social and psychological factors that could also be affecting personality.

Reduct

Strength	Weakness
It allows research to be conducted that can analyse a specific area or behaviour in depth, so how it affects humans	It overlooks other factors that could be affecting the behaviour of people.

3 COGNITIVE PSYCHOLOGY

CORE STUDY 3.1

Mann, Vrij & Bull (2002)

CONTEXT

Early research into the field of lying behaviour had shown mixed results in terms of what people actually do when lying. Some people avert their gaze and become fidgety while others become very still and hardly move at all. However, the designs of these studies meant that the findings were not truly generalisable to real-life lying. They were experimental studies asking people to lie or tell the truth about various issues, perhaps causing unnatural behaviour. Very few participants would feel guilty about deceiving someone as there were no consequences. Therefore, they were simply lying for the sake of the experiment. Very little research had been conducted in field settings using people who could and would lie spontaneously if the stakes were high. Mann, Vrij & Bull found the perfect set of participants for this: suspects in police custody.

> **ASK YOURSELF**
> Can you spot a liar? Do you know how people behave when they are lying to you? List some behaviours that you feel people show when they are lying.

AIM

To investigate the lying behaviours of suspects in police custody – a high-stake situation that is real life so would generate real lying.

METHOD

Design

Detectives from Kent Constabulary in the United Kingdom were asked if they could recollect any videotaped interviews where the suspect had definitely lied but also told the truth. The relevant case files were requested. A researcher looked through these to find forensic evidence or independent witness statements that could easily corroborate the lie and truth in the interview. For example, a videotape might show the suspect lying about any involvement then being presented with clear forensic evidence and confessing. Any case that did not have corroboration was not used. The cases chosen for the study were then re-recorded onto another videotape. Overall, this became a one-hour video with clips from all 16 suspects. For a better comparison, the truths had to be comparable in nature to the lies for inclusion (e.g. a suspect's truthful response to confirm name and age is not comparable to a lie about whether the suspect had committed a murder). A total of 65 clips were used (27 truths and 38 lies). Each participant had a minimum of two clips (one truth and one lie) and the maximum was eight clips. The length of clips ranged from 41.4 seconds to 368.4 seconds. Previous studies had shown that length of time telling the truth or lying has little effect on the behaviour of those telling the truth or lying.

Control

13

Eight behaviours were looked for in the clips:

Behaviour	Coded by:
Gaze aversion	the number of seconds that the suspect looked away from the interviewer
Blinking	frequency of eye blinks
Head movement	frequency of head nods (upward and downward were counted separately); head shakes (side to side) were also counted
Self-manipulations	frequency of head scratching, scratching the wrist
Illustrators	frequency of arm and hand movements (that either modified or complemented what the suspect was talking about)
Hand/finger movements	any movements of the hands or fingers without moving the arms
Speech disturbances	frequency of saying things like "ah" or "mmm" between words, frequency of word and/or sentence repetition, sentence change, sentences not completed, stutters, etc. – any deviation from the official English language as well as the use of slang was not counted
Pauses	the number of seconds where there was a noticeable pause in the suspect's monologue, when the suspect stopped talking for more than 0.5 seconds when the conversation was free flowing.

Reliable

Control Each of the eight coded behaviours was changed into a format in which suspects' truths and lies could be directly compared. For gaze aversion and pauses when telling the truth or lying, the total length of time recorded for these coded behaviours was divided by the total length of time of the truthful clips, then multiplied by 60 to give a total length per minute. This was repeated for when the suspect was lying. The frequency of blinks, head, arm or hand movements while telling the truth or lying was divided by the total length of time for each truthful or lying clip and multiplied by 60 to give a frequency per minute score. The total **Quant** number of speech disturbances during the truthful and lying clips was divided by the total number of words spoken during the truthful and lying clips then multiplied by 100 to give a "per 100 words" frequency score.

TEST YOURSELF
Outline two of the behaviours that the observers were looking for. How were they coded?

Participants

Participants were 16 police suspects (13 males and 3 females). Four of these were juveniles (three were aged 13 years and one 15 years). One was Asian and 15 were Caucasian. The crimes the participants were being interviewed about were theft (n = 9), arson (n = 2), attempted rape (n = 1) and murder (n = 4). At least 10 of the 16 were already known to the police for previous offences.

Procedure

Two observers independently coded the eight behaviours under investigation. They did not know which clips showed suspects telling the truth and which showed lies. They were not told the purpose of the study or any hypotheses so they never knew when **Reliable** a suspect was telling the truth or lying. The first observer coded every clip. The second observer coded a random sample of 36 clips covering all 16 suspects so inter-rater reliability could be measured. Partially due to the sensitive nature of the clips, the fewer people who saw them other than the police the better. The inter-rater agreement was high for all eight coded behaviours.

RESULTS

Table 3.1 shows the scores for six of the coded behaviours split by truth and lying.

Behaviour	Truthful		Deceptive	
	M	SD	M	SD
Gaze aversion	27.82	9.25	27.78	11.76
Blinks	23.56	10.28	18.50	8.44
Head movements	26.57	12.34	27.53	20.93
Hand/arm movements	15.31	14.35	10.80	9.99
Pauses	3.73	5.14	5.31	4.94
Speech disturbances	5.22	3.79	5.34	4.93

▲ **Table 3.1** Scores – truthful and deceptive

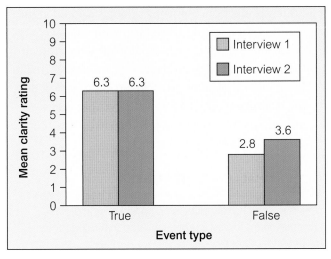

▲ Figure 3.2 Clarity ratings

However, some were still dubious it was a false event despite choosing it at debrief!

CONCLUSION

Some people can be misled into believing a false event happened to them in their childhood through the suggestion that it was a true event. Therefore, in some people, memories can be altered by suggestion.

TEST YOURSELF
Outline four main findings from this study. How useful are these findings?

EVALUATION

Since Loftus & Pickrell collected quantitative data, we can use the general evaluations from Chapter 2, pages 9–10 and apply them directly to the study:

Evaluation	General evaluation (quantitative)	Related to Loftus & Pickrell
Strength	The data are objective and can be analysed statistically to draw conclusions.	The data such as the confidence ratings, word length of recollections and clarity ratings were numerical and could be analysed by calculating the mean scores for true and false events. From these objective data, suitable conclusions could be drawn.
Strength	As the data are numerical, comparison and statistical analysis are easier (e.g. the average score of two different groups of participants can easily be compared so there is very little bias or misinterpretation).	Loftus & Pickrell could calculate the number of true and false events people recalled as being "factual" so comparisons could be made – there could be very little misinterpretation as it was based on participants' initial recall in the booklet. Comparisons between the true and false events could give a factual conclusion.
Weakness	Numerical data miss out on valuable information. If the answer is simply yes/no or on a rating scale we do not know *why* participants chose the answer they did.	The confidence ratings were numerical. While they appeared low for true and false events at both interviews, we do not know why participants felt unconfident. The same applies to the clarity ratings.

Other points that can be used to evaluate this study include the following:

▶ Ethics: deception. Some psychologists could argue that this study breaks the ethical guideline of deception as participants were clearly deceived in the attempt to make them believe that they had been lost in a shopping mall or department store when they were 5 years old. However, Loftus & Pickrell could argue that the deception was *crucial* for their study to have any validity and that they did debrief participants at the end and explain the deception.

▶ Ethics: protection. Some psychologists could argue that this study breaks the ethical guideline of deception as participants did not leave the study in the same psychological state as when they started it. Remember that some participants did not pick out the false event and may now believe that they were indeed lost in a shopping mall department store when they were 5 years old.

CHALLENGE YOURSELF
Evaluate this study in terms of it being a small-scale longitudinal study and on its usefulness. You may want to use a table similar to that used for the quantitative data evaluation.

Exam centre

Try the following exam-style questions.

Paper 1

1. In the Loftus & Pickrell study, outline how the sample was recruited. (2 marks)

2. Outline **two** aspects of the first interview in the Loftus & Pickrell study. (4 marks)

3. Outline **how** confidence *or* clarity was measured in the Loftus & Pickrell study. (2 marks)

4. Evaluate the Loftus & Pickrell study in terms of **two** strengths. (10 marks)

Paper 2

1. Outline what quantitative data were collected in the Loftus & Pickrell study. (3 marks)

2. Outline how the interview method was used in the Loftus & Pickrell study. (3 marks)

3. Discuss the strengths and weaknesses of ethical guidelines in research using Loftus & Pickrell as an example. (10 marks)

CORE STUDY 3.3

Baron-Cohen et al (2001)

CONTEXT

Back in 1997, a "Reading the mind in the eyes" test was developed to assess a concept called theory of mind. This refers to the ability to attribute mental states to oneself and other people. The test appeared to discriminate between adults with Asperger syndrome (AS) and high functioning autistic (HFA) adults from control adults. The AS and HFA groups scored significantly worse than others in the test, which asked participants to look at a pair of eyes on a screen and choose which emotion the eyes best conveyed, from a forced choice of emotions. However, the research team were not happy with elements of the original version and wanted to "upgrade" their measure to make it better (these problems and solutions are outlined in the design section).

ASK YOURSELF
How do you read the emotion that is conveyed by another person's face? What do you look for?

AIM

1. To test a group of adults with AS or HFA on the revised scale of the eyes test. This was to check whether the same deficits seen in the original study could be replicated.

2. To test a sample of normal adults to see whether there was a negative correlation between the scores on the eyes test and their autism spectrum quotient (AQ).

3. To test whether females scored better on the eyes test than males.

METHOD

Design

The researchers redesigned the questionnaire to overcome problems with the original test (see Core study table 3.2).

Original problems	New design element (if applicable)
Forced choice between two response options meant just a narrow range of 17–25 correct responses (out of 25) to be statistically above chance. The range of scores for parents of those with AS were lower than normal but again there was a narrow range of scores to detect any real differences.	Forced choice remained but there were four response options. There were 36 pairs of eyes used rather than 25 – this gives a range of 13–36 correct responses (out of 36) to be statistically above chance. These means individual differences can be examined better in terms of statistics.
There were basic and complex mental states so some of the pairs of eyes were "too easy" (e.g. happy, sad) and others "too hard" making comparisons difficult.	Only complex mental states were used.
There were some pairs of eyes that could be "solved" easily because of eye direction (e.g. noticing or ignoring).	These were deleted.
There were more female pairs of eyes used in the original test.	An equal amount of male and female pairs of eyes was used.
The choice of two responses were always "semantic opposites" (e.g. happy/sad) which made it too easy.	"Semantic opposites" were removed and the "foil choices" (those that were incorrect) were to be more similar to the correct answer.
There may have been comprehension problems with the choice of words used as the forced choice responses.	A glossary of all terms used as the choices on the eyes test was available to all participants at all times.

▲ Table 3.2 Problems and attempts to solve them

The "correct" word and the "foils" were chosen by two authors of the study and were piloted on eight

21

Control judges (equal sex). For the correct word and its foils to be used in the new eyes test, five judges had to agree with the original choice. Also, if more than two judges picked a foil over the correct word, the item had a new correct word generated with suitable foils and was retested. The data from groups 2 and 3 (see below) were merged as they did not differ in performance. This was also a **Reliable** check that the "correct" words had some consensus – at least 50% of the group had to get the correct word and no more than 25% had to select a foil for it to be included in the new eyes test. From the original 40 pairs of eyes, 36 passed these tests and were used.

TEST YOURSELF
Outline two problems with the original version of the eyes test and then describe how the research team attempted to overcome them.

Participants

There were four groups of participants:

1. One group consisted of 15 males formally diagnosed with either AS or HFA. They were recruited via a UK National Autistic Society magazine or support group. Therefore, these participants were volunteers.

2. In this group there were 122 normal adults recruited from adult community and education classes in **Sample** Exeter or a public library in Cambridge – a broad range of people.

3. This group consisted of 103 normal adults (53 male and 50 female) who were undergraduates at Cambridge University (71 in sciences and 32 in other subjects). All were assumed to have a high IQ.

4. This group was formed from 14 randomly selected adults who were matched for IQ with group 1.

Procedure

All participants, irrespective of group, completed the **Control** revised version of the eyes test. Each participant completed it individually in a quiet room. Participants in group 1 were asked to judge the gender of each image. Groups 1, 3

and 4 completed a questionnaire to measure their AQ. All participants were asked to read through a glossary and indicate any words were unsure of – and they could revisit the glossary at any time during the test.

▲ **Figure 3.3** Example of male pair of eyes used in the test

RESULTS

Core study table 3.3 shows the mean and standard deviation scores for the new eyes test and AQ by group.

Quant

Group	Eyes test	AQ
AS/HFA adults	21.9 (6.6)	34.4 (6.0)
General population	26.2 (3.6)	N/A
Students	28.0 (3.5)	18.3 (6.6)
Matched	30.9 (3.0)	18.9 (2.9)

▲ **Table 3.3** Mean and standard deviation (in parentheses) scores for the new eyes test and AQ by group

The AS/HFA group performed significantly worse than the other three groups on the eyes test. In general, females scored better on the eyes test than males. Unsurprisingly, the AS/HFA group scored significantly higher on AQ than the other groups. The correlation between the eyes test and AQ was negative. The distribution of scores for the eyes test (all groups merged) formed a normal bell curve.

TEST YOURSELF
Outline two differences between the different sets of participants used in this study in terms of their performance on the eyes test.

CONCLUSION

The revised version of the eyes test could still discriminate between AS/HFA adults and controls from different sections of society as it replicated previous findings. The new eyes test appeared to overcome the initial problems of the original version and the research team stated "... this therefore validates it as a useful test with which to identify subtle impairments in social intelligence in otherwise normally intelligent adults" Baron-Cohen *et al* (2001: 246).

EVALUATION

As Baron-Cohen *et al* used a psychometric measure, we can use the general evaluations from Chapter 2, page 10 and apply them directly to the study:

Evaluation	General evaluation (psychometrics)	Related to Baron-Cohen *et al*
Strength	Comparisons can be *useful* as people's results are being compared on the same, standardised scale.	The revised eyes test was used in all participants – this means that all comparisons between the groups have some validity as we are comparing on the same set scale using the same questions, etc.
Strength	As they are standardised, they are reliable measures – we can use them again and again to see if we get similar results.	The revised eyes test can be used by other research teams to see if they can replicate findings and test for reliability. This study did find reliable results in terms of performance of AS/HFA (low scores in both studies).
Weakness	There may be issues with validity. Is the test actually measuring the behaviour it is supposed to be measuring?	Some psychologists could query whether the revised eyes test is still actually measuring theory of mind traits or just the ability to complete the eyes test.

There could be some evaluations based around usefulness:

▶ The main advantage is that it is can be used to improve human behaviour in some way. As it is showing that AS/HFA adults appear to lack theory of mind, psychologists could now create therapies (or training) to help these people improve their social communication and social emotional skills to help them integrate better into society.

▶ However, the eyes test does not take into account the "full picture" of understanding emotions – in reality there are subtle cues such as body language alongside other facial cues

Useful

that can help people to understand the emotions of others. A study that assessed the same as the eyes test but using a full face or a moving image with verbalisation might be even more useful to assess theory of mind.

> **CHALLENGE YOURSELF**
> Evaluate this study in terms of it being a snapshot study and also in terms of reductionism. You may want to use a table like that used for the psychometrics evaluations.

Exam centre

Try the following exam-style questions.

Paper 1

1. In the Baron-Cohen *et al* study, identify **two** of the groups of participants used. (2 marks)

2. Outline how the eyes test was used in the Baron-Cohen *et al* study. (4 marks)

3. Outline **two** reasons why the Baron-Cohen *et al* study was conducted. (4 marks)

4. Evaluate the Baron-Cohen *et al* study in terms of **one** strength and **one** weakness. (10 marks)

Paper 2

1. Outline how quantitative data were collected in the Baron-Cohen *et al* study. (3 marks)

2. Outline **one** finding from the Baron-Cohen *et al* study. (3 marks)

3. Discuss the strengths and weaknesses of using psychometric tests using Baron-Cohen *et al* study as an example. (10 marks)

CORE STUDY 3.4

Held & Hein (1963)

CONTEXT

Psychologists have debated for a very long time over nature and nurture. Previous studies had examined the role of exposure to stimuli and movement around stimuli as a way of developing part of our perceptual system. Both may be necessary to enable an organism to perceive its world correctly and comfortably. Riesen proposed an idea of sensory–sensory associations as vital for the optimal development of an organism's perceptual system. That is, one sense alone is not enough to develop perceptual skills, so in this case visual and kinaesthetic associations might be necessary. What happens when an organism is deprived of these associations was the crux of this study.

 ASK YOURSELF
How do you perceive the world around you? How much have you been taught and how much was natural to you?

AIM

To investigate whether kittens have to see and move to be able to develop skills such as depth perception.

METHOD

Design

Held & Hein created a "kitten carousel" for their study as shown in figure 3.4. Each kitten had a distinct role. The one labelled A (active) was allowed to walk around the carousel to explore. The one labelled P (passive) was placed in a device where its paws could not touch the ground, preventing kitten P from walking. However, the device that connected the two kittens meant that kitten P moved in all of the same directions as kitten A but without engaging in any walking. The distance between the kittens was 36 inches. Therefore, kitten A could move

walk freely (with its neck in a holding device) whereas kitten P got moved by the motion of kitten A. Kitten P could move its legs within the device but was never in control of its own movements.

Lab

▲ **Figure 3.4** The kitten carousel

The kittens undertook three main tasks: **Control**

1. Visually-guided paw placement. Each kitten was held in a researcher's hands by the body so that the head and forelegs were free. The kitten was slowly moved forwards and downward towards the edge of a table (horizontal surface). If its perceptual system has developed in the usual way, then the kitten should reach with its paws to touch the surface.

2. Avoidance of a visual cliff. The apparatus has a "deep side" which is a patterned surface about 30 inches below a large plate of glass and a "shallow side" where the patterned surface is attached to the underside of the glass. It was lit from below to make the glass almost invisible. The kittens' behaviours were noted.

3. Blinking to an approaching object. Each kitten was placed in a device similar to that used by the A kitten. A large sheet of Plexiglass was placed in front of the kitten. A hand would be moved quickly towards the kitten, stopping just before the Plexiglass.

There were other tests performed on the kittens: pupillary reflex to light being shone into it, how they reacted to having their paws placed on the top of a table and visual pursuit of a moving object.

 TEST YOURSELF
Outline two of the tasks that the kittens had to perform in this study.

Participants

The participants were kittens. There were 10 pairs of kittens used (so a total of 20) and each pair came from a different litter. They were all aged between 8 and 12 weeks.

Procedure

The ten pairs of kittens were split into groups X and Y:

▶ The X group (eight of the pairs) were reared in darkness from birth until the kitten assigned as A was at the minimum size to be used in the kitten carousel (age varied from 8 to 12 weeks). They were then exposed to the apparatus for three hours per day.

Reliable

▶ The Y group (two of the pairs) had three hours of exposure to the patterned interior of the carousel from about two weeks old until ten weeks old. After this they began a three hour per day exposure to the kitten carousel. When not on the apparatus they were kept in "lightless" cages with their mother and litter mates.

▶ There were six paw-placement assessments each day after the exposures noted above.

▶ As soon as one of the pairs of kittens showed the ability to "paw-place" both of the pair were tested on the visual cliff (placed in the central part and observed). They were then both retested on the following day. Then, the P kitten of each pair was placed in a continuously lit room for 48 hours. They were then retested. This applied to the X group.

▶ The Y group did something slightly different. On the first day that the A kitten showed paw-placement skills, it was tested on the visual cliff and then retested the day after. However, the P kitten simply kept getting exposed to the carousel for 3 hours per day until it reached 126 hours. Only then was it tested for paw-placement and on the visual cliff.

RESULTS

Quant Table 3.4. shows findings from the visual cliff task.

Pair number	Age in weeks*	Ratio of descents shallow/deep	
		A	P
1X	8	12/0	6/6
2X	8	12/0	4/8
3X	8	12/0	7/5
4X	9	12/0	6/6
5X	10	12/0	7/5
6X	10	12/0	7/5
7X	12	12/0	5/7
8X	12	12/0	8/4
1Y	10	12/0	6/6
2Y	10	12/0	8/4

*At the beginning of exposure in the experimental apparatus

▲ **Table 3.4** Results of the visual cliff task

All the A kittens went to the shallow side but it was almost "random" for the P kittens which side they preferred. This indicates that the P kittens had not developed depth perception even in the Y group.

As soon as the A kitten could show paw-placement, the paired P kitten's ability was noted. None of them passed this test. The A kittens could also pass the remaining tests but the P kittens all failed. Following the 48 hours of continually lit living arrangements for the P kittens, when retested on the visual cliff they all went to the shallow side and they could all pass the paw-placement test.

CONCLUSION

To develop "typical" perceptual development, kittens need to be able to move around by themselves with simultaneous visual feedback.

TEST YOURSELF
Outline two key results from this study. How ethical was this study?

EVALUATION

Since Held & Hein used a laboratory experiment, we can use the general
evaluations from Chapter 1, pages 1–2 and apply them directly to the study:

Evaluation	General evaluation (laboratory experiments)	Related to Held & Hein
Strength	Laboratory experiments have high levels of control and so can be replicated to test for reliability.	The amount of time the kittens got exposed to the apparatus, the tasks the kittens had to do and the kitten carousel were all solid controls in this study. Therefore, a different set of researchers could replicate this study to test for reliability (however, whether this *should* be done is arguable – see animal ethics below).
Strength	As laboratory experiments have high levels of control, researchers can be more confident it is the IV directly affecting the DV.	With the controls in place (e.g. the kitten pairings, the conditions in which they were raised and the kitten carousel) Held & Hein could conclude with confidence that the use of vision *and* movement affects the perceptual development of kittens.
Weakness	As laboratory experiments take place in an artificial setting, some say they lack ecological validity.	Group X kittens were brought up in darkness and all kittens spent time in a kitten carousel which are not usual environments for kittens. Therefore, it could be said that the study lacked ecological validity.
Weakness	Many laboratory experiments can make participants take part in tasks that are nothing like real-life ones so they lack mundane realism.	The tasks that the kittens had to perform (e.g. the visual cliff and the paw-placement) are not tasks that kittens in the natural environment would have to perform. Therefore, it could be said that the study lacked mundane realism.

This is the only AS-Level study that used animals as participants;
therefore we can assess the study on animal ethics:

General evaluation (animal ethics)	Related to Held & Hein
Number of animals – this should be a kept to the minimum amount to make statistical analysis meaningful.	Only 20 kittens were used for the entire study which allows for statistical analyses but is also a small number of kittens overall.
Caging – housing in cages should not lead to overcrowding and increased stress levels.	Eight pairs of kittens were reared in darkness and two in lightless cages which are not usual conditions. This could have increased the stress levels of the entire litter (not just the kittens used in the study) and the mother.
There should be general protection from psychological and physical harm.	The findings did show impaired perceptual development in the P kittens which can be seen as being harmful. Also, being raised in darkness could be seen as not protecting the kittens. The kitten carousel could have been stressful for the P kittens as they had no control; the neckbrace for the A kittens could have been stressful too. However, some psychologists might argue that the stress was transient (short-lived) as the P kittens began to overcome their perceptual deficiencies once placed in lit conditions.

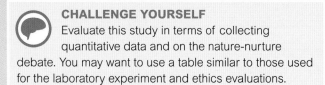

CHALLENGE YOURSELF
Evaluate this study in terms of collecting quantitative data and on the nature-nurture debate. You may want to use a table similar to those used for the laboratory experiment and ethics evaluations.

Exam centre

Try the following exam-style questions.

Paper 1

1. In the Held & Hein study, name **two** of the tests the kittens had to perform after being in the kitten carousel. (2 marks)

2. Outline **two** controls that Held & Hein used in their study. (4 marks)

3. Outline how group X kittens were raised in the Held & Hein study. (2 marks)

4. Evaluate the Held & Hein study in terms of **one** strength and **one** weakness. (10 marks)

Paper 2

1. Outline one finding from the Held & Hein study. (3 marks)

2. Outline how qualitative data *could have been* collected in the Held & Hein study. (3 marks)

3. Discuss the strengths and weaknesses of using animals in psychological research using the Held & Hein study as an example. (10 marks)

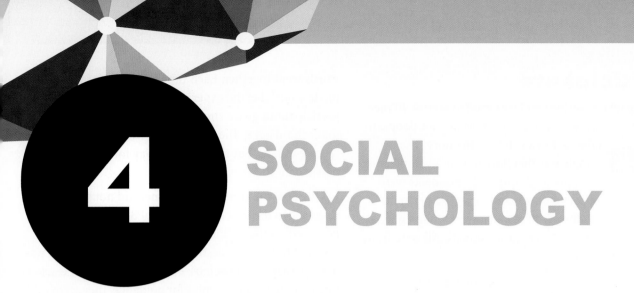

4 SOCIAL PSYCHOLOGY

CORE STUDY 4.1

Milgram (1963)

CONTEXT

Most of the time we are told that obedience is a good thing. But what if you were ordered to do something that caused harm or distress to another person? This type of obedience is called destructive obedience. Social psychologists such as Stanley Milgram have been particularly interested in destructive obedience.

As a member of a European Jewish family that had left Europe for the United States, Milgram was profoundly affected by the atrocities committed by Nazi Germany. A key feature of these atrocities was the extent to which ordinary people obeyed destructive orders that led to the systematic mass murder of minority groups, including Jews, Romanies, Communists, trade unionists and people with disabilities.

Early psychological research into the Holocaust focused on the idea that something distinctive about German culture or personality led to the high levels of conformity and obedience necessary for genocide to take place. This is known as the dispositional hypothesis. While Milgram was interested in this idea, he was also interested in the social processes that take place between individuals and within groups. The idea that we can explain events such as the Holocaust by reference to the social processes operating in the situation, rather than the characteristics of the individuals involved, is called the situational hypothesis. In his early work Milgram worked with another social psychologist, Solomon Asch. Together they studied people's tendency to conform to group pressure.

ASK YOURSELF
Why do you think the Holocaust happened? Can you think of any modern-day examples of such atrocities?

AIM

To investigate how obedient people would be to orders from a person in authority that would result in pain and harm to someone. Specifically, the aim was to see how large an electric shock participants would give to a helpless man when ordered to by a scientist in a laboratory.

METHOD

Design

Milgram described his original study as a laboratory experiment. Technically it might more accurately be called a pre-experiment, because it had only one condition. The results from this condition then served as a baseline for a number of variations in follow-up studies. Obedience was operationalised as the maximum voltage given in response to the orders.

Lab

Participants

A newspaper advertisement was used to recruit 40 men aged 20–50. The advertisement was asking for people to take part in a study on memory. The sample was therefore mostly a volunteer or self-selecting sample. Respondents were from a range of backgrounds and jobs: 37.5 per cent were manual labourers, 40 per cent were white-collar workers, 22.5 per cent were professionals. All were from New Haven, Connecticut, USA.

Participants were recruited using a newspaper advertisement, so were a volunteer or self-selecting sample. They were promised $4.50 for turning up to the study; payment was not conditional on completing it.

Procedure

When each participant arrived at Yale University he was introduced to a man he believed to be another participant. The two men were then briefed on the supposed purpose of the experiment, which was described to them as to investigate the effect of punishment on learning.

In fact the other man was working for Milgram. He was a 47-year-old Irish-American accountant, selected for the role because he was mild-mannered and likeable. People who help with experiments in this way are known as confederates or stooges.

The naïve participant and the confederate were told that one of them would play the role of teacher and the other the learner. They drew slips of paper from a hat to allocate the roles, but this was fiddled so that the naïve participant was always the teacher and the confederate was always the learner. They were then immediately taken to another room where the learner was strapped into a chair and electrodes were attached to him. They were shown the electric shock generator. This had switches labelled with a voltage, rising in 15-volt intervals from 15V up to 450V. Teachers were told that the shocks could be extremely painful but not dangerous; they were each given a 45V shock to demonstrate.

There was a wall between the teacher and learner, so that the teacher could hear but not see the learner. The procedure was administered by an experimenter, played by a 31-year-old male biology teacher. The participant (in the role of teacher) read out word pairs to test the confederate (in the role of learner) on his recognition of which

words went together. Each time the confederate-learner made a mistake, the experimenter ordered the teacher-participant to give a shock. The shock got larger by 15V for each mistake. The confederate-learner did not really receive shocks, but there was no way for the teacher-participant to know this.

Up to 300V the confederate-learner did not signal any response to the shocks. However, at 300V and 315V, he pounded on the wall. He was then silent and did not respond to further questions. This suggested that he was hurt, perhaps unconscious, or even dead. When teachers turned to the experimenter for guidance, they were told to treat this as an incorrect response and to continue to give the shocks. When they protested, they were given a series of verbal prods to encourage them to continue:

Prod 1 – say 'Please continue' or 'Please go on'.

Prod 2 – say 'The experimenter requires you to continue'.

Prod 3 – say 'It is absolutely essential that you continue'.

Prod 4 – 'You have no other choice, you must go on'.

Teachers were considered to have completed the procedure when they refused to give any more shocks, or when they reached the maximum of 450V. They were then interviewed and asked to rate on a scale of 0–14 how painful the last few shocks were. Then they were told that the shocks were not real, the learner was unharmed, and the real purpose of the study was to investigate obedience.

TEST YOURSELF
Try to get the procedure down to eight "vital parts" that are essential for you to understand what the participants had to do.

RESULTS

Quantitative and qualitative data were gathered. The "headline figures" were quantitative, in the form of the average voltage that participants went up to, and the number of participants giving each voltage. The average voltage given by participants was 368V; 100 per cent of participants gave 300V or more; 65 per cent gave the full 450V. Psychology students had estimated that only 3 per cent of participants would do this. In their post-experiment interviews, participants' average rating of how painful the shocks were was 13.42 out of a maximum of 14.

also impersonal (e.g. ID number). A total of five "prisoners" had to be released because of "extreme emotional depression" which included crying, rage and high anxiety. Some of these symptoms were seen on day 2 of the simulation in four of the prisoners. The fifth prisoner had to be released after being treated for a psychosomatic rash that had developed. Of the remainder, only two would not give up their $15 per day to be "paroled". The simulation had to be terminated on day 6 and the remaining prisoners were "delighted by their unexpected good fortune" (Haney, Banks & Zimbardo, 1973: 10). The guards however were the complete opposite. They were enjoying the extreme control and power and did not want to give it up so soon. One of them did state that he felt upset about how the prisoners were being treated and was going to ask to swap roles. He never did. All guards came to work on time and on numerous occasions they worked extra hours after their assigned shift had ended. There were some individual differences reported in the behaviours of people in each group. Half of the prisoners did endure the situation and not all guards were hostile. Some of the guards stuck within the rules they had created while others went beyond them.

Reality of the simulation: So how "real" was the simulation? There were aspects that had to be absent from this for ethical and legal reasons such as involuntary homosexuality, racism, physical beatings and threats to life. Also, the prisoners had been given a two-week sentence (which would not happen in reality).

The marked psychological effects the simulation had on participants was clear, especially as some of these developed after just two days (see above). The research team were clear in wanting to report behaviours and incidences that occurred when participants believed they were not being observed (to decrease the potential effects of demand characteristics). One example was

Quant the private conversations between prisoners. Of these conversations 90 per cent centred on prison life (e.g. food, punishments and harassments). This, of course, meant participants were truly "caught up" in the situation as they rarely *did not* talk about it. The same happened with the guards during relaxation breaks – they spent the majority of their time talking about prison life. From data analysed post-simulation, when the guards were out of view of recording equipment the harassment of prisoners was greater than in the yard, which was monitored. The

amount of aggression from guards continued to increase even when prisoners had stopped resisting the demands placed on them – this was seen as a consequence of simply being put in a uniform of power. One guard placed a prisoner in solitary confinement and kept him in there overnight (against the rules) as he felt the researchers were being too soft! When questioned about their behaviours after the study was stopped, guards stated that they became increasingly aggressive because they were simply playing their role. A Catholic priest visited the simulation and even then the prisoners referred to themselves by number rather than name. When some were interviewed by a public defender, many of the remaining prisoners demanded to be bailed out. Some prisoners would have given up the $15 per day to be released. When they were told that this would have to be discussed they simply allowed themselves to be escorted back to their cells with no attempt at arguing. The prison consultant, priest and public defender all stated that the simulation was pretty "real".

Pathology of power: Those assigned to the guard role held high social status in the prison, had a group identity of the uniform and had the freedom to control prisoners. The aggression appeared to get stronger when prisoners became a perceived threat (initially). Those who were the most hostile tended to become the leaders of the guards. Even though guards spent 16 hours away from the prison every day, the level of aggression intensified and the different ways of showing aggression increased. It was seen as a sign of a guard's weakness not to show hostility to prisoners. After day 1 guards had changed prisoners' rights into privileges that had to be earned for being obedient.

The pathological prisoner syndrome: Initially, prisoners could not believe what was happening, how they had lost their privacy, how they were being constantly watched and the oppressiveness of the whole simulation. This soon passed and their next response was rebellion. This direct force changed to subtle methods including setting up a grievance committee. When all of this failed to change anything, prisoners turned to self-interests at the expense of any group behaviour. It did not take long for any prisoner cohesion to dissolve. Prisoners seemed to choose one of two ways to cope: become sick or become obedient. For example, the obedient ones sided with the guards when one prisoner went on hunger strike and labelled him a "trouble-maker". Three elements to this syndrome that were seen in the prisoners:

1. Loss of personal identity. Prisoners wore the same uniforms, rarely spoke about life outside the simulation and all referred to each other by their ID number not name. They had become deindividuated.

2. Arbitrary control. Prisoners found it increasingly difficult to cope with the increasing stronger control by guards, especially via the often "mixed message" approach (e.g., smiling at a joke could initiate as much punishment as ignoring a joke). As the prison became more and more unpredictable, prisoners just went along with everything (similar to a behaviour called learned helplessness. See section 8.4, page 130 and section 11.3, page 218).

3. Dependency and emasculation. Prisoners had to depend on guards for virtually everything from toilet breaks (they were handcuffed and blindfolded), to

lighting a cigarette and cleaning their teeth. All of these were "privileges" and required permission. In terms of emasculation, the smocks resembled dresses and guards would often call prisoners "sissies" or "girls". Without underwear, prisoners had to sit like females which increased their emasculation.

TEST YOURSELF
Outline four key findings from this study.

CONCLUSION

The situation that people find themselves in has a stronger effect on behaviour than individual (dispositional) factors. In a novel situation, people adapt to what they think they should do in that situation rather than acting on internal factors.

EVALUATION

As Haney, Banks & Zimbardo used observations as the research method, we can use the general evaluations from Chapter 1, pages 3–4 and apply them directly to the study:

Evaluation	General evaluation (observations)	Related to Haney, Banks & Zimbardo
Strength	If participants are unaware that they are being observed they should behave "naturally". This increases the ecological validity of the observation.	Although all participants knew they were in a simulation, many appeared, rather quickly, to produce "natural" behaviour depending on their role. Remember that the prison consultant noted how "real" the situation was as well as the behaviour of prisoners and guards. Therefore, the study could be argued to have some ecological validity.
Strength	As behaviours are "counted" and are hence quantitative, the process is objective and the data can be analysed statistically with minimal bias.	The observers could easily count the number of times certain behaviours occurred and double-check with the recorded footage of the simulation. The data are objective and can be analysed statistically so there is minimal chance of misinterpretation.
Weakness	If participants are aware that they are being observed then they may not act "naturally" but instead show socially desirable behaviours. This reduces the validity of findings.	Even though the prison consultant said the situation felt "real", all participants were aware they were being observed by cameras and a research team. Some participants were acting in a way so as not to be judged by the research team. Therefore, they were not displaying true behaviour.

Below are other points that could be used for evaluation:

▶ Ethics: protection of participants. Even though the study was stopped early, participants assigned as prisoners were subjected to harassment, mental abuse and having to earn basic rights (e.g. food and a bed) for five days. It was very clear from all of the qualitative data collected that participants did not leave in the same psychological and physical state as they started. The simulated arrest alone at the beginning of the study would have also stressed participants assigned to the prisoner role.

Ethics

▶ Individual versus situational explanations: the idea was to see whether "bad" people make prisons "bad" (e.g. it is dispositional). This study supports the idea that the situation we find ourselves in can dramatically affect our behaviour as all participants had been found to be psychologically stable.

Ind vs sit

CHALLENGE YOURSELF
Evaluate this study in terms of individual versus situational explanations and it being useful. You may want to use a table similar to the one used for the observation evaluation.

Exam centre

Try the following exam-style questions.

Paper 1

1. Outline the induction procedure for **either** the prisoners **or** the prison guards. (4 marks)

2. Outline **one** advantage of using observations in the Haney, Banks & Zimbardo study. (2 marks)

3. Outline **one** qualitative result from the Haney, Banks & Zimbardo study. (2 marks)

4. Evaluate the Haney, Banks & Zimbardo study in terms of **two** weaknesses. (10 marks)

Paper 2

1. Outline how observations were used in the Haney, Banks & Zimbardo study. (3 marks)

2. Outline **one** finding from the Haney, Banks & Zimbardo study. (3 marks)

3. Discuss the strengths and weaknesses of individual and situational explanations of behaviour using Haney, Banks & Zimbardo as an example. (10 marks)

CORE STUDY 4.3

Piliavin, Rodin & Piliavin (1969)

CONTEXT

This study is concerned with bystander behaviour. Bystanders are people who witness events and have to choose whether to intervene or not. Recently there has been a lot of debate over "have-a-go heroes" who put themselves at risk to intervene and attempt to stop crimes taking place. Most of the time, bystanders can help without putting themselves at risk. However, surprisingly often we do not choose to act to help people in need.

ACTIVITY

The Kitty Genovese murder
Psychological research into bystander behaviour was triggered by a murder that took place in New York in 1964. Read the excerpts from the *New York Times* article describing the incident.

ACTIVITY

Thirty-Eight Who Saw Murder Didn't Call the Police by Martin Gansberg

For more than half an hour 38 respectable, law-abiding citizens in Queens watched a killer stalk and stab a woman in three separate attacks in Kew Gardens. Twice their chatter and the sudden glow of their bedroom lights interrupted him and frightened him off. Each time he returned, sought her out, and stabbed her again. Not one person telephoned the police during the assault; one witness called after the woman was dead.

That was two weeks ago today. Still shocked is Assistant Chief Inspector Frederick M. Lussen, in charge of the borough's detectives and a veteran of 25 years of homicide investigations. He can give a matter-of-fact recitation on many murders. But the Kew Gardens slaying baffles him – not because it is a murder, but because the 'good people' failed to call the police.

This is what the police say happened at 3:20 A.M. in the staid, middle-class, tree-lined Austin Street area: Twenty-eight-year-old Catherine Genovese, who was called Kitty by almost everyone in the neighborhood, was returning home from her job as manager of a bar in Hollis. She parked her red Fiat in a lot adjacent to the Kew Gardens Long Island Railroad Station, facing Mowbray Place.

Miss Genovese noticed a man at the far end of the lot, near a seven-story apartment house at 82–40 Austin Street. She halted. Then, nervously, she headed up Austin Street toward Lefferts Boulevard, where there is a call box to the 102nd Police Precinct in nearby Richmond Hill. She got as far as a street light in front of a bookstore before the man grabbed her. She screamed. Lights went on in the 10-story apartment house at 82–67 Austin Street, which faces the bookstore. Windows slid open and voices punctuated the early-morning stillness.

Miss Genovese screamed: 'Oh, my God, he stabbed me! Please help me! Please help me!' From one of the upper windows in the apartment house, a man called down: 'Let that girl alone!' The assailant looked up at him, shrugged, and walked down Austin Street toward a white sedan parked a short distance away. Miss Genovese struggled to her feet. Lights went out. The killer returned to Miss Genovese, now trying to make her way around the side of the building by the parking lot to get to her apartment. The assailant stabbed her again. 'I'm dying!' she shrieked. 'I'm dying!'

Windows were opened again, and lights went on in many apartments. The assailant got into his car and drove away. Miss Genovese staggered to her feet. A city bus, 0–10, the Lefferts Boulevard line to Kennedy International Airport, passed. It was 3:35 A.M. The assailant returned. By then, Miss Genovese had crawled to the back of the building, where the freshly painted brown doors to the apartment house held out hope for safety. The killer tried the first door; she wasn't there. At the second door, 82–62 Austin Street, he saw her slumped on the floor at the foot of the stairs. He stabbed her a third time—fatally.

Some of the details of the story as it was reported at the time have since been challenged. Given the layout of the block, it would not have been possible for anyone to have seen the whole incident, so each person would have seen just fragments of the event. Also, the area was not actually as quiet as the article implies – one neighbour said that rows between couples leaving a local bar were common late at night. Given these facts, we cannot be sure that 38 people really saw, correctly interpreted, and chose to ignore the murder. However, the Genovese murder captured the public imagination and stimulated psychological research into bystander behaviour.
Source: New York Times, *March 27, 1964*

1. How could you explain these events according to the individual and dispositional hypotheses?
2. What do you think you would have done?

CORE STUDY 5.2

Freud (1909)

ASK YOURSELF
Why do you think people develop things such as phobias? Could it be because of childhood experiences or are there other factors involved?

CONTEXT

Sigmund Freud remains the most famous psychologist, even more than 70 years after his death. Freud wrote from the 1890s until the 1930s. His approach to psychological theory and therapy – called psychoanalysis – forms the basis of the psychodynamic perspective to psychology. Freud had a number of important ideas, some more controversial than others. Most controversially of all he proposed that childhood can be seen as a series of psychosexual stages. Each stage is characterised by a fixation on an area of the body and a distinct pattern of relationships to parents.

The oral stage takes place in the first year of life. The mouth is the main focus of pleasure at this stage, as children are suckling and weaning. At this stage, they are totally dependent on their main carer, and they acquire the ability to accept nurture and have close relationships. From around 1 to 3 years of age, a child goes through the anal stage. Here the focus of pleasure is the anus, as the child learns to retain and expel faeces at will. This is also the time at which the parents start to exert control over the child's behaviour through potty-training, and this is when the child acquires a pattern of relating to authority.

The third and most crucial Freudian stage of development is the phallic stage (from the word phallus, meaning penis), which lasts from around age 3 to 6 years. In the phallic stage, children go through the Oedipus complex. This involves the development of a strong attachment to the opposite-sex parent, and a sense of the same-sex parent as a rival for their affection. Freud came to this conclusion after a period of self-analysis. He revealed his own Oedipus complex in a letter to a friend:

"I have found in my own case too being in love with my mother and jealous of my father, and now I consider it a universal event in early childhood."

One of Freud's most famous cases is that of Little Hans, a young boy Freud believed to be going through the Oedipus complex.

AIM

To give an account of a boy who was suffering from a phobia of horses and a range of other symptoms, and to use this case to illustrate the existence of the Oedipus complex.

METHOD

Design

The study was a clinical case study. This means that the participant is a patient undergoing therapy. In this case, Freud's direct input in the therapy was very limited. Accounts of how often Freud saw Little Hans vary a little, but it almost certainly was not more than twice. Hans' father conducted regular discussions with Hans and passed these on to Freud, who analysed them in line with his theory. The results consist of Freud's analysis.

Case

Participant

The participant was a Jewish boy from Vienna, Austria. He was 5 years old at the start of the study, although some events were recorded from a couple of years earlier. He was called Little Hans in the study; however, his real name, Herbert Graf, was well known. Little Hans was suffering from a phobia of horses. His father, a fan of Freud's work, referred the case to Freud and went on to provide much of the case information.

Case history

From around 3 years of age, Hans developed a great interest in his penis – his "widdler" as he called it – and it was reported that he played with it regularly. Eventually, his mother became so cross that she threatened to cut it off if he didn't stop. Hans was very disturbed by this and developed a fear of castration. At around the same time, Hans saw a horse collapse and die in the street, and he was very upset as a result. When Hans was 3 and a half years old, his baby sister was born and he was separated from her for a while when she was hospitalised.

Shortly after this, when Hans was 4 years old, he developed a phobia of horses. Specifically, he was afraid **Qual** that a white horse would bite him. When reporting this to Freud, Hans' father noted that the fear of horses seemed to relate to their large penises. At around the same time as the phobia of horses developed, a conflict developed between Hans and his father. Hans had been in the habit for some time of getting into his parents' bed in the morning and cuddling his mother. However, his father began to object to this. Hans' phobia worsened to the extent that he would not leave the family house. At this point, he also suffered attacks of generalised anxiety.

In addition, he reported the following dream: "In the night there was a big giraffe in the room and a crumpled one: and the big one called out because I took the crumpled one away from it. Then it stopped calling out: and I sat down on top of the crumpled one."

By the time Hans was 5 years old his phobia of horses lessened, initially becoming limited to fear of white horses with black nosebands, then disappearing altogether. The end of the phobia was marked by two fantasies:

- Hans fantasised that he had several children. When his father asked who their mother was Hans replied "Why Mummy, and you're the Granddaddy" (Freud, 1909: 238).

- The next day, Hans fantasised that a plumber had come and removed his bottom and penis, replacing them with new and larger ones.

RESULTS

Freud interpreted the case as an example of the Oedipus Complex. More specifically, he noted these points:

- Horses represented Hans' father. White horses with black nosebands were the most feared because they resembled the moustached father. Horses also make good father symbols because they have large penises.

- The anxiety Hans felt was really **Qual** castration anxiety triggered by his mother's threat to cut off his "widdler" and fear of his father caused by his banishing Hans from the parental bed.

- The giraffes in Hans' dream represent his parents. The large giraffe that cried out represented Hans' father objecting to Hans. The crumpled giraffe represented Hans' mother, the crumpling representing her genitals. The large giraffe, with its erect neck, could have been a penis symbol.

- The children fantasy represents a relatively friendly resolution of the Oedipus complex in which Hans replaces his father as his mother's main love object, but the father still has a role as grandfather.

- The plumber fantasy represents identification with the father. By this we mean that Hans could see himself growing a large penis like his father's and becoming like him.

TEST YOURSELF
Outline a few results that appear to confirm that Little Hans was going through the Oedipus complex. How reliable are the results?

CONCLUSION

Hans suffered a phobia of horses because he was suffering from castration anxiety and going through the Oedipus complex. Dreams and fantasies helped express this conflict and eventually he resolved his Oedipus complex by fantasising himself taking on his father's role and placing his father in the role of grandfather.

EVALUATION

Since Freud used a case study, we can use the general evaluations from Chapter 1, page 3 and apply them directly to the study:

Evaluation	General evaluation (case studies)	Related to Freud
Strength	As the psychologist is focusing on one individual (or unit of individuals) he or she can collect rich, in-depth data that have details. This makes the findings more valid.	The focus of the study was on Little Hans. Data were collected though letters from Hans' father which were detailed and contained a lot of information from Little Hans himself. Therefore, the findings could be valid as they are based on looking at the whole situation in depth.
Strength	Participants are usually studied as part of their everyday life which means that the whole process tends to have some ecological validity.	Little Hans continued to be a little boy throughout the study and lived his life "as normal". His father would ask him questions about things such as his dreams and feelings and many parents would do that in everyday life so the findings have some ecological validity. (Little Hans was never take on out of his own home to be "studied".)
Weakness	As the psychologist is focusing on one individual (or unit of individuals), the case may be unique. This makes generalisations quite difficult.	The way that Little Hans developed his phobia of horses may be unique to him, making generalisations difficult as it may not help to explain horse phobias in other boys of a similar age.
Weakness	As participants are studied in depth, an attachment could form between them and the psychologist which could reduce the objectivity of the data collection and analysis of data. This could reduce the validity of findings.	There was no such bond between Freud and Little Hans, but Hans' father was a "fan" of Freud's work. This could have made Hans' father only report aspects of the case study to Freud that fitted in with Freud's own ideas about child development.

Other points that can be used to evaluate the study include these:

▶ Alternative explanation – some psychologists argue that Little Hans' phobia was *not* due to the Oedipus complex. They argue that when young, Little Hans witnessed a horse collapse and die in the street in front of him. He therefore associated the horse with death and this then made him fearful of horses.

▶ Qualitative data – all of the information from Hans' father was qualitative (in the form of letters of correspondence). Therefore, the data are in depth and can be used to explain why Little Hans was suffering from his phobia. Remember that this cannot be done with quantitative data. However, there may have been interpretation bias by Hans' father (who wrote the letters) and Freud (who interpreted the letters) to fit in with Freud's ideas.

CHALLENGE YOURSELF
Evaluate the Freud study in terms of it being a longitudinal study and how useful the case study is. You may want to use a table similar to that used for the case study evaluations.

Exam centre

Try the following exam-style questions.

Paper 1

1. Outline **two** examples that Freud believed showed Little Hans was experiencing the Oedipus complex. (4 marks)

2. How did Freud obtain the information about Little Hans? (2 marks)

3. Outline the dream that Little Hans reported. (2 marks)

4. Evaluate the Freud study in terms of using case studies in psychological research. (10 marks)

Paper 2

1. Outline what qualitative data were collected in the Freud study. (3 marks)

2. Outline how generalisable Freud's study was. (3 marks)

3. Discuss the strengths and weaknesses of case studies using Freud as an example. (10 marks)

CORE STUDY 5.3

Langlois et al *(1991)*

CONTEXT

Here is one question that a lot of people want the answer to: is attractiveness relative or absolute? That is, is attractiveness individually specific in humans or do we all find the same faces more attractive? When do we begin to show any preference to attractive faces? Earlier studies had shown that young infants appear to be drawn to faces that adults have rated as being attractive over those rated not so attractive. This had surprised psychologists as they had not expected any form of discrimination based on attractiveness at such a young age. One aspect of this that had not been tested was whether this phenomenon extended across faces of difference races and ages too.

>
> **ASK YOURSELF**
> What makes someone attractive? Is it the person's face or is there more to it than simply physical features?

AIM

To investigate whether infant preferences for attractive faces extended beyond those for adult female faces on to other types of faces (e.g. male and female adult White faces, adult Black female faces and other young infants). The aims of each study appear in its Design section.

Three studies were conducted.

METHOD

Design (study 1)

Control This first study investigated whether infants show preference to attractive male and female adult faces compared to those rated unattractive.

This study used 16 slides of women's faces and 16 slides of men's faces. The researchers had used them before; half were rated attractive and half unattractive. The final slides had been **Quant** selected from 275 women's and 165 men's faces that had been rated for attractiveness by 40 undergraduates. All of the slides that were rated attractive and unattractive were then looked at further. The final slides that were chosen had to show facial expressions, hair length and hair colour roughly evenly distributed across the attractive and unattractive groups. All the males were clean shaven. Any clothing was masked and the person pictured had to have a neutral pose. The mean ratings for attractiveness (out of 5) were 3.46 (female attractive), 3.35 (male attractive), 1.44 (female unattractive), 1.40 (male unattractive).

Participants (study 1)

A total of 110 infants, who were 6 months old, were recruited via the Children's Research Laboratory at the University of Texas. A total of 50 of these were eliminated from the final sample for **Sample** the following reasons: fussing too much (n = 41), computer failure (n = 3), experimenter error (n = 3) parent looked at the slides (n = 2) and child was premature (n = 1). This left 60 children (35 boys and 25 girls) with an average age of 6 months and 6 days. Fifty three of the children were White, five were Hispanic, one was Black and one was Asian. All were tested within three weeks of their sixth birthday.

Procedure (study 1)

Two faces, one attractive and one unattractive, were projected onto a screen next to each other. Each child sat on his or her parent's lap around 35cm from the screen. The parent wore occluded glasses so he or she could not see the faces. This prevented any of the parent's preferences being seen by the child. A light and buzzer sounded to grab the child's attention every time a new pair of faces was presented. Once the child had focused on the centre of the screen the pair of faces would appear. The trial was labelled "began" when the child first looked at one of the slides. Each trial lasted for ten seconds.

Reliable Two sets of 16 slides were used per child. Each set was divided into eight trial blocks of two slides each. In an attempt to control for "side bias" in the child (e.g. prefers to look to the right naturally), slide pairs were alternated throughout the procedure. All slide pairs were both male or both female. Slides were presented in one of two ways: alternating (pairs of males then females then males, etc.) or grouped (all male then all female). After every eight trial block there was a five- to ten-minute break to stop the child getting tired or bored. The order in which slides appeared was randomised for each child. Trial length, slide movement and recording of data were controlled by a computer.

The experimenter observed the visual fixations of each child in each trial on a video monitor connected to a video camera mounted just under the screen the slides were projected onto. The direction of looks and their duration were recorded. Using this televised image of the child, the experimenter did not have to look at the projection screen and therefore did not know which of the two slides was the attractive or unattractive one. Reliability was checked via a randomly selected sample of recordings. As some of the infants' data were excluded as a result of them "fussing", the research team had to agree that the child had been engaged in this behaviour before withdrawing the data for that trial.

Finally, to examine whether the child's preference might be influenced by the attractiveness of the mother, photographs of each mother were rated by 72 undergraduates.

 TEST YOURSELF
How were the faces on the slides chosen? How easy would it be to replicate this study? Why?

Design (study 2)

Control The design was similar to that for study 1 but with the following changes:

▶ The slides were of 16 Black women from a pool of 197 faces rated for attractiveness by 98 White and 41 Black undergraduates.

▶ Amount of hair and skin colour were evenly distributed across conditions.

▶ Mean attractiveness for attractive group was 3.41 (White raters) and 3.42 (Black raters) and for the unattractive group it was 1.44 (White raters) and 1.54 (Black raters). **Quant**

Participants (study 2)

A total of 43 infants, who were 6 months old, were recruited via the Children's Research Laboratory at the University of Texas. Three of these were eliminated from the final sample for the following reasons: fussing too much (n = 2) and equipment failure (n = 1). This left 40 children (15 boys and 25 girls) with an average age of 6 months and 5 days. Thirty six of the children were White, two were Hispanic and two were Black.

Procedure (study 2)

The procedure was similar to that for study 1 but with the following changes:

▶ Presentation was not alternating versus grouped as children only looked at Black women's faces.

▶ Each trial block consisted of four pairs of slides.

▶ The faces of the infants' mothers were rated for attractiveness by 49 undergraduates.

Design (study 3)

The design was similar to that for study 1 but with the following changes: **Control**

▶ The slides were of 16 infants who were 3 months old selected from a pool of 60 boys and 62 girls rated for attractiveness by 40 undergraduates.

▶ Slides showing four males and four females who had been rated attractive were used, as were slides of four males and four females rated unattractive.

▶ On the slides all clothing was masked and the faces had neutral expressions. Amount of hair was equally distributed across the attractiveness conditions.

▶ The mean attractiveness ratings were 3.02 for the attractive group and 1.69 for the unattractive group. **Quant**

Participants (study 3)

A total of 52 infants, who were 6 months old, were recruited via the Children's Research Laboratory at the University of Texas. A total of 11 of these were eliminated from the final sample for fussing too much (n = 11). Two more were excluded as they were not tested within three weeks of their sixth birthday. This left 39 children (19 boys and 20 girls) with an average age of 6 months and 15 days. Thirty seven of the children were White and two were Hispanic.

Procedure (study 3)

This was the same as for study 2 except attractiveness ratings for the infants' mothers taken.

RESULTS (COMBINED)

Quant For all studies, the time looking at each slide for each child was calculated. This was done by adding together the looking time for the right-side presentation and the left-side presentation of each face. Table 5.2 shows the results.

Type of face	High attractiveness		Low attractiveness	
	M	SD	M	SD
Study 1: Male and female faces	7.82	1.35	7.57	1.27
Study 2: Black female faces	7.05	1.83	6.52	1.92
Study 3: Children's faces	7.16	1.97	6.62	1.83

▲ **Table 5.2** Mean fixation times for high- and low-attractiveness slides

Study 1: Children looked significantly longer at attractive faces unattractive ones. Sex of face had no effect – children looked longer at any attractive face.

They tended to look at same-sex faces for longer (only significant for males) – see Table 5.3. No significant relationship was found between mother's attractiveness and the child's preference.

Sex of infant	Male face		Female face	
	M	SD	M	SD
Male	7.95	1.45	7.36	1.31
Female	7.69	1.35	7.81	1.33

▲ **Table 5.3** Mean fixation times for sex of child participant × sex of face interaction

Study 2: Children looked longer at the attractive Black woman's faces than the unattractive ones. Children looked for longer at any face on their first two trials compared to all of the other trials. There was no significant effect of maternal attractiveness.

Study 3: Children looked longer at the attractive baby faces than the unattractive ones. As with study 2, children looked for longer at any face on their first two trials compared to all of the other trials.

TEST YOURSELF
Outline three main findings from these studies. How valid are the findings? Why?

CONCLUSION

All three studies show that infants prefer attractive faces compared to unattractive faces irrespective of gender, colour of skin and age. Therefore, it would appear that children can discriminate from an early age between attractive and unattractive faces. As the children had not been exposed to much media depicting what is attractive, it could be argued that these preferences are inbuilt into humans.

EVALUATION

Since Langlois *et al* used a laboratory experiment, we can use the general evaluations from Chapter 1, page 1 onwards and apply them directly to the study:

Evaluation	General evaluation (laboratory experiments)	Related to Langlois *et al*
Strength	Laboratory experiments have high levels of control and so can be replicated to test for reliability.	There were many controls in this study (e.g. the standardised procedure followed, the time the slides were projected for and the masking of other cues in the slides). Another research team could easily replicate this study to test for reliability using a different sample.
Strength	As laboratory experiments have high levels of control, researchers can be more confident it is the IV directly affecting the DV.	As there were controls (e.g. the time the slides were projected for and how the slides were chosen) Langlois *et al* could be confident it was attractiveness of the face that was causing the child to look at them for longer.
Weakness	As laboratory experiments take place in an artificial setting, it is said that they can lack ecological validity.	Looking at a projector and having computer and video equipment nearby is not a usual setting for young children so it is difficult to know if they would prefer attractive faces in a more natural setting. Therefore, the study has low ecological validity.
Weakness	Many laboratory experiments make participants take part in tasks that are nothing like real-life ones so they lack mundane realism.	In this study the child sat on the parent's lap, the parent wore occluded glasses and then pairs of faces were shown to the child who was monitored on what he or she was looking at. These things do not happen to children in everyday life so the study lacks mundane realism.

Other points that can be used to evaluate the study include these:

▶ Quantitative data: mean fixation times were taken (and assessed via reliability tests) so the findings are objective. The mean fixation times across all three studies could be reliably compared to draw objective conclusions (e.g. young children do fixate more often on faces that have been rated attractive than those rated unattractive). However, we do not know the reasons *why* this happened as the data were quantitative and the young children could not tell us anyway.

Quant

▶ Ethics: use of children in research. Even though the parents gave permission for their children to be used in the study (they were from a bank of children who could be used in research) we do not know how distressed, etc. it made the children looking at lots of pictures – remember quite a few younger children (especially in study 1) were eliminated as they were "fussing too much".

Children

CHALLENGE YOURSELF
Evaluate this study in terms of the nature-nurture debate and usefulness. You may want to use a table like those used for the laboratory experiment and evaluation above.

Exam centre

Try the following exam-style questions.

Paper 1

1. In the Langlois *et al* study, how were the faces chosen for the final slides? (2 marks)

2. Outline **two** controls that Langlois *et al* used in their study. (4 marks)

3. Identify **two** features of the any sample used in the Langlois *et al* study. (2 marks)

4. Evaluate the Langlois *et al* study in terms of **one** strength and **one** weakness. (10 marks)

Paper 2

1. Outline what quantitative data were collected in the Langlois *et al* study. (3 marks)

2. Redesign the Langlois *et al* study using self-report (e.g. questionnaires) or interviews as the research method. (10 marks)

3. Discuss the strengths and weaknesses of the nature-nurture debate using Langlois *et al* as an example. (10 marks)

CORE STUDY 5.4

Nelson (1980)

CONTEXT

Psychologists interested in the development of moral behaviour have created theories that attempt to explain how children develop a sense of right and wrong. Piaget noted that in children under 10 years of age there appeared to be no solid role of the motive behind the behaviour in judging how "morally correct" a behaviour is. After the age of 10 years, children seemingly develop a skill in morally judging behaviour based on its motive. However, research after Piaget developed these initial ideas showed that children as young as 6 years old would often look at the motive behind a behaviour before morally judging it. Studies had already tried to see whether children as young as 3 years old use motives to judge behaviours but they had been methodologically flawed, according to Nelson. They had not allowed children to show whether they understood the motive behind behaviour before judging. Children this young might believe that motives are important but fail to interpret them correctly or remember them when questioned – they may misinterpret the intentions of the motive as set out by an adult.

> **ASK YOURSELF**
> How do people develop a sense of what is right and wrong? Are we born with morals or do we learn them through experiences?

AIM

To investigate whether children as young as 3 years old use motives and outcomes when morally judging behaviours that are explicit and relevant to them (and are available when judging).

METHOD

Two studies were conducted.

Design (study 1)

Four versions of a story were used. Each involved a boy throwing a ball (chosen as pilot research had seen this as a neutral act). However, the motive and outcome differed:

> **Control**

Story (IV)	Content
Good motive	The boy was playing with a ball. His friend did not have anything to play with. He wanted to throw the ball to his friend so they could play.
Bad motive	The boy was playing with a ball. He was angry with his friend. He wanted to throw the ball at his friend to hit him on purpose.
Good outcome	The boy threw the ball, his friend caught it and they played happily.
Bad outcome	The boy threw the ball but his friend did not catch it. The ball hit his friend on the head and made him cry.

In addition to the story, there were two sets of drawings to accompany each story. They were 25cm by 23cm illustrating the motive, behaviour and outcome. An example is shown in Figure 5.1.

▲ **Figure 5.1** Drawings to accompany the story

Each set conveyed the motive in different ways. One set conveyed emotion via facial expressions only (implicit motive) while the other set conveyed it explicitly by connecting cartoon-like representations of the goal to the head of the boy throwing the ball (explicit motive).

Children who judged the boy throwing the ball as being "good" had to point at one of three smiling faces (5.5 to 7.5cm in size) which represented "a little bit good" to "very good".

> **Control**

This technique was also used, but with frowning faces, if a child judged the boy throwing the ball as being "bad". A seventh face, 4.5cm in size, represented "just okay" (a term used as many children in a pilot used it to convey a neutral judgment). All of these were combined to create a numerical score per judgment from 1 (very bad) through to 7 (very good).

Participants (study 1)

There were 60 pre-school children used for study 1, with a roughly equal split between males and females. They

were all 3–4 years old (average 3.4 years). In addition, 30 "second grade" children were used aged between 6 and 8 years (average 7.4 years). There was a roughly even split between males and females. They were mostly white, middle-class and living in urban areas. Parents gave consent for their children to take part.

Procedure (study 1)

Children of each age group were randomly assigned to one of the three presentations (verbal, motive implicit

and motive explicit). There were 20 children per group in the young group and 10 per group in the older group. Each child heard all four stories. They were randomised per child.

Each child was tested individually by the interviewer. Before the stories were told, children familiarised themselves with the 7-point faces scale via two stories (one about being very good and one about being very bad). Children in the picture groups were also familiarised with how the pictures worked.

In the actual study, children were told to listen very carefully to each story as they would be expected to tell it

Reliable

again later. After each story had been told, children were asked whether the boy had been a good boy, a bad boy or just okay. Then they were asked to indicate via the faces how good or bad the boy had been. If children were in one of the picture conditions, the pictures were introduced at the appropriate time in the story. They remained in front of children until they made their judgment.

After children had made their judgments, the pictures were removed (in the picture condition groups) and children were asked to re-tell the story aloud to the interviewer. If the motive or outcome was missing from their account, specific questions were asked such as "Why did the boy throw his ball?"

TEST YOURSELF
Who were the participants in study 1 and how were they recruited? Are there any ethical issues raised by study 1? Why?

RESULTS (STUDY 1)

Table 5.4 shows the mean ratings per combination by age.

	3-year-olds (n = 60)		7-year-olds (n = 30)	
	Good motive	Bad motive	Good motive	Bad motive
Good outcome	6.55	2.27	6.20	3.46
Bad outcome	4.17	1.60	4.47	1.56

▲ Table 5.4 Mean ratings per combination by age

Overall, the main character in the good motive conditions combined had an average score of 5.35 whereas for the main character in the bad motive conditions it was 2.27. This was statistically significant. There was a similar pattern for outcomes: good outcomes scored 4.70 on average and bad outcomes only 2.92. When the motive or outcome was bad (especially so for the motive) it had a larger effect on judgments than if anything was seen as being good. Also, when the motive information was explicit (good *or* bad) it had a greater effect on judgments than when it was implicit or verbal only. Children appeared to use the outcome information in the good motive stories under all three conditions, but for the bad motive stories this was only for those who saw pictures. Children in the younger group made more errors in recall for motives and outcomes than those in the older group. There was no effect of presentation (verbal or picture) on outcome recall errors, but for motive recall errors there were fewer errors when pictures were presented. Additionally, there were significantly more errors of recall in the younger group when the motive and the outcome were incongruent (e.g. good motive but bad outcome). Finally, 40 per cent of the younger group rated the boy throwing the ball negatively whenever there was just one negative cue, irrespective of its source (motive or outcome). A further 28.33 per cent of the younger group ignored the outcome information and based their judgment on the valence of the motive only.

 These findings may well suggest that younger children understand the concept of bad before they understand the concept of good.

Design (study 2)

This study was based on the idea that in study 1 children in the younger group in the verbal-only story condition were basing their entire judgment on the motive but not the outcome, perhaps because the motive was always presented before the outcome. So, if younger children are more interested in valence (e.g. good, bad, positive, negative) rather than its source (motive or outcome) then reversing the order (so outcome comes before motive), should mean younger children should disregard the motive whenever there is a bad outcome. This is what study 2 tested. The design was exactly the same as study 1 *but* the outcome came before the motive in the stories.

Participants (study 2)

Twenty-seven pre-school children with a mean age of 3.8 years participated in study 2. Each child was randomly assigned to one of the three presentation types (verbal only, motive-implicit picture and motive-explicit picture). Everything was identical to study 1 but the description of the outcome came *before* that of the motive.

RESULTS (STUDY 2)

Table 5.5 highlights the mean ratings per combination of presentation, outcome and motive.

	Good outcome		Bad outcome	
	Good motive	Bad motive	Good motive	Bad motive
Verbal only	6.11	3.56	2.67	1.78
Picture – motive implicit	7.00	2.11	2.33	1.11
Picture – motive explicit	7.00	3.56	4.22	1.11

▲ Table 5.5 Mean rating per combination of presentation, outcome and motive

The main finding was that children in the verbal-only condition were less influenced by motive than those in both picture conditions (see the scores above). Also, even with the outcome *preceding* the motive, the effect of motive on judgments was not less than that of outcome (remember in study 1 the motive came first and children could just have been basing judgments on the first thing they heard). Children also made more errors of recall when the motive and outcome were incongruent (e.g. bad motive, good outcome).

TEST YOURSELF
Outline one main finding from both studies. What do the studies tell us about moral development (e.g. are they useful)?

CONCLUSION

Motive is a powerful tool used by younger children to make a moral judgment. Also, the mode of presentation affects the judgments of younger children with verbal-only presentation of material; as soon as a child hears something "bad" any further information has limited impact on judgments. However, if the presentation involves pictures the judgments are based on a combination of both outcome (good and bad) and motive (good and bad). Younger children are more likely to recall information on moral judgments more accurately if congruence is experienced (e.g. good motive and good outcome) rather than incongruence.

CORE STUDY 6.2

Dement & Kleitman (1957)

CONTEXT

The topics of sleep and dreaming are clearly hard to investigate because the participant is necessarily asleep and so cannot communicate with the researcher. Even when participants are awake, only self-report data can be obtained about dream content and these alone might not be valid, as they are subjective. The study of sleep and dreaming became more scientifically rigorous with the invention of physiological techniques to measure brain activity that indicated dreaming (the electro-encephalograph, or EEG) and allowed the electrical recording of eye movements (the electro-oculogram, or EOG) rather than their direct observation. These techniques were used by Dement & Kleitman to trace the cyclical changes that occur in brain activity and eye movements during a night's sleep. The cycle alternates between a stage in which there are eye movements, and several stages during which there are none.

In the dream or rapid eye movement (REM) sleep stage, our eyes move under the lids (hence "rapid eye movement"). In Aserinsky & Kleitman's (1955) study, participants woken from this stage were more likely to report a vivid, visual dream, than participants woken from non-rapid eye movement (nREM) sleep. Non-REM sleep can be broken down into four stages (1 to 4), of which 1 is the lightest and 4 the deepest.

REM sleep resembles wakefulness in some ways: our eyes move, we often experience vivid (if bizarre) thoughts in the form of dreams, and our brains are active. However, in other ways it is very different from wakefulness: we are quite difficult to wake up, we are fairly insensitive to external stimuli, and we are paralysed. As REM sleep presents these contradictions, it is also known as paradoxical sleep.

An electro-encephalograph (EEG) detects and records tiny electrical changes associated with nerve and muscle activity. The EEG machine produces a chart (an encephalogram) that shows brain waves (see Figure 6.1). These change with the frequency and amplitude (i.e. the "height", which indicates the voltage) of electrical output from the brain over time. In REM sleep, the EEG is relatively low voltage, high amplitude. Non-REM sleep has either high voltage and slow (low amplitude) waves, or frequent "sleep spindles", which are short-lived high-voltage, high-frequency waves.

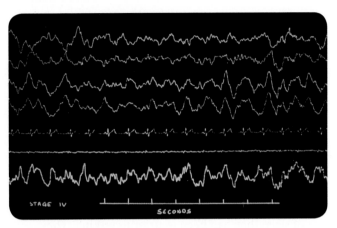

▲ **Figure 6.1** Measures such as frequency and amplitude of brain waves measured with an EEG are ratio scales.

Modern EEG machines are entirely computerised, whereas Dement and Kleitman's EEG had continuously running paper. The faster the paper moved, the more detail could be recorded. The paper was usually moving at 3mm or 6mm per second, although a faster speed of 3cm per second was used for detailed analysis.

To remember the meaning of EEG it can help to break the word down:

▶ electro (electric)

▶ en cephalo (in head)

▶ graph (writing).

The same EEG electrodes and machine can also be used to record eye movements. The output – called an electro-oculogram (EOG) – indicates the presence or absence of eye movements, their size and their direction (horizontal or vertical).

 ASK YOURSELF
Do you remember your dreams? Do you always remember certain types of dream?

AIM

To investigate dreaming in an objective way by looking for relationships between eye movements in sleep and the dreamer's recall. These included whether dream recall differs between REM and nREM sleep, whether there is a positive correlation between subjective estimates of dream duration and the length of the REM period and whether eye-movement patterns are related to dream content.

METHOD

This study included several laboratory investigations with different designs. Three specific approaches were used to test the three aims:

▶ To test whether dream recall differs between REM and nREM sleep: participants were woken either in REM or nREM, but were not told which stage of sleep they had been in prior to waking. They confirmed whether they had been having a dream and, if so, described the content into a recorder.

▶ To test whether subjective estimates of dream duration are related to the length of the REM period: participants were woken following either 5 or 15 minutes in REM sleep. They were asked to choose whether they thought they had been dreaming for 5 or 15 minutes. Longer REM periods were also tested. Again, they gave a report of dream content and the number of words in the dream narrative was counted.

▶ To test whether eye-movement patterns represent the visual experience of the dream content or whether they are simply random movements arising from the activation of the central nervous system during dream sleep: the direction of eye movements was detected using electrodes around the eyes (EOG). Participants were woken after exhibiting a single eye-movement pattern for longer than one minute. Again, they were asked to report their dream.

Design

Dement & Kleitman described this series of studies as experiments. Approach 1 was a natural experiment in a laboratory setting and approach 2 was a true experiment, with each participant being tested

Lab

in both conditions, i.e. they used a repeated measures design. Approach 2 also included a correlation:

Design

▶ Approach 1: the levels of the IV were REM sleep/non-REM sleep and the DV was whether a dream was reported and, if so, the detail.

▶ Approach 2: the data were used in both experimental and correlational designs.

Experimental analysis: the levels of the IV were waking after 5 or 15 minutes, and the DV was the participant's choice of 5 or 15 minutes.

Correlational analysis: the two variables were the participant's time estimate and the number of words in the dream narrative.

▶ Approach 3: the IV of eye-movement pattern type could not be manipulated by the researchers, so this was also a natural experiment (conducted in a laboratory). The DV was the report of dream content.

Participants

Nine adult participants were used in this study (seven male and two female). Four of these were mainly used to confirm the data from five who were studied in detail. Those studied in detail spent between 6 and 17 nights in the laboratory and were tested with 50–77 awakenings. Those used to confirm the findings stayed only one or two nights and were awoken between four and ten times in total. Each participant was identified by a pair of initials.

TEST YOURSELF
Outline how the three approaches in this study were designed.

Procedure

During the daytime prior to arrival at the laboratory, participants ate normally (excluding drinks containing alcohol or caffeine). They arrived at the laboratory just before their normal bedtime and were fitted with electrical recording apparatus. This included electrodes attached near the eyes (to record eye movements) and on the scalp (to record brain waves). Once the participant was in bed in

EcoV

a quiet, dark room, wires from the electrodes (which fed to the EEG in the experimenter's room) were gathered into a "pony tail" from the person's head, to allow freedom of movement. The EEG ran continuously through the night to monitor the participant's sleep stages and to inform the experimenters when the participant should be woken up. Participants were woken by a doorbell that was loud enough to rouse them from any sleep stage. This meant that the experimenter did not have to enter the rooms to wake participants, and thus they were all treated in exactly the same way. The doorbell was rung at various times during the night and participants indicated whether they had been dreaming prior to being woken and, if so, described their dream into a voice recorder. They then returned to sleep (typically within five minutes). Occasionally, the experimenter entered the room after the participant had finished speaking, in order to ask questions. When the narrative was analysed, it was considered to be a dream only if it was a coherent, fairly detailed description of the content (i.e. vague, fragmentary impressions were not scored as dreams).

The patterns of REM and nREM wakings differed between different participants, whose initials are used here. For PM and KC, wakings were determined randomly to eliminate any possibility of an unintentional pattern. WD was treated in the same way, although he was told that he would be woken only from dream sleep. DN was woken in a repeating pattern of three REM followed by three nREM awakenings. The waking of IR from REM or nREM was chosen by the experimenter.

RESULTS

Quantitative and qualitative data were gathered in response to approaches 1 and 2. Only qualitative data were gathered for approach 3.

Results for approach 1

Does dream recall differ between REM and nREM sleep?

Participants described dreams often when woken in REM but rarely from nREM sleep (although there were some individual differences). This pattern was consistent over the night. When awakened from nREM, participants tended to describe feelings (e.g. pleasantness, anxiety, detachment) but this did not relate to specific dream content.

Table 6.4 shows dream recall following wakings from REM and non-REM sleep.

Sleep stage (level of IV)	REM-sleep awakenings		Non-REM-sleep awakenings	
	Dream recall	No recall	Dream recall	No recall
Number of times participants reported the presence or absence of a dream (DV)	152	39	11	149

▲ **Table 6.4** Instances of dream recall following waking from REM and non-REM sleep

Waking pattern did not affect recall. Specifically, WD was no less accurate despite being misled, and DN was no more accurate even though he might have guessed the pattern of wakings. Recall of dreams during nREM sleep was much more likely when the participant was woken soon after the end of a REM stage.

So, REM and nREM sleep differ as the vivid, visual dreams are reported only from waking during, or a short time after, REM sleep.

Results for approach 2

Are subjective estimates of dream duration related to the length of the REM period?

Initially, the researchers had attempted to wake participants after various REM durations to ask them to estimate these. Although participants' responses weren't wildly wrong, the task was too difficult. When asked instead whether they had been in REM sleep for 5 or 15 minutes, participants responded more accurately. They were 88 per cent and 78 per cent accurate respectively for 5- or 15-minute REM durations (see Figure 6.2).

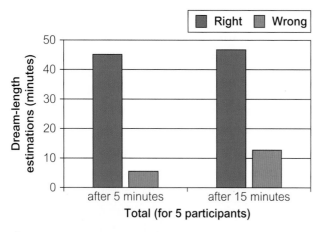

▲ **Figure 6.2** Accuracy of dream-length estimations after 5 or 15 minutes of REM sleep

Although most of the participants were highly accurate (with only 0–3 incorrect responses), one was not. Participant DN frequently found he could recall only the end of his dream, so it seemed shorter than it actually was. Therefore, he consistently underestimated dream duration, often choosing 5 minutes instead of 15. This meant he was accurate on short REM estimates (making only two errors over ten wakings), but inaccurate after 15 minutes' of REM (making five errors over ten wakings).

Using REM periods over a range of durations, narratives from 152 dreams were collected. However, 26 of these could not be used as they were too poorly recorded for accurate transcription. For the remaining dreams (15–35 per participant) the number of words in the dream narrative was counted. Even though this was affected by how expressive the participant was, a significant positive correlation was found between REM duration and number of words in the narrative. The values varied between 0.4 and 0.71 for different participants.

Quant

Dream narratives for very long durations (e.g. 30 or 50 minutes) were not much longer than those for 15 minutes. Participants did report, however, that they felt as though they had been dreaming for a long time, suggesting that they could not recall the early part of the dream.

Results for approach 3

Do eye movement patterns in REM sleep represent the visual experience of the dream?

The researchers found that participants' narratives were not sufficiently accurate to be matched exactly to the changes in eye-movement patterns over the length of a REM sleep period. Instead, participants were woken after periods of specific eye-movement patterns (vertical, horizontal, both of these or little movement).

Three of the nine participants showed periods of predominantly vertical eye movements, and each was allied to a narrative about vertical movement. In one, the participant dreamed about standing at the foot of a tall cliff, using a hoist (a kind of winch or pulley). The person reported looking up at climbers at various levels on the cliff, and down at the hoist machinery. A single dream followed predominantly horizontal movements. Here, the participant reported dreaming about two people throwing tomatoes at each other.

Qual

On ten occasions participants were woken after little or no eye movement. Here, they reported either watching something in the distance or staring with their eyes fixed on a single object. In two cases, participants had been dreaming about driving. Their eyes had been very still, then made several sudden movements to the left just before being woken up. One participant reported a pedestrian standing on the left who hailed him as he drove by, and the other had been startled by a speeding car appearing to his left as he arrived at a junction.

There were 21 wakings following mixed eye movements. In these instances, participants reported looking at people or objects nearby (rather than far away) – e.g. in fighting or talking to a group of people.

Dement & Kleitman also recorded the eye movements of people when they were awake (including the five original participants and some other, naïve ones). These findings confirmed that, when awake, our eyes are relatively stable when we are focused on objects in the distance, and show movements of similar amplitude to when we are dreaming of viewing nearby objects (i.e. many small but frequent and predominantly horizontal movements). Few vertical movements were recorded except when the experimenter threw a ball in the air for participants to watch (and when they blinked).

	Time of waking after REM stage	
	Within 8 minutes	After 8 minutes
Number of wakings conducted	17	132
Number of dreams recalled	5	6
Percentage of occasions on which dreams recalled	29	5

▲ **Table 6.5** Number of dreams recalled following wakings from nREM sleep after an REM stage

Table 6.5 shows that when woken from nREM sleep, participants returned to nREM and the next REM stage was not delayed. When woken from REM sleep, participants generally did not dream again until the next REM phase.

quant

TEST YOURSELF
Outline four different results from this study.

CONCLUSIONS

Dement & Kleitman drew three main conclusions from this study, one in relation to each approach:

1. Dreams probably (although not certainly) occur only during REM sleep, which occurs regularly throughout each night's sleep. Dreams reported when woken from nREM sleep are ones from previous REM episodes. As the REM phases are longer later in the night, dreaming is more likely at this time. Earlier research found that dreams did not occur every night. This study suggests three possible explanations for this difference:

  (a) If previous recordings were not continuous, they may have failed to "catch" instances of dream sleep in every participant (if short REM periods occurred between sampling intervals).

  (b) Equipment might not have detected small eye movements.

  (c) Participants in whom no dreaming was identified might have had dreams that led to few eye movements, such as those about distant or static objects.

2. It is often believed that dreams happen in an instant. If the length of REM periods is proportional to subjective estimates, this would help to confirm that the two are related and would provide some information about the rate at which dreaming progresses. The finding that the length of an REM period and its estimation by the participant are very similar shows that dreams are not instantaneous events but rather they are experienced in "real time".

3. Eye movements during REM sleep correspond to where, and at what, the dreamer is looking in the dream. This suggests that eye movements are not simply random events caused by the activation of the central nervous system during dream sleep, but are directly related to dream imagery. Furthermore, they correspond in amplitude and pattern to those we experience when awake.

EVALUATION

Since Dement & Kleitman used a laboratory experiment, we can use the general evaluations from Chapter 1, page 1 and apply them directly to the study:

Evaluation	General evaluation (laboratory experiments)	Related to Dement & Kleitman
Strength	Laboratory experiments have high levels of control and so can be replicated to test for reliability.	Dement & Kleitman controlled many variables (e.g. pre-study levels of caffeine and alcohol, the doorbell sound, the EEG monitoring). This means that another researcher could easily replicate this study to test it for reliability.
Strength	As laboratory experiments have high levels of control, researchers can be more confident it is the IV directly affecting the DV.	The high level of control of variables (see above) meant that for each part of the experiment, Dement & Kleitman could confidently conclude cause and effect (e.g. that dream recall is affected by stage of sleep).
Weakness	As laboratory experiments take place in an artificial setting, it is said that they can lack ecological validity.	Participants had to sleep in an artificial setting (in a laboratory, with electrodes on their head). Therefore, the study has low ecological validity.
Weakness	Many laboratory experiments make participants take part in tasks that are nothing like real-life ones so they lack mundane realism.	Being woken up and then asking to recall dream content or estimate dream length is not a normal activity for people. Therefore, the study lacks mundane realism.

Other points that can be used to evaluate the study include these:

▶ Generalisability: only five people were studied "in detail" and four more used to confirm the findings. This could make it difficult to generalise **Gen** beyond the sample of people because of the sample size. These five + four people may not represent a wide cross-section of society in terms of how we dream and what we dream about.

▶ Reductionism: the findings are all based around biological mechanisms affecting our dreaming state. Some psychologists may see this as being reductionist as there are psychological mechanisms that could be affecting dream content.

> **CHALLENGE YOURSELF**
> Evaluate the Dement & Kleitman study in terms of it being a snapshot study and that it collected quantitative and qualitative data. You may want to use a table similar to that used for the laboratory experiment.

Exam centre

Try the following exam-style questions.

Paper 1

1. Outline **two** aims of the Dement & Kleitman study. (4 marks)

2. Outline **one** quantitative finding of the Dement & Kleitman study. (2 marks)

3. Evaluate the Dement & Kleitman study in terms of **one** strength and **one** weakness. (10 marks)

Paper 2

1. Outline how qualitative data were collected in the Dement & Kleitman study. (3 marks)

2. Outline how the Dement & Kleitman study is testing the physiological approach to psychology. (3 marks)

3. Redesign the Dement & Kleitman study using self-report as the research method. (10 marks)

4. Discuss the strengths and weaknesses of laboratory experiments using the Dement & Kleitman study as an example. (10 marks)

CORE STUDY 6.3

Maguire, Frackowiak & Frith (1997)

CONTEXT

Psychologists conducting research about memory are finding that different types of memory system are located in different parts of the brain. One of these memory system has only recently begun to be studied: topographical memory, which consists of memories that allow us to navigate and find our way around familiar environments. Thinking of a route you take quite often with all of the landmarks that you pass activates topographical memories. If the route has some meaning to you it is called a topographical semantic memory. As you are visualising your route, you are using what psychologists call a cognitive map – a "mental map" that helps you visualise your route before you embark on your journey. It also allows you to recollect your route after your journey and you may add to it if a new landmark becomes part of the route. All of this takes place in your brain and until this study little was known about which specific area(s) of the brain allow you to use cognitive maps, remember routes or visualise a route from A to B even though you never have travelled that route before – the latter is what taxi drivers do on a regular basis.

ASK YOURSELF
How do you find your way home or to some other place? Do you use landmarks or visualise the route?

AIM

To investigate: whether there are specific brain regions that are responsible for semantic topographical memory (in this study, routes that had been or could be used by taxi drivers in London); whether there were brain functioning differences between tasks that involved topographical or non-topographical memories; and if these two types of memories were affected by whether the memory was a sequence of logical events or not.

METHOD

Design

Participants had to complete six tasks. Each task was performed twice. Five were relevant to the current study. It was a repeated measures design with all participants completing all tasks (counterbalanced too). The whole design was a 2 × 2 design with topographical/non-topographical being factor 1 and sequencing/non-sequencing being factor 2. Table 6.6 shows the set-up.

Design

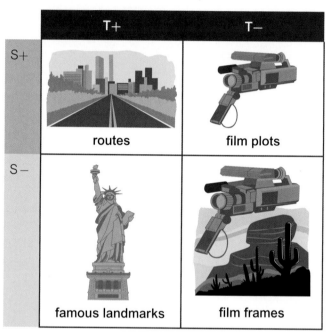

▲ Table 6.6 T+ means it is testing topographical; S− means it is testing non-sequencing

These were the five tasks:

1. Describe the shortest route between a starting point and a destination in the City of London. (Topographical and sequencing.)

2. Describe a landmark known to the taxi drivers (all world-famous ones) in terms of features, appearance, etc. (Topographical and non-sequencing.)

3. Describe the plot of a film (familiar to the participant) between two given points in the film. (Non-topographical and sequencing.)

4. Describe individual frames of some famous films (familiar to the participant) – not the plot but the imagery, characters, etc. (Non-topographical and non-sequencing.)

Procedure

Each participant sat on a chair that was 70cm from a computer screen. A chin rest was used keep the person's head stable. Figure 6.3 shows the order of events for one trial.

EcoV

The order of events was as follows:

1. Participants were told to look at a cross on the screen.

Reliable

2. They were told to exhale as soon as they heard a quiet tone.

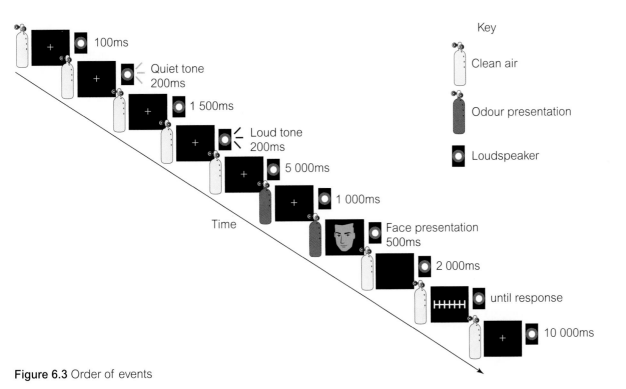

Key

🛢 Clean air

🛢 Odour presentation

◉ Loudspeaker

- 100ms
- Quiet tone 200ms
- 1 500ms
- Loud tone 200ms
- 5 000ms
- 1 000ms
- Face presentation 500ms
- 2 000ms
- until response
- 10 000ms

Time

Figure 6.3 Order of events

3. They were told to inhale through the nostrils as soon as they heard a loud tone.

4. 500ms after they had performed step 3, one of the four odours (or clean air) was delivered.

5. Participants had to decide if an odour had been presented or not.

6. 1 000ms after the odour had been delivered, the cross disappeared on the monitor and a face appeared for 500ms. When the face disappeared any odour that was being delivered was replaced with clean air.

7. The screen then turned black for 2 000ms then participants were presented with a 9-point rating scale. They had to rate the face for attractiveness (1 being least attractive and 9 being most attractive).

8. As soon as the response had been logged, the fixation cross reappeared 10 000ms before the next trial began.

9. There was a rest period of 5 minutes after each block of 40 trials.

At the end of each session, participants had to rate each odour on three dimensions (intensity, pleasantness and familiarity). They used a labelled magnitude scale (LMS) – a line with 0 at one end and 100 at the other for them to mark with a pen where their response lay. The order of presentation of the scale and the odour was randomised between participants.

Quant

TEST YOURSELF
What was the sample used in this study? How was the attractiveness of the faces rated? What were the two "pleasant odours" used in the study?

RESULTS

Table 6.7 shows the mean attractiveness ratings across all odours.

Quant

Statistical analysis showed that faces were rated less attractive when an unpleasant odour was presented compared to a pleasant odour. However, there was no significant difference in attractiveness ratings for pleasant odours compared to clean air.

When the scores for both pleasant odours and both unpleasant odours were merged, the average ratings for attractiveness were as follows: clean air (4.90), pleasant odours (4.85) and unpleasant odours (4.42).

The LMS data showed that the pleasant and unpleasant odours were more intense than clean air (as expected). The unpleasant odours were indeed rated less pleasant than the pleasant odours.

TEST YOURSELF
Describe the study to a friend or family member in terms of a brief aim, what the researchers did, what the key findings were and what it all means.

CONCLUSION

It appears that olfactory cues can regulate perception of facial attractiveness. Participants consistently rated faces as less attractive when presented with an unpleasant odour.

Ind vs Sit

CHALLENGE YOURSELF
The researchers chose to use a laboratory experiment for this study. Redesign the study as a case study of one participant. Include who will be taking part, what design decisions you need to make, how you will run the study, and when and where it will take place.

Quant

Facial attractiveness	Odour	Mean (SD)			
	Clean air	Geranium	Gravity	Body odour	Rubber
High	5.70 (0.21)	5.40 (0.23)	5.73 (0.24)	5.39 (0.21)	4.96 (0.25)
Low	4.10 (0.16)	4.06 (0.20)	4.15 (0.20)	3.64 (0.21)	3.72 (0.23)

▲ Table 6.7 Mean attractiveness ratings

EVALUATION

Since Demattè, Österbauer & Spence a laboratory experiment, we can use the general evaluations from Chapter 1, pages 1–2 and apply them directly to the study:

Evaluation	General evaluation (laboratory experiments)	Related to Demattè, Österbauer & Spence
Strength	Laboratory experiments have high levels of control and so can be replicated to test for reliability.	Controls for this study include the pre-rating of faces for attractiveness, the odour concentrations and the trials' standardised presentation. Therefore, the study could be replicated to test for reliable results (e.g. using a different sample).

Strength	As laboratory experiments have high levels of control, researchers can be more confident it is the IV directly affecting the DV.	The standardised procedure including the delivery of the different smells means the researchers can be confident it was the odour presented that affected the ratings of attractiveness.
Weakness	As laboratory experiments take place in an artificial setting, it is said that they can lack ecological validity.	The setting was artificial as participants sat on a chair with their chin on a chin rest.
Weakness	Many laboratory experiments can make participants take part in tasks that are nothing like real-life ones so they lack mundane realism.	Having an odour released near your face and then having to rate a picture on attractiveness is not something that would happen in everyday life.

Demattè, Österbauer & Spence collected quantitative data only. This also has strengths and weaknesses:

Evaluation	General evaluation (quantitative data)	Related to Demattè, Österbauer & Spence
Strength	The data are objective and can be analysed statistically to draw conclusions from them.	The ratings given by participants were numerical (on a scale of 1–9) so averages could be calculated to show the difference between the attractiveness ratings per odour presented.
Strength	As the data are numerical, comparison and statistical analysis are easier (e.g. the average score of two different groups can easily be compared so there is very little bias or misinterpretation.	The ratings were given by participants and analysed for a mean score per presented odour. There was no room for misinterpretation of results or drawing the wrong conclusion. This made comparisons easy.
Weakness	Numerical data miss out on valuable information. If the answer is simply yes/no or on a rating scale we do not know *why* participants chose the answer they did.	The researchers do not know the *reasoning* behind participants' ratings of the faces so lose some rich detail that could have been collected via qualitative data.
Weakness	Social desirability and/or demand characteristics can affect quantitative data as it is simply a number that is recorded.	Some participants may have worked out the aim of the study and recorded ratings that fitted in with the study aims (demand characteristics), e.g. they may have rated faces more attractive when pleasant odours were delivered because they felt that was expected. This reduces the validity of the study.

This is another point that can be used to evaluate the study:

▶ Use of repeated measures means that any participant variables have been controlled for. This is because all participants rated all pictures under unpleasant odour, pleasant odour and clean air conditions. This controlled for things such as personal views on attractiveness.

▶ However, as they did rate all pictures under unpleasant odour, pleasant odour and clean air conditions, participants may have been able to work out the aim of the study and give ratings based on that rather than their own personal judgments (demand characteristics). This reduces the validity of the study.

CHALLENGE YOURSELF
Evaluate this study in terms of it being a snapshot study. You may want to use a table like those used for the laboratory experiment and quantitative data evaluations.

Exam centre

Try the following exam-style questions.

Paper 1

1. In the Demattè, Österbauer & Spence study, what were the pleasant odours? (2 marks)

2. Outline **two** controls that Demattè, Österbauer & Spence used in their study. (4 marks)

3. Identify **two** features of the sample used in the Demattè, Österbauer & Spence study. (2 marks)

4. Evaluate the Demattè, Österbauer & Spence study in terms of **one** strength and **one** weakness. (10 marks)

Paper 2

1. Outline how quantitative data were collected in the Demattè, Österbauer & Spence study. (3 marks)

2. Redesign the Demattè, Österbauer & Spence study using self-report as the research method. (10 marks)

3. Discuss the strengths and weaknesses of laboratory experiments using Demattè, Österbauer & Spence as an example. (10 marks)

Exam centre

Try the following exam-style questions.

Paper 1

1. Outline who the pseudopatients were and how they got admitted to the hospitals. (4 marks)

2. Outline **one** finding from the Rosenhan study. (2 marks)

3. Outline **one** aim of the Rosenhan study. (2 marks)

4. Evaluate the Rosenhan study in terms of **one** strength and **one** weakness. (10 marks)

Paper 2

1. Outline what quantitative data were collected in the Rosenhan study. (3 marks)

2. Outline how Rosenhan was testing out the individual differences approach to psychology. (3 marks)

3. Discuss the strengths and weaknesses of observations using Rosenhan as an example. (10 marks)

CORE STUDY 7.2

Thigpen & Cleckley (1954)

ASK YOURSELF
Can someone really have, for example, three different personalities that think and reason in different ways?

CONTEXT

Most of us experience forgetfulness on a regular basis. We might forget something when distracted and later recall the information we were trying to access. Some psychologists believe that this dissociation occurs on a continuum, with all of us experiencing occasional, mild dissociative episodes. However, the following study involves a woman with extreme dissociation, known as multiple personality disorder (MPD).

MPD is a rare psychological condition. So little is known about the disorder that some professionals doubt its existence. MPD is known as dissociative identity disorder (DID) in the *Diagnostic Statistical Manual of Mental Disorders* (DSM).

DID is defined by DSM-IV as the presence of two or more distinct identities, or distinct identities that each have their own way of perceiving and thinking about the environment and self. According to the diagnostic criteria, at least two of these personality states recurrently take control of the individual's behaviour. Although plural identities are present, it is important to remember that they all exist as manifestations of one person.

Two or more personalities coexist, but only one is "in control" of the person at a given time. The different personalities might not be aware of one another's existence and experience. This means those with the disorder might experience dissociative fugues, and be unable to recall important personal information.

MPD is a neurotic disorder – it is not a form of schizophrenia, although many people confuse the two conditions. Schizophrenia is a psychotic disorder characterised by the impairment of one's sense of reality, and can be accompanied by visual or auditory hallucinations or delusions. MPD is a neurotic disorder, where the sufferer does not lose contact with reality.

The existence of MPD is highly contested. Not only is it very rarely diagnosed, but its treatment often involves the use of hypnosis (a controversial technique in itself). Some cases have become notorious, as the psychiatrists involved have been accused of exploiting their patients for their own purposes.

AIM

To give an account of the psychotherapeutic experience of someone thought to have multiple personalities.

METHOD

Participant

The participant was a 25-year-old married mother with a 4-year-old daughter. Her real name was changed in Thigpen & Cleckley's report to Eve White to preserve her anonymity. She was the oldest of three siblings and was employed as a telephone operator. She was initially referred to Thigpen for therapy after complaining of severe and blinding headaches. At her first interview she also mentioned experiencing blackouts following these headaches.

Case

Design and procedure

This research is a classic case study. It focuses on one individual, Eve White, and explores her background, symptoms and therapy in great depth. Case studies employ a range of different methods for studying participants. The case of Eve was explored primarily through psychotherapeutic interviews. Some of these were done under, or following, hypnosis, in order to "draw out" different personalities. The study took place over a period of 14 months, and material was gathered from approximately 100 hours of interviews.

In addition, background information was obtained through interviews with family members and Eve's husband. These were carried out to back up Eve's account of events from her childhood to adulthood. Quantitative measures were taken of Eve White and the second personality, Eve Black, including psychometric tests of memory and IQ. Eve also underwent two projection tests analysed by the researchers. These included an exercise drawing human figures, and interpreting Rorschach ink blots. Later, when the third personality "Jane" appeared, all three were given an electroencephalogram (EEG).

Qual

Quant

RESULTS

Eve White

Initially, the therapists report some slight progress in treating Eve White's (EW's) symptoms following discussion of some of her emotional problems. EW was thought to have personal frustrations and difficulties with her husband (from whom she was currently separated). During a session EW was unable to recall details of a recent trip she had made. Hypnosis was induced and her memory was restored. Several days later, a letter arrived from EW about this session, written in her handwriting with the exception of the final paragraph, which was written in a childish scrawl.

The letter was the first indication that anything was unusual about EW's case, as she had presented herself as a self-controlled and truthful person. At the next session, EW denied sending the letter, but was distressed and agitated and asked whether hearing an imaginary voice would indicate she was "insane". She said she had occasionally heard a voice other than her own addressing her over recent months. Before any response was made, EW held her hands to her head as if in pain and suddenly her entire manner and voice changed. She smiled and said "Hi there, Doc!", and when asked who she was, introduced herself as "Eve Black". "Black" was later found to be Eve's maiden name. Her IQ was 110.

Qual

Eve Black

Eve Black (EB) now appeared mischievous, light-hearted and playful as she continued to be interviewed. She seemed to have existed independently from EW since childhood. She was found to have separate thoughts and feelings from EW, but also had awareness and access to EW's life while she herself was absent. Despite this access to EW's thoughts, EB had little sympathy for her. While EW loved and missed her daughter (from whom she was also separated), EB was unconcerned and glib about EW's suffering. EW was totally ignorant of EB's existence, but came to be aware that she existed through the course of therapy. Initially, persuading EB to "come out" required hypnosis, but over time this was no longer necessary. However, EB was never hypnotisable, and attempts to "call out" both personalities simultaneously were unsuccessful and distressing to Eve.

While EB did not seem deliberately cruel, in early childhood she would emerge and cause trouble. EW was forbidden from playing in the woods as a child; one day EB took over and broke her parents' strict rule. Upon her return, EW was whipped for her disobedience, much to her confusion and dismay. Her parents corroborated this story and also expressed their puzzlement at such out-of-character behaviour in their normally obedient and honest daughter.

Similar instances occurred in Eve's adulthood. Her husband recalled an incident where he discovered she had spent an enormous sum of money on clothes; he had abused her for being so careless and indulgent. As it was EB who had indulged in the expensive shopping trip, EW was deeply bewildered about this irresponsible lapse in her behaviour. The therapists note that although it is unlikely Eve's marriage would have been successful even without her condition, there is no doubt EB's difficult behaviour contributed to the couple's difficulties.

To explore the extent of the psychological differences between the two personalities, Eve underwent several psychometric and projective tests. These revealed differences in IQ and memory, as well as key differences in the defence mechanisms of repression and regression that were underlying Eve's two different personas.

EB's other distinctive behaviours included drinking to excess, hooking up with strange men and, allegedly, even committing to a prior secret marriage. EB claimed to be able to erase certain occurrences from EW's memory: "I just start thinking about it very hard and after a while … it doesn't come back to her anymore".

After eight months of therapy, EW was no longer experiencing headaches or blackouts. EB had been causing less trouble and EW had had some encouraging successes in her work and social life. But suddenly all this changed. The headaches, blackouts and fugues returned with greater frequency, and were now experienced by both EW and EB. The therapists feared she might be about to experience an episode of psychosis. Her IQ was 104.

Jane

In a session after the headaches had restarted, EW was discussing a painful childhood memory when suddenly her head dropped back and her eyes closed. Two minutes later she looked around the room confusedly and asked where she was. Another transformation had taken place, with mannerisms and characteristics highly distinct from either EW or EB. "Jane" – as she called herself – was more confident, interesting and assertive than timid EW, but without the personality faults of EB. She was aware of the behaviour of the other two personalities, but could not access their memories prior to her emergence.

The EEG conducted several weeks later on all three personalities traced 33 minutes of recording, including intervals of at least 5 minutes of each personality, and some transitions between individuals. Tenseness was most pronounced in EB, next in EW, and least of all Jane. Muscle tension was greatest in EB, and the test indicated it was easiest to transpose from EB to EW. EB's results were only borderline normal, with some records showing an association with psychopathic personality. Both EW and Jane's records were normal.

Jane continued to emerge through EW only, but became stronger over time. She took over many of EW's duties both at work and at home in an effort to help her, but was reluctant to take over fully as a maternal figure to EW's daughter as she did not wish to interfere with their relationship.

TEST YOURSELF
Outline at least three differences between Eve White and Eve Black.

CONCLUSIONS

Despite the debate over the existence of MPD, Thigpen & Cleckley concluded that they had not been tricked by a skilful actress but had observed the existence of three distinct personalities in one individual.

There will undoubtedly continue to be controversy over the existence of MPD/DID. Thigpen & Cleckley argue that what they witnessed was genuine because the length of time spent with EW, EB and Jane meant that at least some mistakes or inconsistencies would have been noticed.

EVALUATION

Since Thigpen & Cleckley used the case study method, we can use the general evaluations from Chapter 1, page 3 and apply them directly to the study:

Evaluation	General evaluation (case study)	Related to Thigpen & Cleckley
Strength	As the study focuses on one individual (or unit of individuals) the psychologist can collect rich, in-depth data that have details. This makes the findings more valid.	The researchers focused on just the one person (Eve) and ran many psychological and physical tests to assess the three "distinct" personalities: a lot of data were collected to help differentiate between the three. This makes the findings more valid.
Strength	Participants are usually studied as part of their everyday life which means that the whole process tends to have some ecological validity.	It could be argued that the study has some ecological validity as Eve was in therapy and the assessment followed what could happen in a therapeutic setting.
Weakness	As the psychologist is focusing on one individual (or unit of individuals), the case may be unique. This makes generalisations quite difficult.	As Thigpen & Cleckley were only studying one actual person, she may be a unique case. This would make generalising difficult as she may not represent any other person who claims to have more than one personality.

Evaluation	General evaluation (case study)	Related to Thigpen & Cleckley
Weakness	As participants are studied in depth, they could form an attachment with the psychologist. This could reduce the objectivity of the data collection and analysis of data and so the validity of the findings.	Some psychologists could argue that Thigpen & Cleckley got attached to Eve as a patient and lost objectivity because they wanted to find differences between the three personalities. This could obviously reduce the validity of findings as they may have only reported data that confirm their ideas.

Thigpen & Cleckley collected some qualitative data we can evaluate too. These data also have strengths and weaknesses:

Evaluation	General evaluation (qualitative data)	Related to Thigpen & Cleckley
Strength	The data collected are in-depth and in the words of the participant so they are rich and in detail and represent what the participant believes. Therefore it can be argued that it is not reductionist.	The interviews and psychometric testing was in depth so a lot of detail was recorded. All of it represents what was actually happening to Eve in her three personality "states" so Thigpen & Cleckley were looking at as much data as possible. Therefore, the study is not reductionist.
Weakness	Interpretation of the data could be subjective as we are dealing with words not numbers: psychologist could misinterpret what the participant meant to say or be biased against some of the person's views.	The researchers may have only reported data that confirmed what they believed as some of the data collected were subjectively analysed (the interview transcripts and what Eve was feeling). They may have also misinterpreted some of what Eve was trying to get across in her interviews.

CHALLENGE YOURSELF
Evaluate this case study in terms of it being longitudinal and its ethics. You may want to use a table similar to those used for the case study and qualitative data evaluations.

Exam centre

Try the following exam-style questions.

Paper 1

1. Outline **two** differences between Eve White and Eve Black in the Thigpen & Cleckley study. (4 marks)

2. What was the aim of the Thigpen & Cleckley study? (2 marks)

3. Evaluate the Thigpen & Cleckley study in terms of **one** strength and **one** weakness. (10 marks)

Paper 2

1. Outline how qualitative data were collected in the Thigpen & Cleckley study. (3 marks)

2. Outline what quantitative data were collected in the Thigpen & Cleckley study. (3 marks)

3. Discuss the strengths and weaknesses of case studies using Thigpen & Cleckley as an example. (10 marks)

CORE STUDY 7.3

Billington, Baron-Cohen & Wheelwright (2007)

CONTEXT

Psychologists have long been interested in why there are gender differences in the rates of people studying certain subjects at school, college and university. There has always been a marked difference in the number of males and females choosing to study subjects such as mathematics and sciences. Performance in these subjects has also shown some gender differences even from an early age. However, psychologists have questioned whether there is a true gender divide or whether there are other factors, such as how we process information, that could account for the imbalance of males and females studying science and mathematics. This research team were interested in "cognitive style" and if they could explain gender differences (rather than finding that males are better than females in these subjects). Two examples of cognitive style are empathisers (those who have the ability to identify another person's mental state and respond using a range of correct emotions) and systemisers (who have the ability to analyse the rules underlying a system in order to predict a behaviour – systems include machines, weather systems, mathematics, maps, etc.). The research team had already developed a psychometric test to measure people's empathy quotient and systemising quotient.

ASK YOURSELF
Why are you taking Cambridge AS level Psychology? What other subjects are you taking? Do you feel that certain types of people only study certain types of subject at school and college?

AIM

1. To see whether there is still a gender difference in the number of people studying the physical sciences and humanities.

2. To see whether males are more likely to be systemisers and females more likely to be empathisers.

3. To see whether physical science students are more likely to be systemisers and humanities students more likely to be empathisers.

4. To see whether cognitive style is a better predictor than gender in explaining enrolment onto physical science courses compared to humanities courses.

METHOD

Design

There were two questionnaires and two performance tasks. All were accessible and completed via a secure university website.

▶ Questionnaire 1: Systemising quotient-revised scale (SQ-R). It consists of 75 items. The score range on the questionnaire is 0–150.

Quest

▶ Questionnaire 2: Empathy quotient (EQ). It consists of 40 items. The score range is 0–80.

From these questionnaires, participants could be classified as one of five brain types: type S (systemiser), type E (empathiser), type B (balanced), extreme type S and extreme type E. The extreme groups were those in the top 2.5 per cent when the difference was calculated between the SQ-R and EQ scores for each participant.

▶ Task 1 was the embedded figures task (FC-EFT). This task involves seeing a series of 12 pairs of diagrams like the pair shown in Figure 7.1. Participants had to choose which of the two more complex diagrams contained the smaller shape within it. It was a forced-choice task so participants had to choose just one of the more complex shapes. If the participant failed to respond in 50 seconds then the task automatically moved on to the next pair of shapes. Every time participants got the answer correct they were awarded 1 point. There was an additional bonus point added to participants' scores every time they were in the fastest 25 per cent for that pair of shapes. Therefore, the range of scores was 0 to 24.

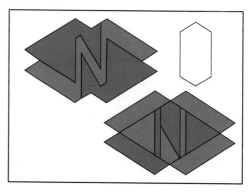

▲ **Figure 7.1** Embedded figures task (FC-EFT)
Source: Based on Billington, Baron-Cohen & Wheelwright, 2007

Task 2 was the eyes test. This task assesses cognitive empathy by showing participants a pair of eyes conveying a pre-chosen emotion. The participant was given four choices of emotions and asked to choose the one that is the closest to the emotion that the eyes are conveying. An example is shown in Figure 7.2. If the participant failed to respond in 20 seconds then the task automatically moved on to the next pair of eyes. There are 36 pairs of eyes to rate and 1 point is awarded for each correct choice – the same bonus point system was used here as in the FC-EFT. Therefore, the range of scores is 0 to 72.

 Quant

apologetic | friendly

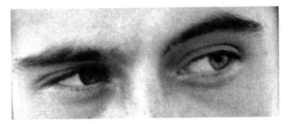

uneasy | dispirited

▲ **Figure 7.2** Eyes test

TEST YOURSELF
What were the various measures that were taken of each participant? Choose one and outline how the data were collected.

Participants

For this study 415 participants were recruited. They were either studying for a physical sciences degree or a humanities degree. Physical science subjects included mathematics, physics, engineering and astronomy. Humanities subjects included classics, law, theology and history. The average age of the participants was 21 years (standard deviation of 2.51 years). Of the participants, 87.7 per cent of the participants were right-handed, 10.6 per cent were left-handed and 1.7 per cent were ambidextrous. They were recruited through an email post and advertisements across the university with a prize draw incentive. Therefore, participants volunteered to take part. Table 7.1 shows the distribution of participants per degree per sex.

 Sample

Sex	Degree	N	% of total N
Female	Physical	108	26
	Humanities	104	25.1
	Total	212	51.1
Male	Physical	160	38.6
	Humanities	43	10.4
	Total	203	48.9
Total	Physical	268	64.6
	Humanities	147	35.4
	Total	415	100

▲ **Table 7.1** Percentage of participants studying each degree category, by sex

Procedure

Those who volunteered to take part in the study could visit the secure university website and complete the questionnaires and tasks in any order. They did not have to complete both questionnaires and tasks in the same sitting but they could only attempt each task and complete each questionnaire once.

RESULTS

Overall, there was a significant gender difference in degree choice: 59.1 per cent of physical science students were male and 70.1 per cent of humanities students were female.

Table 7.2 shows the mean and standard deviation scores for each gender split by degree choice for the two questionnaires. **Quant**

	Female physical science	Female humanities	Male physical science	Male humanities
SQ-R	61.23 (20.60)	51.54 (19.18)	65.46 (18.17)	58.65 (21.17)
EQ	43.48 (12.56)	46.82 (12.07)	35.59 (10.39)	40.56 (10.33)

▲ **Table 7.2** The two questionnaires – mean and standard deviation scores for each gender split by degree choice. Standard deviations are in parentheses

Table 7.3 shows the mean and standard deviation scores for each sex split by degree choice for the two tasks.

	Female physical science	Female humanities	Male physical science	Male humanities
FC-EFT	15.05 (3.05)	14.07 (2.40)	15.03 (3.14)	14.14 (2.63)
Eyes test	32.86 (6.65)	46.82 (12.07)	31.83 (7.23)	33.79 (8.00)

▲ **Table 7.3** The two tasks – mean and standard deviation scores for each sex split by degree choice. Standard deviations are in parentheses

These were the main results based on these figures:

▷ There was a significant relationship between gender and cognitive style: 66 per cent of males were categorised as type S or extreme type S (only 28.8 per cent of females); 36.8 per cent of females were categorised as type E or extreme type E (only 10.3 per cent of males).

▷ Females performed significantly better than males on the eyes test.

▷ There was no significant gender difference in participants' performance in the FC-EFT.

▷ Of the physical science students, 56.3 per cent of them had type S or extreme type S profiles (only 29.4 per cent of humanities students). With the humanities students, 41.5 per cent had type E or extreme type E profiles (only 14.2 per cent of physical science students).

▷ Physical science students performed significantly better on the FC-EFT compared to humanities students.

▷ Overall, males tended to be categorised more as systemisers whereas females tended to be categorised more as empathisers.

▷ Overall, physical sciences students tended to be categorised more as systemisers whereas humanities students tended to be categorised more as empathisers.

The research team conducted a logistic regression analysis to examine which of the factors was the best predictor of degree choice. All of the main predictors could predict degree choice but there was a rank order:

1. Brain type was the strongest predictor (type E, type S, etc.).

2. Performance on the FC-EFT task was the next predictor.

3. Performance on the eyes test was the next predictor.

4. Gender was the weakest predictor (but was still significant).

 TEST YOURSELF
Outline the differences between the students who studied humanities and those who studied physical sciences.

CONCLUSION

It would appear that the "gender differences" in degree choice between physical sciences and humanities is less of an actual "gender difference" but of a cognitive style difference. Students with certain brain types (systemisers and empathisers) tend to pick their degrees differently – systemisers pick physical sciences in the main while empathisers pick humanities subjects in the main.

EVALUATION

As Billington, Baron-Cohen & Wheelwright used questionnaires, we can use the general evaluations from Chapter 1, page 2 and apply them directly to the study:

Evaluation	General evaluation (questionnaires)	Related to Billington, Baron-Cohen & Wheelwright
Strength	Participants may be more likely to reveal truthful answers in a questionnaire as it does not involve talking face to face with someone.	Participants completed the questionnaires by themselves and did not have to answer questions in front of anyone so were more likely to give truthful answers.

Evaluation	General evaluation (questionnaires)	Related to Billington, Baron-Cohen & Wheelwright
Strength	A large sample of participants can answer the questionnaire in a short time span which should increase the representativeness and generalisability of the findings.	A total of 415 participants took part in the study over a short period of time giving a wide spread of results that could be applied to students of physical sciences and humanities.
Weakness	Participants may give socially desirable answers as they want to look good rather than giving truthful answers – this lowers the validity of findings.	As they completed the questionnaires by themselves, some participants may have chosen answers that made them "look good" rather than how they truly process information (e.g. as a systemiser).
Weakness	If the questionnaire has a lot of closed questions participants might be forced into choosing an answer that does not reflect their true opinion.	There may have been some questions that participants had to choose an answer for that was not how they truly process information but was the closest answer to how they do it – therefore, it may not be a fully true representation of their cognitive style.

Volunteer or self-selected sampling can be evaluated as follows:

Evaluation	General evaluation (volunteer sampling)	Related to Billington, Baron-Cohen & Wheelwright
Strength	Large numbers of participants can be obtained relatively quickly and easily.	A total of 415 participants came forward to participate (the researcher simply advertised) and they could complete the study when it was convenient for them (so they were more likely to complete it).
Strength	People are more likely to participate if they have already volunteered so the drop-out rate should be lower.	No drop-out rate figures were given so we can assume that most participants completed all four tasks.
Weakness	Gaining a wide variety of participants to allow for generalisation is unlikely (for opportunity you will go for one type of person in the main whereas for volunteer it is only a certain type of person who will volunteer to do research for a particular study).	Only motivated students of physical sciences and humanities would have come forward to participate, so it might make generalisation a bit difficult for those who are less motivated to take part in a study but are completing similar degree programmes. We cannot be certain that those who chose not to participate followed the same general patterns for systemisers and empathisers.

The following other points could be used in evaluation:

▶ The researchers use psychometric tasks in the study which means comparisons can be *useful* as people's results are being compared on the same, standardised scale – therefore, the differences found by cognitive style and gender are meaningful and more likely to be valid.

Psychom

▶ The study can be easily replicated using the same standardised psychometric tests

(FC-EFT and the eyes test) to test for reliability with a different sample.

> **CHALLENGE YOURSELF**
> Evaluate the Billington, Baron-Cohen & Wheelwright study in terms of it being a snapshot study and also in terms of individual versus situational explanations. You may want to use a table like those used for the questionnaire and volunteer sampling evaluations.

Exam centre

Try the following exam-style questions.

Paper 1

1. In the Billington, Baron-Cohen & Wheelwright study, what were the two questionnaires completed by all participants? (2 marks)

2. Outline **one** psychometric task used in the Billington, Baron-Cohen & Wheelwright study. In your answer include how it was scored. (4 marks)

3. Outline **one** reason why the Billington, Baron-Cohen & Wheelwright study was conducted. (2 marks)

4. Evaluate the Billington, Baron-Cohen & Wheelwright study in terms of **two** weaknesses. (10 marks)

Paper 2

1. Outline how quantitative data were collected in the Billington, Baron-Cohen & Wheelwright study. (3 marks)

2. Outline **one** finding from the Billington, Baron-Cohen & Wheelwright study. (3 marks)

3. Discuss the strengths and weaknesses of volunteer sampling using Billington, Baron-Cohen & Wheelwright as an example. (10 marks)

EXAM CENTRE (AS LEVEL)

The questions, example answers, marks awarded and/or comments that appear in this book/CD were written by the author. In examination, the way marks would be awarded to answers like these may be different.

Unit 1 (Core studies 1)

This unit constitutes 50 per cent of the AS level qualification and 25 per cent of the A level qualification. Students need to have studied all 20 core studies alongside methodology, approaches and perspectives, and issues and debates. For the core studies, students need to know the following:

1. Background to the study
2. The aim(s) of the study
3. The method and procedure of the study
4. The results of the study
5. The conclusions drawn from the study.

For each core study, there have to be some evaluations based around:

1. The methodology used
2. The approach or perspective the study belongs to
3. Issues and debates surrounding the study.

The exam lasts for 1 hour 30 minutes and is marked out of 80. The structure of the exam is as follows:

▶ Section A – there are 15 short-answer questions based around 15 core studies. They are marked out of 2 or 4 depending on the question being asked. This section carries 60 marks.

▶ Section B – there are two structured essays and both need answering. Each is based around a methodology or issues/debates. There are three core studies listed *per essay* and the student has to use one core study to answer the question. This section carries 20 marks (10 *per essay*).

Section A

Example questions could be as follows:

1. Outline two results from the … study (4 marks)
   (a) How was the sample recruited in the … study? (2 marks)
   (b) Outline one disadvantage of recruiting a sample in that way. (2 marks)

When asking for one result, ensure that there is a comparison (if possible). If the question states "as used in the X study" in the question, then this link *has to be made*. If the question is asking for a "result" then this is usually quantitative or qualitative data. If the question is asking for a "conclusion" then this is whether the study fulfilled its aims or not (written in general terms).

Section B

Example questions could be as follows:

1. Evaluate one of the studies below in terms of validity. (10 marks)

2. Discuss the strengths and weaknesses of self-reports using one of the studies below as an example. (10 marks)

If the question states "strengths and weaknesses" note that this is *plural* and two of each (minimum) are required to be likely to get towards the top band of marks (6+ marks). The question will have a focus on a study chosen from a list by the student. This study must be used in the answer to be likely to reach the top-end marks available (6+ marks).

Unit 2 (Core studies 2)

This unit constitutes 50 per cent of the AS level qualification and 25 per cent of the A level qualification. Students need to have studied all 20 core studies alongside methodology, approaches and perspectives, and issues and debates. For this unit, the focus is more on the methodology used in each study, which approach or perspective the study belongs to, and which issues and debates are relevant to each study. The examination lasts for 1 hour 30 minutes and is marked out of 70. The structure of the examination is as follows:

Section A

This is split into two parts.

Part A has one question on methods (sometimes via a named core study) plus students must *redesign* a core study using a *different research method*. They must then evaluate their own study. This part carries 25 marks (5 + 10 + 10). Example questions could be as follows:

1. (a) Outline what is meant by a case study using Freud as an example. (5 marks)

(b) Redesign the Piliavin, Rodin & Pilivain study using self-report as the research method and describe how it can be conducted. (10 marks)

(c) Evaluate this alternative way of studying aggression in practical and ethical terms. (10 marks)

For (a) students could gain 1 mark per correct point up until the maximum of 5 marks. For (b) students must consider the what, how, who, where and when (if applicable). The study must be ethical. Usually, the what, how and who are major aspects that need covering so if they are missing, the answer is likely to be classed as having "major omissions". For (c) the issues under debate need to be directly linked back to the study students have designed in (b) to be likely to gain 5+ marks.

Part B has one structured question based on an approach, issues and debates or methods (some are similar to section B for unit 1). This part carries 25 marks (2 + 3 + 10 + 10). Example questions could be as follows:

2. (a) What is meant by quantitative data? (2 marks)

(b) Outline one quantitative finding from the Milgram (1963) study. (3 marks)

(c) Discuss the strengths and weaknesses of collecting quantitative data using Milgram as an example. (10 marks)

(d) Discuss the advantages and disadvantages of ethical guidelines in research using Milgram as an example. (10 marks)

For (a) the answer will be likely to score 1 mark if it is a partial answer and 2 if it is a full answer. For (b), to gain 3 marks the answer would normally have to specifically address what is being asked for in a clear and concise way. For (c) and (d) the evaluation or discussion is *plural* and two advantages and disadvantages (minimum) are required to be likely to get towards the top band of marks. (7+ marks). Just one of each would probably only gain a maximum of 6 marks.

Section B

There is a choice here – students answer one question from the two given. The questions will have focus on an approach, issue and debate or method and students have to use three named core studies to answer part of the question. This part of section B carries 11 marks (2 + 9). There is also a final question that tests the evaluation skills of students for a named method, issue and debate or approach and perspective. This part of section B carries 9 marks. Therefore, overall, section B carries 20 marks. Example questions could be as follows:

3. (a) Outline what is meant by the "social approach" to psychology. (2 marks)

(b) Using the studies from the list below … describe how the data were collected in each of these studies. (9 marks)

For (a) the answer will be likely to score 1 mark if it is a partial answer and 2 if it is a full answer. For (b) there are 3 marks available *per study listed*. Expect to gain 3 marks for any study the answer would have to be in sufficient detail to get across what the question is asking for (e.g. *how* were data collected).

There is also a final question that tests the evaluation skills of students for a named method, issue and debate or approach and perspective. This part of section B carries 9 marks. Therefore, overall, section B carries 20 marks. Example questions could be as follows:

(c) What are the disadvantages of using psychometric testing? (9 marks)

(d) What are the strengths of using longitudinal studies in psychology? (9 marks)

For (c) there are 3 marks available which would normally be allocated *per relevant point* raised by the student. The same point made again but using a different example or study would *not be expected to gain any extra marks*.

▶ 1 mark = identifying a point that is relevant

▶ 2 marks = the above plus some description

▶ 3 marks = 2 marks + linked to a study.

The best three relevant points would be taken forward to give a score out of 9.

Refer back to the example evaluations at the end of each core study and ensure that you have completed the extra evaluations highlighted. These will help you improve your exam skills.

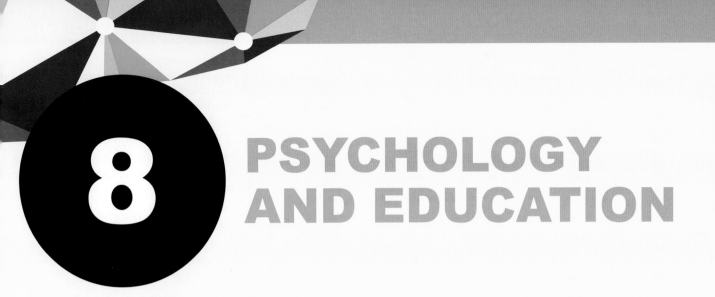

8 PSYCHOLOGY AND EDUCATION

There are many different ways in which humans and animals learn skills and behaviours. In terms of the Cambridge A level Psychology specification, there are two main behaviourist ways plus a humanistic and a few cognitive approaches to learning.

BEHAVIOURIST APPLICATIONS TO LEARNING

The behaviourist perspective was covered in the section for AS level (see page 47). Remember that it is about observing the observable and how we learn things through our environment and the organisms within it.

Classical conditioning

This follows the idea of learning through association. It was Pavlov who introduced this idea after experimenting with laboratory dogs. He trained dogs to salivate to the sound of bell without any food being present. He had conditioned that behaviour into the dogs. We will come back to *how* he did this after we have looked at the principles of classical conditioning.

There are three main stages to classical conditioning:

1. pre-conditioning

2. the conditioning process

3. post-conditioning.

Pre-conditioning requires associations to already be "in place" that can then be used to help to condition the organism. A pre-programmed biological relationship has to already be in existence (e.g. food naturally produces a response for saliva in many animals). The food is called the unconditioned stimulus (UCS) and the salivation is called the unconditioned response (UCR). A neutral stimulus (NS) must be chosen that does not elicit any biological response and this can be used to condition a new behaviour in the organism.

The conditioning process requires the UCS and the NS to be presented at the same time so that the organism can *associate* the two things. The UCR will still happen as the UCS is still present.

Post-conditioning is when the NS can be presented on its own and it produces a response similar to the UCR. The NS has now turned into a conditioned stimulus (CS) and the UCR has turned into a conditioned response (CR). The organism has now been classically conditioned.

Figure 8.1.1 shows how the process works.

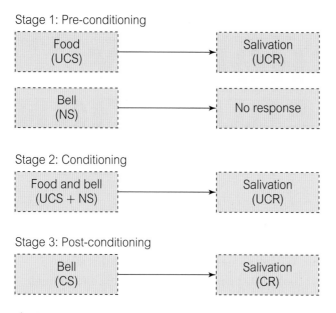

Stage 1: Pre-conditioning

| Food (UCS) | → | Salivation (UCR) |
| Bell (NS) | → | No response |

Stage 2: Conditioning

| Food and bell (UCS + NS) | → | Salivation (UCR) |

Stage 3: Post-conditioning

| Bell (CS) | → | Salivation (CR) |

▲ **Figure 8.1.1** Classical conditioning (Pavlov's experiment)

With the original Pavlov experiment, the food was the UCS and the salivation was the UCR. He had introduced a bell as the NS. He then rang the bell every time the dogs were presented with food (UCS + NS) – the dogs would still salivate (UCR) as the food was present. After several associations he would just ring the bell (now a CS) and the dogs would salivate (CR).

Higher-order conditioning

This is more relevant to the processes of learning in education. This is when there is an established CS-CR link but a new NS is presented every time the CS is presented. Again, after several associations, the new NS also becomes a CS (given the code CS2 as it is a new CS – a second one). This then produces a CR.

Operant conditioning

This follows the idea of learning through consequences. The idea first began with the law of effect – we are more likely to repeat a behaviour if we find it pleasurable. However, as pleasure cannot be directly observed, Skinner then proposed operant conditioning based around the idea of reinforcement and punishment. Table 8.1.1 shows the four mechanisms that can be used to help an organism learn a behaviour.

	Positive	Negative
Reinforcement	Positive reinforcement is when a behaviour results in the *addition of something nice* happening so the probability of repeating that *behaviour is increased.*	Negative reinforcement is when a behaviour results in the *removal of something not nice* so the probability of repeating that *behaviour is increased.*
Punishment	Positive punishment is when a behaviour results in the *addition of something not nice* so the probability of repeating that *behaviour is decreased.*	Negative punishment is when a behaviour results in the *removal of something nice* so the probability of repeating the *behaviour is decreased.*

▲ **Table 8.1.1** Four mechanisms that can help an organism learn a behaviour

An example linked to education is shown in Table 8.1.2.

	Positive	Negative
Reinforcement	A child shows friendly behaviour in the classroom so the child is awarded a gold star and a sweet. The child is more likely to show the friendly behaviour again.	A child has not been behaving very well in class and keeps getting detentions. However, the child begins to behave well and so the detention is removed. The child is more likely to behave well in the future.
Punishment	A child is not behaving very nicely to another child. The child is given a detention which means the child arrives home late. The child is less likely to repeat the behaviour.	A child is not behaving very nicely to another child. As a result, the child's "golden time" of having extra playtime is removed and the child has to sit in the classroom alone. The child is less likely to repeat the behaviour.

▲ **Table 8.1.2** Two mechanisms in an example linked to education

exercise or an exercise matching terms to definitions by connecting them with a line. The fill-in-the-gaps exercise might have all of the words given to students in a box; they then place each one in the correct gap.

▶ "Templates" that break information down could be provided for students. An example would be templates for the AS level core studies you looked at last year. You would be given a template that has sections for *you* to write the aim, design, participants, etc. This would ensure that you look at each section in turn.

▶ Students might be asked to write an essay-style answer to a question. A handout would be provided giving some guidelines on how to write it. For example, the handout may hint at what the question is asking, what material is useful and even give an example evaluation to show students how it is done. However, students would still have to write the essay themselves as this is the skill that is being taught.

EVALUATION

cognitive   useful   ind vs sit

8.2 SPECIAL EDUCATIONAL NEEDS

DEFINITIONS, TYPES AND ASSESSMENT OF SPECIAL EDUCATIONAL NEEDS (INCLUDING GIFTED CHILDREN)

Definitions of special educational needs and giftedness

The Department for Education in the United Kingdom defines special educational needs as follows:

> Children have special educational needs if they have a learning difficulty which calls for special educational provision to be made for them. Children have a learning difficulty if they:
>
> (a) have a significantly greater difficulty in learning than the majority of children of the same age; or
>
> (b) have a disability which prevents or hinders them from making use of educational facilities of a kind generally provided for children of the same age in schools within the area of the local education authority
>
> (c) are under compulsory school age and fall within the definition at (a) or (b) above or would so do if special educational provision was not made for them. Children must not be regarded as having a learning difficulty solely because the language or form of language of their home is different from the language in which they will be taught. Special educational provision means:
>
> (a) for children of two or over, educational provision which is additional to, or otherwise different from, the educational provision made generally for children of their age in schools maintained by the LEA, other than special schools, in the area (b) for children under two, educational provision of any kind.

See Section 312, Education Act 1996

The Department for Children, Schools and Families in the United Kingdom (2008) defined giftedness as:

> Children and young people with one or more abilities developed to a level significantly ahead of their year group (or with potential to develop those abilities).

 ASK YOURSELF
Do you agree with these definitions? Can you think of an example that may not fit into these?

TYPES OF SPECIAL EDUCATIONAL NEEDS

Dyslexia

We will focus on dyslexia here as an example of a special educational need. The British Dyslexia Association's definition is:

> Dyslexia is a combination of abilities and difficulties that affect the learning process in one or more of reading, spelling and writing. It is a persistent condition.

Table 8.2.1 shows a list of characteristics of dyslexia broken down by age.

Age	Symptoms/indicators
Persistent (so not linked to age of child)	Children who have dyslexia: ▶ have "good" and "bad" days for no reason ▶ confuse directional words such as "up" and "down" ▶ can find sequencing difficult (e.g. putting beads in an order) ▶ have problems with numbers and adding up "in their head" ▶ have a short attention span ▶ have problems organising themselves
Pre-school	▶ have delayed speech development ▶ jumble up phrases (e.g. saying "beddy tear" instead of "teddy bear") ▶ have difficulties expressing themselves through speech ▶ have difficulty with rhyming words and phrases ▶ have difficulty in remembering labels for objects (e.g. chair, bed)

8.6 INTELLIGENCE

This section looks at a range of aspects related to intelligence. This has probably been one of the most controversial areas in psychology for many years as there has been a lot of debate as to the origin of intelligence and the best ways to measure it.

 ASK YOURSELF
What is intelligence and how do you think we should measure it?

CONCEPT, TYPES AND TESTS OF INTELLIGENCE

In this first area we look at what intelligence is and what tests are used to measure it.

Concept of intelligence and IQ

There have been many attempts to define intelligence by a range of psychologists. One that appears to sum it up in terms of it being in line with what the majority of psychologists believe is from Sternberg: "...(it is) mental activity directed toward purposive adaptation to, and selection and shaping of, real-world environments relevant to one's life". (1985: 45). Therefore, it is about using the knowledge and skills we have to help us tackle problems and tasks in every day life.

IQ stands for intelligence quotient. It is a quantitative measure of a person's intelligence based on the person's performance on an IQ test which is designed to measure a range of capabilities. The overall score is based on the following equation:

$$IQ = \frac{\text{mental age}}{\text{chronological age}} \times 100$$

Therefore, the average score is 100 no matter what chronological age you are so it is an attempt at finding a standardised measure of intelligence. However, below we will cover different tests that have been created to measure a person's IQ.

Stanford-Binet Test

The French government commissioned Alfred Binet to create a test that would detect which children were "too slow intellectually" to benefit from a regular school curriculum so other measures for them could be out into place (previously those labelled "slow" were kept at home and not allowed to attend school!). He based his test on the idea that intelligence was more to do with mental reasoning and problem solving than motor skills. He devised a test and kept refining it before a final version was released in 1911 to help test children. Children scored on a scale depending on how well they performed in each section of the test to give them a mental age. This could then be compared to their mental age to see who was "slow".

Lewis Terman from Standford University took Binet's ideas and developed them further with a test for US children, hence the Stanford-Binet test. In 1916 he released the US version of the test that could be used in schools to assess children. This test has been continually revised up until its latest version from 1986. All of the test items are devised with the idea that the majority of children, at that age, should be able to answer them. The current version of this test has four components: verbal reasoning, abstract or visual reasoning, quantitative reasoning (ability to "handle" numerical data) and short-term memory.

Weschler (WAIS and WISC)

Weschler developed a new test of intelligence back in 1939 as he felt that the Stanford-Binet test relied too much on language ability, plus it was only for children. The Weschler Adult Intelligence Scale (WAIS) and, some 20 years later, the Weschler Intelligence Scale for Children (WISC) were devised to improve on the Stanford-Binet test.

Both the WAIS and WISC are divided into two parts: a verbal scale and a performance scale. Obviously the WISC version has questions and tasks that are more child appropriate.

The verbal scale consists of the following tests:

▶ Information. This test consists of general knowledge questions about the world.

- Comprehension. This assesses practical information and ability to use past experiences to answer questions.

- Arithmetic. Verbal problems that are number based are given in this test.

- Similarities. This test asks questions about ways in which two objects or concepts are similar.

- Digit span. A series of numbers are presented verbally and then the person must repeat them forwards and backwards in order.

- Vocabulary. This test has questions about definitions of words, etc.

- Letter number sequencing. Letters and number are presented orally in a mixed-up order (e.g. H1F7S9P4). The person has to then recite the numbers in numerical order then the letters in alphabetical order.

The performance scale consists of the following tests:

- Digit symbol. Points on various shapes are given numbers and then the person is asked to recall what shape a certain number is (or part of a shape).

- Picture completion. The missing part of a picture must be discovered and named.

- Block design. Designs seen on pictures must then be built with blocks.

- Picture arrangement. A series of comic-strip pictures must be placed in order to tell a story.

- Matrix reasoning. A geometric shape has to be selected from a range of alternative in terms of similarity.

- Object assembly. Pieces of a puzzle must be assembled into a complete object.

- Symbol search. Paired groups of target symbols are shown to the participant. The person is then shown some search groups of symbols and has to say whether any of the target symbols appear in it.

A person's IQ is calculated based on the individual's performances across all of these tests. However, one advantage of the WAIS and WISC is that you have score for each person on each test – therefore, you can see a person's strengths and weaknesses on certain tasks, which can help with support at school, for instance.

THE BRITISH ABILITY SCALE (BAS)

This is now in its third version and is divided into early years and school age formats. There are three brief assessment scales that are quick measures of number, spelling and reading abilities (see Table 8.6.1). However, the main element of the BAS is its cognitive scales which are divided into two categories:

- The core scales – these are six cognitive tests that measure verbal ability, non-verbal reasoning ability and spatial ability. There are two for each ability. The test scores are simply added together to generate a general conceptual ability (GCA) score. Therefore, an overall score is generated but there are component scores that can be looked at separately.

- The diagnostic scales – these can be used to measure specific cognitive abilities such as object recall, recognition of pictures, speed of information processing and number concepts.

Therefore, like the WAIS and WISC, the BAS gives an overall score (the GCA) but the advantage is you get component scores and if something else needs assessing then there are the diagnostic scales that can help pinpoint the strengths and weaknesses of a child's abilities.

VERBAL

General information
What day of the year is Independence Day?

Similarities
In what way are *wool* and *cotton* alike?

Arithmetic reasoning
If eggs cost 60 cents a dozen, what does 1 egg cost?

Vocabulary
Tell me the meaning of corrupt.

Comprehension
Why do people buy fire insurance?

Digit span
Listen carefully, and when I am through, say the numbers right after me.

       7   3   4   1   8   6

Now I am going to say some more numbers, but I want you to say them backward.

       3   8   4   1   6

PERFORMANCE

Picture completion
I am going to show you a picture with an important part missing. Tell me what is missing.

'85

SUN	MON	TUE	WED	THU	FRI	SAT
1	2	3	4	5	6	7
8	9	10	11	12	13	14
15	16	17	18	19	20	21
22	23	24	25	26	27	28
29	30					

Picture arrangement
The pictures below tell a story. Put them in the right order to tell the story.

Block design
Using the four blocks, make one just like this.

Object assembly
If these pieces are put together correctly, they will make something. Go ahead and put them together as quickly as you can.

Digit-symbol substitution

Code

△	○	▱	×	8
1	2	3	4	5

Test

△	8	×	○	△	▱	8	×	△	8

▲ **Figure 8.6.1** Sample items from the WAIS test

Source: Thorndike & Hagen, 1977

	CLUSTERS				SNC
	Verbal ability	**Non-verbal reasoning ability**	**Spatial ability**		
Recognition of designs			45		45
Word definitions	52				
Pattern construction			45		45
Matrices		34			34
Verbal similarities	51				
Quantitative reasoning		36			36
Sum of T-scores	**103**	**+70**	**+90**	**= 263**	**160**

	Verbal ability	Non-verbal reasoning ability	Spatial ability	GCA	SNC
Standard score	**102**	**74**	**91**	**86**	**79**
Confidence interval (95%)	93–111	68–85	82–102	80–93	73–88
Percentile	55	4	27	18	8

CLUSTER	Standard score	Description of standard score
Verbal ability	102	Average
Non-verbal reasoning ability	74	Low
Spatial ability	91	Average
GCA score	86	Below average
SNC score	79	Low

▲ **Table 8.6.1** BAS cluster scores

TEST YOURSELF
Outline what is involved in either the WAIS, WISC or BAS test of intelligence.

Reliability, validity and predictive validity

We have already covered these concepts in the issues and debates section. Reliability refers to the consistency of something – in this case, testing whether we score the same in an intelligence measure over time. Validity refers to the accuracy of a measure – in this case, whether the test actually measures intelligence. Predictive validity refers to a test's ability to predict a specific behaviour that the test is supposed to be measuring. Therefore, in this case it would be looked at by correlating the score on an intelligence test with intelligent behaviour in real life (e.g. educational performance or job aptitude).

Myers (1998) noted that for the Stanford-Binet test, the WAIS and the WISC, the reliability scores are +0.90 – this means that when retested on the same scale, most people score virtually the same (the maximum reliability score is +1.00).

A way to measure reliability is called a *test-retest* method. For this, you get a sample of participants and test them on the *same* measure one or two months apart. The results are correlated and if there is a strong positive correlation then the measure is said to be reliable. This is because people are scoring roughly the same both times they complete it.

TEST YOURSELF
How would you test the reliability and predictive validity of an IQ test?

Intelligence and educational performance

In terms of predictive validity, can IQ tests and other tests of intelligence and skills predict things such as educational performance?

In a comprehensive review on the field in the 1990s, Sternberg, Grigorenko and Bundy (1991) reported that there may be some kind of link. Studies had shown a correlation of between +0.40 and +0.50 between IQ scores and educational attainment. However, Sternberg was quick to point out that there were vast differences in these correlations depending on the sample, the tests used and what was being used to measure educational performance. Sternberg reviewed 29 studies and found that between 10 per cent and 22 per cent of variance in specific subject achievement at school can be accounted for by IQ. However, the research team did note that there had not been any research that had assessed the link between IQ and academic performance using a representative national sample (outside of samples used to standardise the test). Therefore, we still do not fully know what the relationship is between IQ and educational performance.

More recent research has attempted to link different aspects of intelligence to educational performance. Abu-Hilal and Nasser (2012) noted that there was an indirect link between IQ and mathematics ability for boys and not girls. They found that boys with a high IQ exerted more effort when studying mathematics and this led to better results compared to low IQ boys who did not exert much effort. However, for girls, the high and low IQ groups exerted the same amount of effort but the high IQ group performed better at mathematics. This shows that there may be other factors that interact with IQ that can explain educational performance.

A longitudinal study by Duckworth, Quinn & Tsukayama (2012) reported that IQ predicted changes in standardised achievement test scores over time more than "self-control" factors (e.g. homework and classroom conduct). Emery & Bell (2009) reported that scores on one section of the biomedical admissions test used by the University of Cambridge called "Scientific knowledge" correlated strongly with high examination scores once these students had been accepted and were studying at the university.

EVALUATION

useful   ind vs sit   gen

THEORIES OF INTELLIGENCE

There are many ideas from psychologists about what intelligence actually is. We have looked at ways of measuring it, but what is intelligence anyway?

Factor-analytic approach (Cattell, 1971)

There is a common underlying idea for any factor-analytic approach to intelligence (there are many theories for intelligence): there are different "clusters" of intelligent behaviours and skills that can be measured on any test. Factor-analysis allows a psychologist to interrelate (correlate) aspects of a test to see which items or sub-scales link together strongly. Factor analysis is a complex statistic technique that does that job – it allows psychologists to see which elements of a test relate strongly to each other and from that each "factor" that is found can be named (e.g. verbal intelligence, problem-solving skills).

Spearman originally had an idea that there was one factor within intelligence. He called it *g* for general intelligence. He believed this because he found that virtually all items on an intelligence test correlated with one another strongly, hence there was just one general factor of intelligence. Thurstone did note that the *g* factor was evident through a range of different tests but that they differed in the amount of *g* that was being shown via the correlations. He stated that there were seven factors including numerical ability, spatial ability and verbal fluency.

Cattell (1963, 1971) proposed another theory based on factor analysis. There are just two main forms of intelligence:

▶ Crystallised intelligence – this is intelligence based on previous knowledge and skills. Therefore, tests that include vocabulary and reading comprehension are testing this type of intelligence.

▶ Fluid intelligence – this is intelligence based on novel ways of thinking. Therefore, tests that ask for the next number in a sequence test this type of intelligence.

Cattell believes that crystallised intelligence appears to be maintained in a person throughout life whereas fluid intelligence begins to decline at the age of 40.

Multiple intelligences (Gardner, 1983)

Gardner (1983) took the idea of the factor-analytic theories a stage further by stating that there are seven different *types* of intelligence in a person. They are:

▶ linguistic: speech production, syntax and semantics

▶ musical: our ability to create and understand sounds such as pitch, rhythm and timbre

▶ logical-mathematical: the use of logic and mathematics to help solve problems

▶ spatial: our ability to perceive spatial information and recreate visual images in our "mind's eye" plus our ability to rotate shapes visually

▶ bodily-kinesthetic: our ability to use movement and our body to solve problems (use of motor skills)

▶ intrapersonal: this covers understanding our own feelings and intentions

▶ interpersonal: this covers understanding and recognising the beliefs, behaviours, feelings and intentions of others.

The theory has recently been modified further to incorporate environmental, moral and spiritual intelligences.

Triarchic theory (Sternberg 1988)

While Sternberg (1988) agreed with the ideas of Gardner, he stated that instead of seven areas of intelligence, there are three main areas of "practical" intelligence:

▶ Academic problem-solving – these are skills assessed via tests such as an IQ test. The questions are well structured and there is always a single correct answer.

▶ Practical – these are skills that are often needed for everyday tasks. These tasks may not be very well defined and have multiple solutions where you have to choose which one is best to solve an issue, etc.

▶ Creative – these are the skills and behaviours that we show when trying to cope and tackle with novel situations (we may, for example, draw on previous knowledge that could be applied to a novel situation).

CHALLENGE YOURSELF
Explain to a friend one theory of intelligence highlighting at least one strength and one weakness of your chosen theory.

ALTERNATIVES TO INTELLIGENCE

There may be alternative ways in which we can measure and look at the general concept of "intelligence" – by considering factors such as the emotional side of our intellect, being creative and problem-solving techniques.

Emotional intelligence

Salovey & Mayer (Myers, 1990) identified a part of people's social behaviour that they called emotional intelligence. People who have high levels of emotional intelligence have these characteristics:

▶ They are self-aware – they can manage their emotions well in different circumstances and not be overwhelmed by one single emotion (e.g. depression or anxiety).

▶ They can easily delay any self-gratification in pursuit of a reward – they do not let impulses overcome them.

▶ They have strong empathy skills.

▶ The can handle other people's emotions easily and skilfully. They can handle conflict well.

▶ They succeed in aspects of life that require emotional awareness rather than academic prowess (e.g. marriage and parenting).

TEST YOURSELF
Outline what is meant by emotional intelligence.

Creativity and unusual uses test

Creativity involves finding a solution to a problem that is both unusual *and* novel. It requires an element of "thinking outside of the box" and maybe tackling a problem from a non-logical or non-traditional way. Newell, Shaw & Simon (Matlin, 1963) outlined that one or more of the following criteria have to be met for something to be labelled "creative":

▶ The answer does have novelty and is useful (either to an individual or society).

▶ The answer means that we reject ideas that had previously been accepted.

▶ The answer comes from a period of intense motivation *and* persistence with the task.

▶ The answer clarifies a problem that was originally seen as being vague.

There are many ways of measuring creativity. One is called the divergent production test and some example questions are given below.

Try to answer the following:

1. Here is a simple familiar form: a circle.

How many pictures of real-life objects can you draw in a one-minute period, using the circle?

2. Many words begin with "L" and end with "N". Write down as many as you can, in a one-minute period. The words can have any number of letters between the "L" at the start and the "N" at the end.

3. Imagine that normal height for an adult is 1 metre. In a one-minute period, list as many consequences of this as you can.

4. Look at this list of names:

BETH   HAROLD   GAIL
JOHN   LUCY   SALLY

These names can be classified in many ways. For example, number of syllables could be used: Beth,

Gail and John have only one syllable, the other names in the list have two. In a one-minute period, classify the names in as many ways as you can.

5. Here are four shapes.

Combine them to make: a face, a lamp, a piece of playground equipment, a tree. You can use each shape once, more than once, or not at all in forming each object and each one can be shrunk or expanded to any size.

Another way of measuring creativity is through the unusual uses test. This presents people with various objects (e.g. a brick, a matchbox, a pen) and asks them, in a set period of time, to come up with as many different ways as possible that the objects can be used. Those who think of many ways are said to be creative in the way that they think and reason.

CHALLENGE YOURSELF
You have been asked to devise a test that measures creativity. What sorts of things will you get people to do? Justify the choices of task.

Problem solving: means-end analysis, planning strategies and backwards searching

Problem solving has also interested psychologists for many years.

Means-end analysis is a problem-solving strategy where the problem solver has to divide the problem into a smaller number of "sub-problems" in order to reach the goal. Each "sub-problem" should reduce the difference between the starting point and the end point. Therefore, we figure out the "ends" of a problem and then figure out the "means" by which we will do it – hence means–end analysis. Some psychologists have tried to use

computer simulations to show how a human uses means–end analysis. The computer breaks down a problem to a number of smaller problems and solves each one before moving on to the next. As with humans, the simulations do make a decision at each sub-problem that was identified – so we may process in the same way as a computer. Therefore, means–end analysis is an example of a *planning strategy* that we can use when problem solving.

There are other planning strategies that people may use when attempting to solve problems. One is called *trial and error* in which people try lots of different ways to solve a problem, fail and make errors throughout, but ultimately (they hope) solve the problem this way. We may also use an *analogy* – this is about using the solution to an earlier problem to help us solve a new one. So we use previous experiences and knowledge of something similar (but not same) to help solve a new problem. We also may engage in *lateral thinking* which is about solving a problem creatively (as highlighted above).

Backward searching is another technique that we may use to help us to solve a problem. The problem solver starts at the goal state (e.g. what needs to be solved or the end state) and works backwards from this towards the original (or start) state.

Try the following puzzle using backward searching as it highlights it very well.

A lily pad grows so that each day it doubles its size (area). On the 20th day of its life, it completely covers the pond. On what day of its life was the pond half covered?

Children will often use backward searching when trying to solve a maze. They may start from the exit point and try to move backwards towards the starting point.

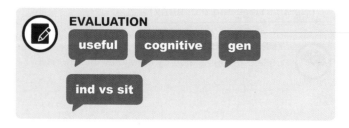

Answer to the lily pad problem

The lily pad covered the pond on the 19th day of its life.

You could have worked it out by noting that the lily pad was doubling in size (area) each day, so if it completely covered the pond on the 20th day, it had to have half covered the pond the day before. All it took to cover the pond was one more day.

EXAMPLES OF HOW TO EVALUATE

For the 12 mark question in Paper 3, you will be asked to evaluate one of the topics covered in this section. You will have noticed that after each topic in this chapter there are the icons for the different issues, debates, approaches, perspectives and research methods that *could* be used to help you answer the 12 mark question in the examination. Below are three examples of the types of things you *could* write in the examination.

You should aim to make *at least* four different evaluation points for the 12 mark question. Our accompanying Revision Guide has a series of student answers with marks and examiner comments attached to them.

Measuring learning styles

Learning styles can be measured using *psychometrics*. This is an advantage as they are standardised on a large sample of people, they can be seen as being more objective and scientific. Therefore, Enwhistle's ASI allows a direct comparison between students in a group or class to directly show which of the 4 dimensions each student is stronger on. There is no need for any interpretation. However, there may be issues with *validity*. Is the test actually measuring the behaviour it is supposed to be measuring? For example, with Kolb, how can we be sure it is exactly measuring accommodators, divergers etc. Also, these measures have to rely on people being honest with their answers. This can affect the validity of the final scores on the scales and therefore a student may be incorrectly labelled with a type of learning style (e.g. accommodator) when in fact

they are something else – this may then affect how they are educated. In addition to this, there could be an issue of validity in terms of people may answer questions in one way on paper that does not really represent how they actually behave when in the classroom or trying to learn. Therefore, *predictive validity* might be low.

Improving motivation

One problem with using praise with children in the classroom is based around its *usefulness*. Whilst behavioural psychologists will argue that using rewards increases the probability of repeating that behaviour, others may argue that this only changes the observable behaviour and not the thought processes that are happening behind the behaviour. Also, if a teacher does not consistently give praise to all students for the same behaviours or level of performance then it will be difficult to implement as it could de-motivate students who are showing good behaviour but do not receive a reward of some form.

Corrective and preventive strategies

Preventive strategies for dealing with disruptive behaviour have been seen to be *useful*. Wang, Berry & Swearer (2013) interestingly noted that having the 'warm' and 'positive' climate appears crucial in the success of a prevention program for bullying. In addition, Cross *et al* (2011) reported on the Friendly Schools Program and how it was successful if everyone was committed to the Program with support from the local community (usually through parents) then there was significantly less bullying even 36 months after the Program started. Therefore, it can be useful within schools to improve student behaviour that is a problem.

Exam centre

Try the following exam-type questions.

Section A

(a) Explain, in your own words, what is meant by the term 'learning style'. (2 marks)

(b) Explain, in your own words, what is meant by the term 'intelligence'. (2 marks)

(c) Describe **two** ways in which you could improve motivation in students. (4 marks)

(d) Outline **one** special educational need. (4 marks)

Section B

(a) Describe what psychologists have discovered about cognitive approaches to learning. (8 marks)

(b) Describe what psychologists have discovered about motivation and education. (8 marks)

(c) Evaluate what psychologists have discovered about intelligence and include a discussion on the use of psychometrics. (12 marks)

(d) Evaluate what psychologists have discovered about corrective and preventive strategies for disruptive behaviour and include a discussion on usefulness. (12 marks)

Section C

(a) Describe one way we can measure learning styles. (6 marks)

(b) Suggest how you would test the reliability and validity of a measurement of learning styles. (8 marks)

(c) Describe **one** strategy that can be used to help children who have been labelled as 'gifted'. (6 marks)

(d) Suggest how you might help a child with dyslexia at school. (8 marks)

and the most common are fevers, infections, bleeding and seizures. However, Turner & Reid state that these patients may go through medical procedures that do not show that they have a "real illness" and many are then "caught out" by inconsistencies in their self-reported medical histories.

In addition to Münchausen syndrome there is Münchausen syndrome by proxy. In these instances the mother or carer of a child deliberately exaggerates and fabricates illness of the child. The caregiver may induce physical and psychological problems into the child. It is now referred to as factitious disorder by proxy. Criddle (2010) noted three levels of this syndrome:

1. Mild (symptom fabrication) – the caregiver may claim the child experiences mild symptoms of an illness the child does not have.

2. Moderate (evidence tampering) – the caregiver may go as far as manipulating laboratory specimens of the child or falsifying the medical records of the child.

3. Severe (symptom induction) – the caregiver induces an illness into the child including diarrhoea, seizures and even sepsis. These methods may also include poisoning with things such as insulin and salt, applying faecal matter to open wounds to infect them and injecting urine into the child.

CASE STUDIES

Zibis *et al* (2010) reported on a case of Münchausen syndrome. A 24-year-old woman had been referred to a surgeon as she had extremely painful, stiff and swollen right hand and arm. She reported having had four previous operations on the same region. Four days into her treatment at the hospital she developed a "fever temperature" that would not react well to any drug. However, diagnostic tests could not locate any infection or fever. It was discovered that she was preheating thermometers to take her own temperature and that she was often heard punching the wall at night (presumably with her right hand). She was also seen reading medical text books about hand diseases and amputations. The medical staff stopped her treatment. Her temperature dropped back to usual levels and 20 days after taking her cast off, her arm was free of any injury.

Faida *et al* (2012) reported on a 40-year-old woman who had injuries to her right leg. She was complaining of arthritis of the right leg with headaches and ulcers. During her hospitalisation, her condition got worse and she could no longer walk on her right leg. Tests to examine why this could be the case showed nothing abnormal about the leg. When a standard x-ray was taken, it revealed that a sewing needle was embedded in her right calf. When the hospital staff questioned her about this she became very aggressive and denied any knowledge of it. She then attempted to jump out of the hospital window to escape but thankfully was stopped. Many of her symptoms resolved spontaneously after this incident.

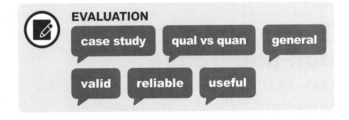

EVALUATION

case study   qual vs quan   general

valid   reliable   useful

CHALLENGE YOURSELF

Produce a leaflet that explains to people why some patients may *misuse* medical health services. Think about the target audience and what message you want to get across.

9.2 ADHERENCE TO MEDICAL ADVICE

Patients visit their doctor for advice about health problems and usually end up with a prescription for drugs or some referral for further tests or treatment. However, as health psychologists are discovering, not every patient follows the medical advice given. This section looks at why patients may not adhere to advice, how to measure adherence to advice and ways to improve patients' adherence.

ASK YOURSELF
Why would a patient not adhere to medical advice? List as many reasons as possible and then see how many turn up in this chapter.

TYPES OF NON-ADHERENCE AND REASONS WHY PATIENTS DO NOT ADHERE

Types and extent of non-adherence

Clarke (2013) noted different types of adherence that we can reverse to discover different types of non-adherence, which are:

- not following short-term advice (e.g. to take three pills per day, five hours apart, for one week)
- failing to attend a follow-up interview or a referral appointment
- not wanting to make a lifestyle change (e.g. to reduce then quit smoking or take more exercise)
- not engaging in preventative measures linked to health (e.g. using contraception).

According to Sarafino (2006), up to 40 per cent of a given population *fail to adhere to the medical advice given to them.* That is, two in five people do not follow their doctor's advice. In addition, the research showed the following:

- When medicine needs to be taken for short-term acute illness, the adherence rate climbs to 67 per cent.
- For longer-term chronic regimes, the figure appears to be around 50 per cent.

- People tend to adhere more just before or just after seeing a doctor.
- There appears to be very little adherence at all to any advice that involves a change in lifestyle.

Sarafino (2006) was quick to note that these are probably overestimates of non-adherence as the data are only based on people who were willing to take part in a study and then *admit* to non-adherence. Also, the data fails to appreciate the range of adherence as some patients will adhere to advice 100 per cent of the time but others' adherence may vary markedly from illness to illness.

Rational non-adherence

There are patients who choose not to adhere to medical advice as it *appears rational for them to do this.* By this, we mean that they have conducted a cost-benefit analysis and it appears to them "costly" to adhere to the treatment being given to them or asked of them. Laba, Brien & Jan (2012) wanted to try to understand rational non-adherence using a community sample of patients in Australia. The patients were given a discrete choice online survey that wanted to estimate the importance of eight medication factors with regard to non-adherence. The factors were:

- immediate medication harm
- immediate medication benefit
- long-term medication harm
- long-term medication benefit
- cost
- regimen
- symptom severity
- alcohol restrictions.

Six of the factors appeared to affect choice of adherence rationally in the sample. The two that did not were symptom severity and alcohol restrictions. Therefore, rational non-adherence is a complex interaction between the six remaining factors with an overall cost-benefit analysis by individual patients finally predicting whether they will adhere or not. It was noted that when a potential health outcome was framed in terms of "side effects" the person quite rationally was more likely not to adhere than if a health outcome was framed in terms of "therapeutic benefits". Therefore, the way that the treatment is, essentially, "sold to them" affects whether patients will adhere (as rational people do not want side effects but do want therapeutic benefits).

EVALUATION

useful ind vs sit valid

TEST YOURSELF
Outline reasons why people may not adhere to medical advice.

Customising treatment

CHALLENGE YOURSELF
Read the improving adherence section at the end of this page, and make notes on how practitioner style, information providing and behavioural treatment can be used to customise treatment for any patient.

MEASURING ADHERENCE AND NON-ADHERENCE

If non-adherence to medical advice is such a widespread problem then psychologists must come up with ways in which they can measure it. Below we look at a number of different ways of assessing non-adherence (and adherence).

Subjective: self-reports

One technique that can be used is for patients to complete self-reports with questions related to how much they are adhering to the treatment. Patients can be given booklets to record when they took certain drugs or engaged in certain behaviours that are asked of them as part of their treatment. Many psychologists are sceptical about the validity and reliability of self-reports as patients can easily lie about what they have done in terms of adhering to treatment. However, Kaplan & Simon (1990) noted that if the questions are direct and simple to answer then this technique can be used successfully to measure rates of adherence. However, patients may give socially desirable answers especially if they have *not* been adhering to the treatment prescribed to them.

Objective: pill counting, biochemical tests, repeat prescriptions

Another way of measuring adherence is by simply counting the amount of pills left in a bottle and working out whether the patient has taken the recommended amount over a certain time period. This can assess whether the patient has followed the correct procedure and taken the specified amount of tablets. However, just because the pills are not in the bottle any more does not mean they have actually been taken. A patient may have thrown the pills away (see Core study 7.1, page 87) or just placed them in a different container, so this is not the most accurate method of measuring *actual* adherence to a treatment regime.

Biochemical tests can be run on the patient to measure adherence. These include urine analysis and blood tests to detect levels of the drug that the patient should have consumed. While some psychologists believe these are the best methods to use after reviewing the research (e.g. Roth, 1987), the methods are very expensive compared to the other choices available. Also, while they do detect drug levels, they still do not show total adherence to a regime, only that the person has ingested enough of the drug for it to be detectable.

Repeat prescriptions have been a relatively new addition to the medical field with patients who are on longer-term treatment having the option of asking for the same amount of drugs again *without* having to see a doctor first. These patients simply request a repeat prescription from their local doctor's surgery and then pick up the drug. Although this means that patients have to have the motivation to do this (so the argument is that they must be adhering to the treatment), they could still obtain the drugs but not consume them (especially if the drugs are free).

EVALUATION

qual/quan questionnaire useful

valid reliable

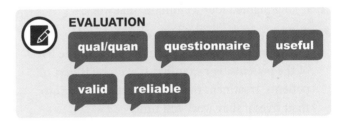

CHALLENGE YOURSELF
A local health charity wants you to help it decide which is the best way to measure adherence to medical advice. In your report to the charity, you must outline at least three ways and highlight the strengths and weaknesses of each technique.

IMPROVING ADHERENCE

Now we will look at techniques that can be used to try to improve adherence levels in patients after they have visited a doctor.

Improve practitioner style, provide information and behavioural techniques

All of these three aspects can be incorporated in an attempt to make patients adhere more to medical advice. The practitioner style and information aspects can be combined as Sarafino (2006) outlined. Practitioners can use a variety of techniques:

- They can ensure that the patient understands the "disease process" and the pros and cons of treatment.

- They can use simplified non-medical language.

- They can use measurable statements for treatment rather than generic (e.g. with people who take exercise by swimming, advising that they should swim 20 lengths each time they go for their regular swim, rather than telling them to take some exercise daily).

- Any key information that is vital to the treatment can be stated more than once.

- They can ensure that any written instructions have no ambiguity whatsoever.

- The patient can be asked to repeat the instructions *at least once*.

Practitioners can also use a range of behavioural methods to try to improve adherence. Burke, Dunbar-Jacob & Hill (1997) highlighted four techniques that work:

- Tailor the regimen – that is, ensure that the treatment programme is compatible with the lives of the patients. For example, if exercise is part of patients' treatment then make sure it can fit into their lives if they work full time.

- Provide prompts and reminders to serve as cues so patients are reminded of the treatment – one example is having the day printed on the drug packaging so patients know whether they have taken the pill on the correct day.

- Arrange self-monitoring – ask patients to keep a written record of what they do. These records act as prompts; also, patients are more likely to stick to the treatment if they have to keep a record.

- Establish a behaviour contract – a "contract" can be drawn up between practitioner and patient for the patient to reach certain treatment goals, with rewards given when this happens.

USE OF TEXT MESSAGING

As the number of mobile phones increasingly grows, healthcare providers may be able to use simple text reminders to improve adherence to treatment. Lewis *et al* (2013) reported on a scheme that sent tailored text messages to people currently undergoing HIV treatment. After being assessed prior to receiving text messages, patients received reminder texts, answered weekly adherence texts and those who adhered to treatment received tailored messages such as "He shoots! He scores! Perfect med adherence. Great job!' (2013: 250). Patients found to be non-adherent were sent reminder texts such as "Stop, drop and pop. Take your meds now!" (2013: 250). Patients reported being very receptive to the text-messaging system and appreciated the messages. The adherence to medication (which was self-reported) improved significantly during the three months receiving the texts especially among those who had begun the study not adhering to treatment. Objective measures of adherence such as viral load confirmed that these patients had been adhering to treatment.

LETTERS

Even with IT dominating people's lives, Zhang & Fish (2012) examined whether a simple letter received by post might improve adherence to a variety of treatments in a healthcare setting. They also wanted to investigate whether different types of treatment were affected in the same way using a reminder letter. Adult patients were followed to check for adherence rates to a variety of health issues (e.g. colonoscopies, general x-rays, vaccines and general eye tests for diabetics). A first reminder letter was sent out one month after the appropriate time frame for treatment for urgent cases and after two months for non-urgent cases. If these were not responded to then a second letter was sent out one month after the first. Table 9.2.1 shows the adherence rates for a variety of treatments followed in the study.

NEGATIVE EFFECTS

Now we will examine whether noise can have a negative effect on the social behaviours of adults and the educational performance of children.

Anti-social behaviour

One anti-social behaviour that could be affected by noise is aggression. It has been predicted that as noise increases arousal, any behaviour that requires arousal will become more intense when noise is present. Geen & O'Neal (1969) tested this by showing participants either a violent boxing film or a non-violent sports film. After watching either film, participants were given an opportunity to be aggressive towards a confederate "victim" using an electric shock apparatus. They were told that the higher-numbered buttons gave a larger shock and that the shock would last for as long as they held the switch down. In reality, no one was actually shocked. During this shock phase the participants were either exposed to whatever noises were naturally in the laboratory or a two-minute blast of 60dB white noise. The participants exposed to the white noise delivered more shocks to the confederate. In addition, those who had watched the violent boxing film *and* were exposed to the white noise gave the highest number of shocks and for the longest duration.

Pro-social behaviour

Mathews & Canon (1975) ran two studies to test whether noise affects pro-social behaviour (behaviours that include, for example, helping others). One study was in a laboratory and one was in the field.

For the laboratory study participants were split into three groups. They were exposed to either 48dB of normal noise or 65dB or 85dB of white noise played through a speaker. When they arrived for the study they were greeted by a confederate who asked them to wait in a laboratory for a few minutes. During this time the confederate sat and read a journal in the same room, with other papers and materials balanced on his or her lap. When the experimenter came into the room to get the participant, the confederate got up and accidentally dropped the materials right in front of the participant. The frequency of helping behaviour was recorded. A total of 72 per cent of the participants helped when the noise was of a normal level. In contrast, 67 per cent helped when the noise was 65dB and only 37 per cent helped when the noise was 85dB.

In the field study a confederate would drop a box of books while getting out of a car. In half of the trials, he wore a cast on his arm. Noise was also manipulated so that half of the trials were under "normal background levels" which were measured to be 50dB whereas in the other half a confederate used a lawnmower that generated 87dB of noise. The amount of passers-by that helped was measured in four conditions. The results showed that noise had little impact on passers-by when the person was not wearing a cast – around 15 per cent of people helped out. However, noise had an impact on helping behaviour when the person wore a cast. When the noise was at background levels, 80 per cent of passers-by helped out. However, when the noise was loud (from the lawnmower), helping behaviour *decreased* to 15 per cent. It would appear that loud noises lead people to *not* pay attention to cues that indicate a person may need help.

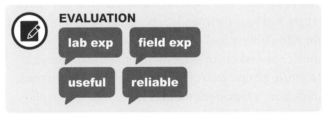

TEST YOURSELF
How does noise affect anti-social *or* pro-social behaviour? Evaluate the evidence you use in your answer.

Performance in children

There have been studies examining whether noise can affect the educational performance of children. Cohen, Glass & Singer (1973) examined children living in a high-rise apartment block that was directly above a highway. Those who lived on the lower floors were obviously exposed to a higher level of noise than those on the upper floors. Unsurprisingly, the children on the lower floors had poorer hearing discrimination than the children on the upper floors. This could have had a direct effect on their reading skills – the children on the lower floors had significantly poorer reading skills for their age. Also, Bronzaft & McCarthy (1975) tested the reading ability of two sets of children from the same school. One class was situated near a railroad track while the other class was on the opposite, quieter, side of the school. Around 11 per cent of teaching time was lost due to noise in the railroad class and the children here had significantly poorer reading ability than the children in the class on the quiet side of the school.

POSITIVE USES OF SOUND (MUSIC)

So far we have looked at noise being unwanted and a nuisance, but have psychologists found ways of using sound and noise in a more positive way?

Consumer behaviour

North, Hargreaves & McKendrick (1999) examined whether in-store music affected wine selections. During a two-week period, a display was set up at the end of an aisle in a supermarket that had four French wines and four German wines displayed in it, matched for affordability and sweetness. Stereotypical French music (played on an accordion) or German music (featuring brass instruments) was played on alternate days from a tape deck on the top shelf of the display. The music could be heard up to 1 metre away. Once customers had placed a bottle of wine from the display in their trolley or basket an experimenter approached them and asked them questions about their purchase. They were asked about their usual preference for wine (French or German) and to rate how much the music made them think of the appropriate country. A total of 82 shoppers purchased wine from the display and 44 of these completed the questionnaire. Table 10.1.1 shows the amount of bottles sold by the type of music being played.

Bottles sold	French music	German music
French wine	40	12
German wine	8	22

▲ **Table 10.1.1** Wine purchases by type of music played

As can be clearly seen, more wine was purchased from the country from which music was being played. However, only one participant actually noted that the music had influenced the person's choice of wine purchased. A further five people did say that the music could have affected their decision. Therefore, it would appear that music can affect how we think, which in turn affects our consumer behaviour.

Yeah & North (2010) examined the role of "musical fit" on the ability of consumers to recall products. By "musical fit" the researchers meant that the music fits in with the product (as above with the wines). A total of 144 students from Malaysia (24 each of Malay, Indian and Chinese) were played either Malay music or Indian music. They were then asked to list as many Malay and Indian foods as they could and were given as much time as they needed to do this. The mean amount of food items recalled can be seen in Table 10.1.2.

Ethnicity of participant	Malay music and Malay food	Malay music and Indian food	Indian music and Malay food	Indian music and Indian food
Chinese	5.12	3.96	4.67	5.54
Malay	7.87	4.12	9.50	4.92
Indian	7.00	7.96	10.29	12.38

▲ **Table 10.1.2** Type of music played and food items recalled

Table 10.1.2 shows that the Chinese participants recalled more food items when the items were linked to the music playing, i.e. they recalled more Malay foods than Indian foods when Malay music was being played, and so on. However, this was not true for the other ethnic groups. Malay students recalled more Malay foods irrespective of the music being played and Indian students recalled more Indian food irrespective of the music being played. This shows that music can affect consumers' ability to recall food items but only if the context is *not* based on one's own culture.

CHALLENGE YOURSELF

A supermarket has approached you to help it to use music to make consumers buy more products. Write a report, based on evidence, that you can present to the manager of the supermarket.

Stress reduction

Han *et al* (2010) reported on the effects that music intervention had on stress responses in patients who were undergoing mechanical ventilation in hospital. A total of 137 patients were randomly assigned to either a group listening to music without headphones, a group wearing headphones or a control group. Physiological measures of heart rate, respiratory rate, oxygen levels and blood pressure were taken pre- and post-intervention. There was a significant reduction in heart rate and respiratory rate in the group listening to music without headphones compared to a significant *increase* in the control group. There were no significant changes in the groups wearing headphones. This shows that music can be used as a short-term "therapy" for patients undergoing mechanical ventilation.

Carr *et al* (2012) examined the role of music therapy for patients who had persistent post-traumatic stress disorder (PTSD). They used a sample of patients with PTSD who had not responded positively to

cognitive behavioural therapy (CBT). A total of 17 patients formed the sample. Nine of these received group music therapy and the remaining eight were the control group (but it should be noted that they were offered the music therapy after completing the study). All patients had previously not responded to CBT. Participants' PTSD symptoms were assessed using the Events Scale (revised version) pre- and post-intervention. The group who underwent music therapy had a significant reduction in the severity of their PTSD symptoms ten weeks after starting the therapy. The patients viewed the music therapy as being very helpful.

Finally, Kushnir *et al* (2012) noted that if women were allowed to choose their favourite music to listen to prior to a caesarean section, their experience was more positive, they perceived less threat from the situation and their blood pressure reduced compared to the control group.

Performance

Shih, Huang & Chiang (2012) examined whether music with or without lyrics affected attention performance. A total of 102 participants from Taipei County University took part in the study. They were randomly allocated to one of two conditions as shown in Figure 10.1.2.

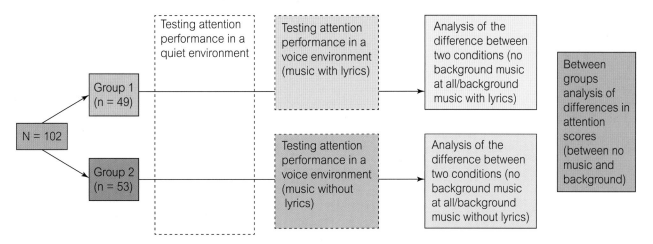

▲ **Figure 10.1.2** Participants in one of two test conditions: group 1 (music with lyrics), group 2 (music without lyrics

Source: Based on Shih, Huang & Chiang (2012)

All participants had to complete the Chu Attention Test, a psychometric measure of attentional performance. This is a 100-item test where participants are asked to indicate the number of times an asterisk (*) appears in a series of scrambled codes. Participants were given ten minutes to go through as many codes as possible. At baseline, the two groups did not differ significantly on their attentional performances. Table 10.1.3 shows the comparison of scores at baseline and with music and also that there was a greater reduction in attentional performance when music was played that contained lyrics than when music with no lyrics was played.

Group	Mean baseline score	Mean score with background music
Music with lyrics	105.5	98.4
Music without lyrics	109.3	106.7

▲ **Table 10.1.3** Mean scores: baseline and with background music

daze or dream and memory problems such as forgetting to do important things. Other differences included difficulty in sleeping, having poor concentration, feeling agitated and restless, and lacking energy. However, these differences had disappeared at the 12-week assessment.

EVALUATION

`useful` `ind vs sit` `ethics`

TEST YOURSELF
Outline ways in which psychologists have helped people who have survived disaster.

Herald of Free Enterprise

This disaster occurred when a ferry capsized and sank off Belgium killing 197 people. Survivors were examined for PTSD. Joseph *et al* (1997) discovered that there was a relationship between emotional expression

three years after the event and PTSD five years after the event. Those who believed, emotionally, that having negative attitudes was a sign of weakness were more likely to show PTSD symptoms. Also, Joseph *et al* (1996) noted that those who scored high on a measure of "have intrusive and avoidant activities" tended to show higher levels of depression and anxiety three years after the sinking.

London bombing

Bombings were carried out in London on 7 July 2005. Rubin *et al* (2007) telephoned 1 010 Londoners 11–13 days after the bombings occurred. The researchers wanted to assess stress levels, perceived threats and travel intentions. Seven months after this, 574 respondents were contacted again and asked similar questions. Around 11 per cent of people in the sample were still feeling "substantial stress" and over 40 per cent still felt personally threatened by the events. Around 20 per cent had reduced their travelling around London as a result. Rubin *et al* (2007) also reported on data from the first phase of the study (answers to questions 11–13 days after the bombings). Around one-third of the sample at this time felt substantial stress and intended to travel less as a result of the bombings. Those who felt the substantial stress tended to be people who would find it difficult to contact friends and family, those who thought that they could have been killed or injured and those who were Muslim. Only 1 per cent of people in the sample felt they needed psychological intervention post-bombings.

Finally, Wilson *et al* (2012) examined the transcripts of 18 people who received cognitive behavioural therapy (CBT) after the bombings to help them with PTSD. The clients tended to focus on recollection of direct experiences during the bombings, the horror of it all and reconnecting with the outside world on the day of the event plus feelings of PTSD and depression the day *after* the bombings.

▲ **Figure 10.3.3** Herald of Free Enterprise

10.4 PERSONAL SPACE AND TERRITORY

DEFINITIONS, TYPES AND MEASURES

ASK YOURSELF

In what situations do you not like your personal space being invaded? Are there times and situations when it is good to invade someone's personal space?

Defining space and territory

Bell *et al* (1996) define personal space as a "…portable, invisible boundary surrounding us, into which others may not trespass. It regulates how closely we interact with others, moves with us, and expands and contracts according to the situation in which we find ourselves" (1996: 275).

Hall (1963) distinguished between zones of personal space, which he called spatial zones, based around interpersonal relationships we may have. This is shown in Table 10.4.1.

Distance	Usual activities and relationships
Intimate (0 to 1½ feet)	Contact is intimate (e.g. comforting another or having sex). Physical sports such as judo and wrestling allow invasion of the intimate zone.
Personal (1½ to 4 feet)	Friends are allowed to get into this zone, especially those who are close to us. Your usual everyday interactions will trespass into this zone too.
Social (4 feet to 12 feet)	People we do not really know personally, but whom we meet quite regularly, are allowed into this zone. Business-like contacts are also allowed here.
Public (more than 12 feet away)	This zone is for formal contact (e.g. someone giving a public speech).

▲ Table 10.4.1 Spatial zones

Source: Hall (1963)

Altman (1975) noted that we have three different types of territory. These are shown in Table 10.4.2.

Type of territory	Occupation of territory/ perception of ownership	Amount we "personalise" the territory
Primary territory (e.g. own home, office space, bedroom)	**High** degree of occupation and perception of ownership: we believe that we permanently own the territory and others believe this too.	The territory is personalised in great detail so that the owner has complete control and others recognise this almost immediately after entering it. Uninvited intrusion can have serious consequences.
Secondary territory (e.g. classroom)	**Medium** degree of occupation and perception of ownership: we believe that we are one of only a limited number of users of the territory.	Personalisation occurs to some extent but only when the occupancy of the territory is legitimate (e.g. within about one month of a new class, each person may stick with the same seat for the rest of the year. That person legitimately owns that seat every lesson).
Public territory (e.g. area on a beach, seat on a bus)	**Low** degree of occupation and perception of ownership: we believe we are one of many people who use this territory.	Personalisation tends to be temporary as we may not revisit the territory for some time. We tend not to defend this territory in the way we would if it were primary or secondary territory.

▲ Table 10.4.2 Three types of territory

Source: Altman (1975)

Bell *et al* (1996) define territoriality as follows: "…(it) can be viewed as a set of behaviours and cognitions a person or group exhibits, based on perceived ownership of physical space" (1996: 304). This may be permanent, as in owning a house, or temporary, as in controlling your office space but not directly owning it.

Alpha space and beta space

Alpha space is the personal space that is objective and can be measured directly (e.g. the actual distance). Beta space is the personal space that is subjective and is how a person feels when being invaded.

Measuring space: simulation

Little (1968) examined cultural differences over 19 different social situations in a sample of Americans, Swedes, Scots, Greeks and Italians. They had to place dolls at distances that reflected where they would stand in real social situations. The situations they had to assess included two good friends talking about a pleasant topic, a shop owner discussing the weather with his assistant, two people talking about the best place to shop and two strangers talking about an unpleasant topic.

The average distances at which participants placed the dolls over the 19 different social situations are shown in Figure 10.4.1.

Stop-distance

This technique involves getting someone to approach a participant from a variety of angles and getting the participant to say "Stop" when the participant begins to feel uncomfortable. The actual distance is measures so that a "picture" of the amount and shape of personal space can be generated. This can then be re-assessed in different situations.

Space invasions

These types of measurements involve directly invading the space of other people and noting how they react or asking them how they felt. The "Invading space and terrritory" section outlines some studies that have used this method.

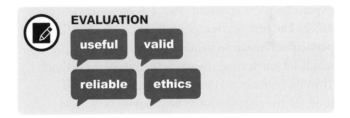

EVALUATION

useful valid

reliable ethics

TEST YOURSELF
Outline and evaluate two ways in which personal space can be measured.

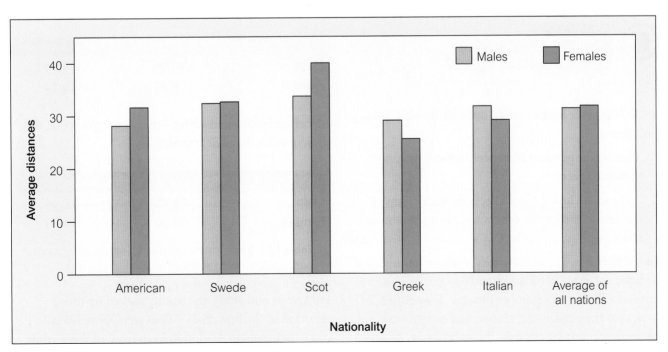

▲ **Figure 10.4.1** Results from the Little (1968) study

INVADING SPACE AND TERRITORY

Invasions

Middlemist *et al* (1976) wanted to investigate the proposal that invasion of personal space produces arousal. The setting was a men's public lavatory. According to the researchers this was an ideal place as "norms for privacy" are already set up (space between the urinals), so the effect that distance had on arousal could be easily measured. The men's public lavatory had three urinals in it. Sixty participants were randomly assigned to one of three conditions: (1) the experimenter stood immediately next to the participant, (2) the experimenter stood at the other end of the three urinals to the participant or (3) the experimenter was absent. Two key measures were taken. The first was a measure of how quickly the participant began to urinate. The second measure was how much time the participant took to urinate. The closer the experimenter stood, the longer it took for the participant to begin urination. Also, the closer the experimenter stood, the less time it took the participant to complete urination. The evidence suggests that invasion of personal space in men produces physiological changes associated with arousal. The more the personal space was invaded, the more aroused the men became.

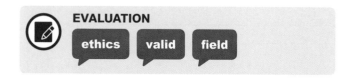

EVALUATION

ethics   valid   field

In 1975 Fisher & Byrne carried out a study with two main aims:

1. To examine gender differences in the invasion of personal space.

2. To examine how gender affects the putting up of barriers to indicate to others where our personal space is.

For the first aim, Fisher & Byrne's confederates invaded the personal space of 62 males and 63 females in a university library in a number of ways. They either sat next to the participant, sat one seat away from the participant or sat opposite the participant. After the invasion had taken place, Fisher & Byrne asked participants to complete a questionnaire about the experience. It asked questions about how participants felt during the invasion of their personal space (e.g. how happy they felt, how attracted they were to the confederate, their perceived level of crowding).

For the second aim, a different researcher was used who was not told the aim of the research (this is called the single-blind technique). This researcher had to observe 33 males and 33 females and record where they placed their personal belongings on a library table.

From the first study, distinct gender differences emerged. Males disliked being invaded by someone approaching from opposite them but did not mind someone invading the space next to them. For females, the opposite results arose; they did not mind people invading the space opposite them but disliked the invasion when someone sat next to them. Table 10.4.3 shows averages that highlight this trend across all measures taken on the questionnaire.

Happiness rating – the higher the score, the more happy participants were:

	Sitting next to	Sitting opposite
Male	29.15	23.57
Female	23.46	26.79

Attractiveness rating – the higher the score, the more attracted participants were to an opposite-sex confederate:

	Sitting next to	Sitting opposite
Male	10.99	9.14
Female	9.87	10.14

Perceived level of crowding – the higher the score, the more participants felt crowded:

	Sitting next to	Sitting opposite
Male	11.48	17.04
Female	16.60	14.76

▲ **Table 10.4.3** Ratings for happiness, attractiveness and perceived level of crowding

For the second study, the results backed up those reported in the first study. Males were more likely to place their personal belongings in front of them while females were more likely to place personal belongings

10.6 ENVIRONMENTAL COGNITION

DEFINITIONS, MEASURES, ERRORS AND INDIVIDUAL DIFFERENCES IN COGNITIVE MAPS

 ASK YOURSELF
Draw a map of the surrounding area of your home or school. Find a real map of the area and see how accurate you have been.

Definitions

Tolman (1948) defined cognitive maps as an internal representation that animals develop about the spatial relationships within their environment.

Measures

The following are different ways in which you can measure cognitive maps.

Sketch maps

Lynch (1960) was one of the first to make people simply sketch maps to see how they were representing their surroundings psychologically. He found five main categories that are used to mentally describe maps:

- paths: shared routes for travel (e.g. footpaths and roads)
- edges: boundaries that are defined (e.g. walls of buildings or coastlines)
- districts: large spaces with a shared characteristic (e.g. The West End in London)
- nodes: points on a map that act as a focus for behaviour (e.g. town squares, roundabouts or major road junctions)
- landmarks: distinctive features used as reference points which are generally visible from a distance (e.g. a place of worship or a tall skyscraper).

Multidimensional scaling

This is a statistical technique that can assess the "cognitive distance" people believe landmarks are separated by. Participants are asked to estimate distances between a number of buildings on a route. Once this is completed, a computer program can process the data and generate a "map" based on these estimations (so that a person's drawing skills are not affecting how the person perceives a map, etc.). If these are compared among a group of participants who have all estimated the distances, if all are consistent then a relatively accurate map should be produced. However, as Bell *et al* (2001) noted, people may well exaggerate the distance between unpleasant landmarks or travel paths they do not usually take.

 **EVALUATION**
ind diffs   valid   useful

 TEST YOURSELF
Outline and evaluate one way of measuring cognitive maps.

Errors

Lloyd and Patton (2011) asked participants to learn locations on one of three cartographic maps that contained true or novel location names. The following recall errors were found:

- There were fewer cognitive distance errors for reference points that were central to the map.
- There were fewer errors in recall when a reference point was part of a cluster.
- Females made fewer errors when learning novel maps.
- Males made fewer errors when learning maps with true names and places.

Steyvers & Koojiman (2009) examined the differences in error rates using cognitive maps of a fictitious zoo between sighted and visually impaired participants. The participants were matched on age, gender and education. The matched pairs were randomly assigned to one "information type":

- Survey-type descriptions such as "the area containing the indoor animal exhibits is north of the children's recreational area" (2009: 226).

▶ Route-type descriptions such as "on your right is the petting zoo. Turn right and then left after passing the petting zoo. The aquarium is now on your right" (2009: 226).

They listened to the tape of information twice and then were asked questions such as "Which animals will you find east of the insect house?" (survey-type) and "Standing on the path with your back to the petting zoo and facing the monkeys, which animals are on your left?' (route-type) (2009: 226).

The visually impaired participants showed no difference in the frequency of errors between survey-type and route-type descriptions. Sighted participants made fewer errors with the survey-type descriptions. Overall, the sighted participants made fewer cognitive map errors.

EVALUATION

lab exp   valid   useful

CHALLENGE YOURSELF
Design a study that would test whether there are any differences in errors using cognitive maps based on the age *or* gender of the participants. Evaluate your idea.

Individual differences

In terms of sketch maps, there appears to be gender difference in what is included in them. Huynh, Doherty & Sharpe (2010) noted that when asked to draw a map, males and females tend not to differ with the initial drawing. However, as the map got more elaborate and detailed, females drew more landmarks on their maps while males drew more pathways.

The Steyers & Koojiman (2009) study can also be used to show individual differences.

COGNITIVE MAPS IN ANIMALS

Squirrels

Jacobs & Liman (1991) investigated the role of the cognitive map in allowing animals to search for food they had stored themselves. Each grey squirrel (*sciurus*

carolinensis) was released into a 45m² area to bury ten hazelnuts. The location of each food item was recorded and the nuts were then removed. The squirrels were returned to the area individually 2, 4 or 12 days later. New hazelnuts had been placed at the individuals' own hiding places and at an equal number of randomly chosen sites which had been used by other squirrels. The squirrels were more likely to find nuts from places where they had buried them even when they had to pass the sites chosen by other squirrels. Although the squirrels clearly could locate buried nuts by smell alone, they were preferentially seeking the ones they had hidden on the basis of recalling each location.

Bees

Capaldi & Dyer (1999) examined the role of orientation flights on the homing performances of honeybees. Previous research had shown that bees do use visual references to help them move from foraging site to foraging site. However, the majority of research had examined bees that were experienced. Capaldi & Dyer wanted to investigate this in naïve bees. The bees were all from the Michigan State University Research Farms. There were three groups of bees:

1. Resident bees – they already lived in the test location.

2. First-flight bees – they had never been outside the nest.

3. Reorienting bees – these were worker bees that had foraging experience at a different site from the test site.

Bees in groups and 3 were allowed on an "orientation" flight that typically lasted less than ten minutes. On the experimental trials after this, homing ability was measured via vanishing bearings and homing speed. When the first-flight bees were tested after the orientation flight, they returned to the hive faster than the reorienting bees. They also had faster homing rates than resident bees. When they were released at a distance, resident bees tended to outperform the other two groups. When there were landmarks near to the target hive, all groups tended to head towards the hive (vanishing bearings were similar). However, when they were released out of sight of any landmarks (and they had to rely on route memory), the first-flight bees performed poorly, whereas the resident bees could still find their way home.

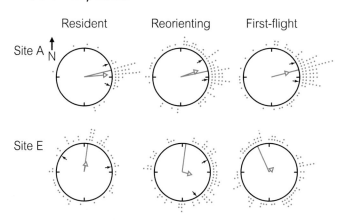

Figure 10.6.1 Bees' homing ability measured via vanishing bearings – site A landmarks were near to the target hives; for site E the bees had no route memory

It would appear that landmarks are used as part of a cognitive map of foraging sites in bees.

Pigeons and magnetite

Walcott has researched the homing abilities of pigeons for many years. It would appear that magnetic fields help pigeons to find their way home. Early studies drugged pigeons and drove them to a place of release (so they could not see any landmarks on their outward journey). Once released, virtually all pigeons found their way home and it was hypothesised that pigeons may use magnetism to way-find (via a substance called magnetite in their brains). Walcott (1977) noted that applying a magnetic field of 0.1 gauss to the heads of homing pigeons increased the scatter of the pigeons as they left their release site. This is shown in Figure 10.6.2.

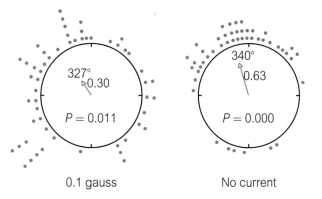

Figure 10.6.2 Scatter of pigeons from the release site

Figure 10.6.3 Pigeon wearing on its head a device that generates a magnetic field

Therefore, it would appear that changes in the magnetic fields that a pigeon experiences affects its ability to way-find.

TEST YOURSELF
Outline and evaluate one study that has looked into cognitive maps in animals.

DESIGNING BETTER MAPS; WAY-FINDING

Map design

Levine (1982) and Levine *et al* (1984) have suggested strategies for improving the usefulness of "you are here" maps. To aid their navigation users need to know where they are in relation to the map. This can be achieved if they can correctly identify a minimum of two features both on the map and in the environment. This is called *structure matching* and enables users to place themselves accurately on the map. For example, a "you are here" dot may pinpoint your position along a road running down the map. However, without indicators of direction, such as buildings that are both visible in the environment and appear on the map, it would be impossible to decide whether your side of the pavement was to the left or right of the map – you would be unable to navigate.

Many passengers travelling from north to south prefer to hold their map upside down to assist navigation. This restores the map to its correct *orientation*, that is, it achieves direct correspondence between the map and the real world – what is ahead on the road is "up" on the map (*forward-up equivalence*) and features to the left on the map are on the left-hand side of the road. Levine *et al* (1984) demonstrated experimentally that if way-finding maps are not displayed with forward-up equivalence they are misleading and will disrupt way-finding even when people are made aware of the non-equivalence. Levine *et al* also found that the presentation of maps in airports and offices often fails to achieve forward-up equivalence. The consequences of this could range from mild inconvenience or delay to a serious threat to life in emergency evacuations.

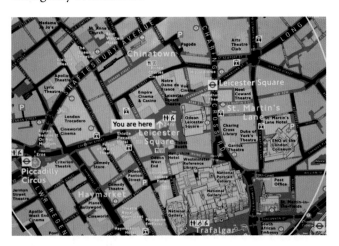

▲ **Figure 10.6.4** An example of a "you are here" map

CHALLENGE YOURSELF
Find a map of your school and identify features that could be improved.

Way-finding

Possession of a cognitive map may neither be necessary for nor guarantee successful way-finding, the process of navigating through an environment. We may use published maps, ask others for directions or obtain other experience or information to help us to find our way. In the absence of these, or an ability to understand them, we may become lost. In reality this is relatively rare. We may indeed "lose ourselves" but this tends to be short-lived. By keeping moving until we find somewhere familiar or by returning to a known location we can re-establish effective way-finding:

▷ Determine the location.

▷ Localise the destination.

▷ Select a route.

▷ Decide how to travel.

Way-finding is also facilitated by a high degree of *visual access*, i.e. being visible from different perspectives. In a hilly town we are likely to be able to obtain different views of buildings and streets, increasing visual access. Conversely, underground, such as in car parks or particularly on tube trains, our visual access is limited and so assimilating information about the relationships between locations is difficult.

How difficult an area is to understand in terms of the amount of detail and its intricacy is referred to as the *complexity of spatial layout*. Way-finding is hampered in environments with a very complicated spatial layout. Within a building this may result from having several floors, unpredictable interconnections both across and between floors and having a different floor plan at each level. Complex spatial layouts such as this may be encountered in large shopping centres. Since it may also be difficult to gain a high degree of visual access and because store fronts are all essentially similar, lowering differentiation, it may be very difficult to learn the way around.

Virtual way-finding

Revisit Core study 6.3 for AS level on page 78. The researchers used virtual way-finding in this study where taxi drivers had to mentally (virtually) plan a route from location A to location B.

11.2 SCHIZOPHRENIA

TYPES, SYMPTOMS AND CHARACTERISTICS

ASK YOURSELF
How would you diagnose schizophrenia in someone? What behaviours and characteristics would you look for?

Schizophrenia was first called "dementia praecox" (premature dementia) as it affects people's thoughts, emotions and behaviours. Below are the types of schizophrenia currently recognised and the characteristics that need to be shown for people to be diagnosed.

Types

Schizophrenia is an umbrella term used to outline a range of different psychotic disorders that affect thoughts, emotions and behaviours. These are the main diagnostic types:

▶ Simple – when people gradually withdraw themselves from reality.

▶ Paranoid – when people have delusional thoughts and hallucinations and may experience delusions of grandeur.

▶ Catatonic – when people have motor activity disturbances that may involve them sitting or standing in the same position for hours.

▶ Disorganised – when people have disorganised behaviour, thoughts and speech patterns. They may also experience auditory hallucinations.

▶ Undifferentiated – when an individual does not fit into one of the types above but is still experiencing affected thoughts and behaviours.

Characteristics

For a diagnosis of schizophrenia, the *Diagnostic and Statistical Manual of Mental Disorders* (DSM) outlines the following:

▶ The person shows two of the following for at least one month: delusions, hallucinations, disorganised speech, disorganised or catatonic behaviour, flattening of emotions; or continual voices in the head giving a running commentary of what is happening.

▶ The person must show social and/or occupational functioning that has declined.

▶ There must be no evidence that medical factors are causing the behaviours.

Symptoms can be split into positive and negative:

▶ Positive refers to the *addition* of certain behaviours. For example, hallucinations, delusions of grandeur or control and insertion of thoughts are all positive.

▶ Negative refers to the *removal* of certain behaviours. For example, poverty of speech, withdrawal from society and flattening of mood are all negative.

Case studies

CHALLENGE YOURSELF
Find two real-life case studies of people being either diagnosed with schizophrenia or living with schizophrenia.

EXPLANATIONS OF SCHIZOPHRENIA

Below we will examine a range of potential causes of schizophrenia, giving evidence.

Genetic

This idea states that there is a link between schizophrenia and inherited genetic material. If this is the case then the closer our genetic link is to someone diagnosed with schizophrenia, the more likely we are to be diagnosed ourselves. Gottesman (1991) examined over 40 studies conducted in Europe to pool data on research focused on genetics and schizophrenia. The results are shown in Table 11.2.1.

Relative	Percentage risk
Nephews or nieces	4
Children	13
Non-identical (dyzgotic) twins	17
Identical (monozygotic) twins	48
In contrast: general population	1

▲ **Table 11.2.1** Link between genetics and schizophrenia (Gottesman, 1991)

It seems that the data support the idea of schizophrenia being inherited because the more genetic material people shared, the more likely they were to be diagnosed too. However, the highest risk was 48 per cent (not 100 per cent, indicating a wholly genetic trait) so it looks as if people may be born with a predisposition to develop schizophrenia and it is some environmental influence that ultimately causes it.

Yang *et al* (2013) analysed ten "candidate" genes that could be responsible for schizophrenia in a sample of 1 512 participants. While there was no single gene that appeared to be associated with schizophrenia, the DAO gene was strongly associated with schizophrenia in comparison to all of the other candidate genes. In addition, Roofeh *et al* (2013) noted that the human leukocyte antigen region of a genome could well be a plausible cause for some types of schizophrenia. It is interesting to note in the Yang *et al* (2013) study the DAO gene may interact with another called RASD2 which may affect dopamine production (the next cause we will look at).

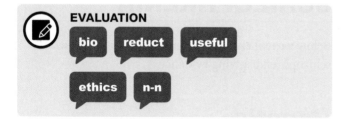

Biochemical (dopamine hypothesis)

This idea is based around the idea that schizophrenia is caused by an excess of dopamine in the brain. This involves two main ideas:

▶ When people experience amphetamine psychosis it resembles certain types of schizophrenia. This is caused by an excess of dopamine.

▶ Drug treatment (e.g. prescribing phenothiazines) does help to treat some of the symptoms of schizophrenia *but* these drugs can bring about symptoms similar to Parkinson's disease which is cause by *low* levels of dopamine.

Linstroem *et al* (1999) used a PET scan to test out the dopamine hypothesis. Ten schizophrenics and ten healthy controls were injected with a radioactively labelled chemical called L-DOPA. This is used in the production of dopamine. The PET scan could trace its usage in all participants. The L-DOPA was taken up significantly faster in the schizophrenics, pointing towards them producing more dopamine. Also, Arakawa *et al* (2010) noted that a drug called perospirone, which has a high affinity to D2 dopamine receptors, had an average 75 per cent usage rate which then blocked the further production of dopamine in schizophrenics. Seeman (2011) reviewed the field and noted that animal models of schizophrenia pointed toward elevation in levels of D2 receptors and that antipsychotics do reverse the elevation in D2 receptors but should only be used in the short term to stop other side effects.

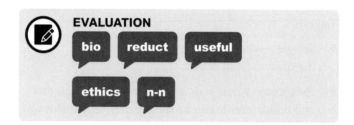

Cognitive

This idea states that schizophrenia is caused by faulty information processing. Frith (1992) noted that schizophrenics might have a deficient "metarepresentation" system – the system that makes people able to reflect on thoughts, emotions and behaviours. It could also be linked to theory of mind (see Core study 3.3 for AS level on page 21) as it controls self-awareness and how we interpret the actions of others. These are characteristics that are lacking in some schizophrenics.

Also, those showing more negative symptoms might have a dysfunctional supervisory attention system. This system is responsible for generating self-initiated actions. Frith & Done (1986) reported that when participants were asked to do things such as name as many different fruits as possible, or generate as many designs for something as possible, those with schizophrenia (with negative symptoms predominant) had great difficulty in managing this.

Frith (1992) also examined a central monitoring system. This allows us to be able to understand and label actions that we do as being controlled by ourselves. Frith had noticed that in some schizophrenics inner speech may not be recognised as being self-generated. Therefore, when they hear "voices" it is their own voice but they are unaware that it is themselves producing inner speech and believe it is someone else.

Finally, Johnson *et al* (2013) tested the cognitive abilities of 99 schizophrenics and 77 healthy controls on a battery of cognitive tests. It was seen that the schizophrenics performed worse across all cognitive tests including those for working memory (which involves tasks such as dealing with inner speech) and that this might be the core determinant of overall cognitive impairment in schizophrenics.

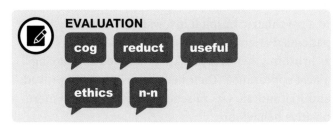

EVALUATION

cog   reduct   useful

ethics   n-n

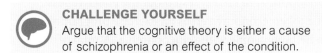

CHALLENGE YOURSELF
Argue that the cognitive theory is either a cause of schizophrenia or an effect of the condition.

TREATMENTS FOR SCHIZOPHRENIA

There are four different treatments that will be covered below.

Biochemical

This treatment centres on using drugs to alleviate the symptoms of schizophrenia. Davison & Neale (1997) noted that, from the 1950s onwards, drugs classed as phenothiazines were commonly used to treat schizophrenia. They were effective as they block dopamine receptors in the brain. However, many had "extrapyramidal side effects" which resemble symptoms of neurological diseases such as Parkinsonian-type tremors, dystonia (muscular rigidity), dyskinesia (chewing movements) and akasthesia (the inability to keep still). Second-generation antipsychotics were developed to also block dopamine receptors *but* produce fewer side effects and there are now third-generation antipsychotics that reportedly produce even fewer side effects.

Contemporary research still shows the effectiveness of antipsychotics in treating schizophrenia. Sarkar & Grover (2013) conducted a meta-analysis on 15 randomised controlled studies testing the effectiveness of antipsychotics on children and adolescents diagnosed with schizophrenia. It was seen that both first- and second-generation antipsychotic drugs were superior to the placebo in alleviating symptoms. Second-generation drugs were superior overall with chlozapine being the most effective of all drugs. Extrapyramidal side effects were seen more in first-generation antipsychotics while side effects that affected metabolism were seen more often in second-generation drugs.

Ehret, Sopko & Lemieux (2010) noted that a third-generation drug called lurasidone had been shown to be effective in four separate clinical trials, reducing both positive and negative symptoms. Noted side effects had only been nausea, vomiting and dizziness (they noted that drugs like clozapine were now showing more metabolic dysfunction side effects plus bone marrow toxicity so newer drugs needed to be developed).

Keating (2013) noted that a first-generation drug called loxapine was now being used again as an effective treatment for agitation in schizophrenic patients by getting them to inhale it as a powder. This meant a rapid onset of effect (usually around 10 minutes) by using a non-invasive method that showed few side effects.

Finally, Motiwala, Siscoe & El-Mallakh (2013) reported on the use of depot aripiprazole for schizophrenia. Depot injections are usually given deep into a muscle and allow the administration of a sustained-action drug formulation for slow release and gradual absorption, so that the active agent can act for much longer periods than is possible with standard injections. Only one study had been published in a peer review journal but it was positive in terms of effectiveness and safety so in the future this method of antipsychotic drug delivery may gain momentum.

Electro-convulsive therapy (ECT)

ECT is basically a procedure where a person receives a brief application of electricity to induce a seizure. Early attempts at this were not pleasant but nowadays patients are anaesthetised and given muscle relaxants. Electrodes are fitted to specific areas of the head and a small electrical current is passed through them for no longer than 1 second. The seizure may last up to 1 minute and the patient regains consciousness in around 15 minutes. There will always be debate about whether ECT should be used for any mental health issue as clinicians and psychologists are divided on the severity of the therapy itself and the longer-term side effects. ECT is now mainly used for depression (we will come back to its effectiveness with this on page 220), but there has been research conducted on the use of ECT with schizophrenics.

Zervas, Theleritis & Soldatos (2012) conducted a review of the use of ECT in schizophrenia. They looked at four issues: symptom response, technical application, continuation/maintenance ECT and its combination with medication. It would appear that ECT can be quite effective with catatonic schizophrenics and in reducing paranoid delusions. There was also evidence that it may improve a person's responsivity to medication. Lengthier courses worked well with catatonic schizophrenics. When combined with medication, ECT worked better than when only ECT was used. Phutane *et al* (2011) also noted that in a sample of 202 schizophrenics who had undergone ECT, the common reason why they had the ECT was to "augment pharmachotherapy" and that the main target was catatonia. Thirthalli *et al* (2009) reported that in a sample of schizophrenics split into catatonic and non-catatonic people, those who were catatonic required fewer ECT sessions to help control their symptoms. Finally, Flamarique *et al* (2012) reported that adolescents who received ECT in conjunction with clozapine had a lower re-hospitalisation rate (7.1 per cent) compared to a group who received ECT and a different antipsychotic (58.3 per cent).

Token economy

As we saw in sections 8.5 and 9.6, token economies are based on the idea of operant conditioning (rewards and learning by consequence). Behaviour is shaped towards something desired by giving out tokens (e.g. plastic chips or a stamp) every time a relevant behaviour is shown. Patients can accrue these tokens and exchange them for something they would like (e.g. money or food vouchers). Therefore, patients continue to show desired behaviours as they want to earn tokens to exchange for primary reinforcers that fulfil a direct biological need such as hunger or enjoyment.

Ayllon & Azrin (1968) introduced a token economy to a psychiatric hospital in a ward for long-stay female patients. Patients were rewarded for behaviours such as brushing their hair, making their bed and having a neat appearance. Their behaviour rapidly improved and staff morale was raised as staff were seeing more positive behaviours.

Gholipour *et al* (2012) tested out the effectiveness of a token economy versus an exercise programme in helping people with schizophrenia. A total of 45 patients were randomly split into three groups – two treatments and a control – (therefore, there were 15 patients per group). All participants were male, had been diagnosed for at least 3 years, were between 20 and 50 years old and had no other mental health illness. Negative symptoms of schizophrenia were measured pre- and post-treatment. The average symptom scores pre- and post-treatment are shown in Table 11.2.2.

Group	Pre-treatment score	Post-treatment score
Exercise	71.07	50.47
Token economy	76.73	41.20
Control	84.67	84.87

▲ **Table 11.2.2** Average symptom scores pre- and post-treatment (Gholipour *et al*, 2012)

As Table 11.2.2 shows, the largest reduction on negative symptom scores was in the token economy group.

Prior to this study, Dickerson, Tenhula & Green-Paden (2005) conducted a review of the field. They found 13 studies and it appeared that there was evidence for the effectiveness of a token economy in increasing the adaptive behaviours of patients with schizophrenia. They noted that many studies had methodological issues that could cast doubt on findings and that long-term follow ups were rare.

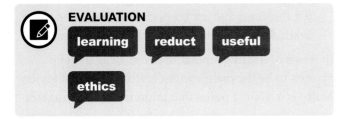

CBT

This type of therapy aims to change or modify people's thoughts and beliefs and also change the way that they process information. A therapist will challenge irrational and faulty thoughts as well as behaviours that are not helping. Patients may be set tasks outside the face-to-face therapy to help challenge faulty thoughts and beliefs. For schizophrenia, the intention of CBT would be to help patients make sense of the psychotic experiences and reduce the negative effects of the condition plus any distress they may be feeling. Patients may also be given help to understand that views, thoughts and interpretations are not facts, then given help to deal with assessing them.

Bechdolf *et al* (2005) assessed the effectiveness of CBT versus group psychoeducation on re-hospitalisation and medication compliance up to 24 months after treatment. A total of 88 patients were randomly assigned to either group and they received 8 weeks' therapy. When followed up six months later, the CBT group were less likely to be hospitalised and be taking their medication. At 24 months post-treatment, the CBT group had 71 days fewer in hospital. In a further study, Bechdolf *et al* (2010) analysed the data collected from their first

study but on quality of life measures taken at six months post-treatment. Both groups reported improved quality of life but there was no significant difference between the two treatment groups.

Ng, Hui & Pau (2008) assessed the introduction of a CBT programme in a hostel for people who had become treatment-resistant to schizophrenia (drug therapy) in Hong Kong. Measures of schizophrenic symptoms, mood, insight and self-esteem were taken pre- and post-treatment. Six months after treatment there was a significant reduction in the symptoms of schizophrenia alongside an increase in self-esteem. Mood and insight remained unchanged.

Davis *et al* (2008) noted that there had been little research into patients evaluating CBT for schizophrenia. Their study used 44 patients with schizophrenia who either underwent CBT or a support-group programme. The study lasted for six months. Irrespective of group, all patients were satisfied with the intervention they had taken part in, rating it either good or excellent. However, those in the CBT group reported higher levels of satisfaction overall especially with the quality of service and the assistance given for problem solving.

Finally, Sarin, Wallin & Widerlöv (2011) conducted a meta-analysis on the use of CBT with schizophrenics. They concluded that there was strong evidence for CBT affecting positive, negative and general symptoms of schizophrenia compared to all other therapies. They also stated that the effects of CBT can be delayed and having 20 sessions or more is better than shorter programmes that are available.

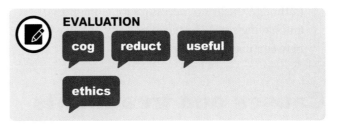

CHALLENGE YOURSELF
You have been asked to choose the most effective programme for dealing with schizophrenia at a local clinic. Which therapy would you choose and how would you run the programme? Justify your choices.

11.3 ABNORMAL AFFECT

TYPES, CHARACTERISTICS, EXAMPLES AND SEX DIFFERENCES

ASK YOURSELF
How would you diagnose depression in someone? What behaviours and characteristics would you look for?

Types

There are two main types of depression:

▶ Unipolar – this is sometimes called a major depressive episode. Symptoms for this type include having a depressed mood for most of the day, diminished pleasure in most activities undertaken, some weight loss, insomnia or hypersomnia, some psychomotor agitation, fatigue, feelings of worthlessness and a reduced ability to concentrate on tasks.

▶ Bipolar – this used to be referred to as manic depression. Symptoms for this type include having episodes of manic behaviour that cannot be accounted for by a physical condition, having some episode that is similar to unipolar depression (although this is not necessary for a diagnosis) and having some change in polarity of behaviour between mania and depression.

Causes and treatments for manic depression

Causes of depression tend to be all biological. The current main ones are as follows:

▶ There may be a genetic cause. Edgunlu, Duvarci & Cetin (2013) noted that bipolar disorder may be caused by a defect on the X-chromosome after examining a case study of a 35-year-old male who had muscular dystrophy and bipolar disorder and

whose mother also had bipolar disorder. Muscular dystrophy is transmitted by the X-chromosome hence the link to bipolar disorder. Also, Chang *et al* (2013) reported on initial work on a BD gene project to try to pinpoint the genetic cause of bipolar disorder. Currently there are 43 BD core genes that require further investigation.

▶ Another possible cause is brain structure. Nery, Monkul & Lafer (2013) reviewed the field and reported on isolated cases where people with bipolar disorder had decreased grey matter in the left thalamus and left hippocampal regions of the brain. However, findings are currently inconsistent.

In terms of treating bipolar disorder, drug therapy appears to be the main method used. In a recent review Malhi *et al* (2013) noted that lithium has been used for over 50 years as an effective treatment. It works well at stabilising manic moods but does not affect depression much. It also possesses anti-suicidal properties that no other drug has managed to achieve yet.

Joshi *et al* (2013) noted that a drug called paliperidone was effective in treating acute bipolar disorder in children and adolescents after an eight-week randomised trial where all participants took the drug. The only side effect seen was significant weight gain (average 4.1 lbs).

Finally, Katagiri *et al* (2013) conducted a study to test the efficacy and safety of using olanzapine for bipolar disorder. There were 156 participants of which 104 were allocated to the olanzapine group and 52 to the placebo (it was a double-blind study). Patients in the drug group showed greater improvement in symptoms across a range of questionnaire measures but also showed greater weight gain and cholesterol levels compared to the placebo.

EVALUATION
bio reduct useful ethics

Sex differences in depression

Nolen-Hoeksema (1987) conducted a review of sex differences in depression in terms of prevalence and potential explanations. Virtually all studies reported a gender bias. Females were up to 4.6 times more likely to be diagnosed with depression compared to males and this was seen across many nationalities and cultures. Also, these figures were across a range of different types of depression. There were three potential explanations for the gender differences reported:

- ▶ It is about income not gender. However, two studies in the review did look at income differences and found no significant effect.

- ▶ There may be reporting bias. There had been an idea that females are more likely to reveal symptoms and therefore more likely to be diagnosed. Studies did not appear to support this idea.

- ▶ The kind of symptoms shown might provide an explanation. Depression in men usually takes a form of acting out behaviours such as sadness and crying. Males act in ways to dampen their mood when depressed whereas women are much more likely to amplify their mood by "thinking things over too much".

As a result of the last point above, men's reactions tend to be more active, making theirs a more adaptive response compared to women's reactions which tend to be less active and more cognitive. This could go some way to explain sex differences in rates of depression as men actively work through their depression and tend not to seek help compared to females.

EXPLANATIONS OF DEPRESSION

Below we look at at how three different approaches attempt to explain the causes of unipolar depression.

Biological: genetic and neurochemical

The genetic argument follows the idea that depression may well run in families and be encoded in genetics. One way of testing this is to conduct twin studies using monozygotic (MZ: identical) and dizygotic (DZ: non-identical) twins. McGuffin et al (1996) examined 214 pairs of twins where at least one of them was being treated for depression. They reported that 46 per cent of MZ and 20 per cent of DZ twins of the patients also had

a diagnosis of depression. This hints at a part-genetic component for depression but a drawback is that twins tend to be brought up together and treated in the same way so we cannot rule out environmental influences.

Following on from this, Silberg et al (1999) wanted to assess whether it was genetics, the environment or a combination of the two that could be causing depression. A total of 902 pairs of twins completed psychiatric interviews to assess levels of depression alongside data about life events and from parents. In general, females were diagnosed more often with depression than males. This was more marked when life events were negative. However, there were individual differences seen among the females, and those who were diagnosed with depression after a negative life event were more likely to have a twin who was also diagnosed with depression. Therefore, it would seem both genetics and the environment interact to cause depression.

Earlier studies had also shown a part-genetic component of depression. Bertelsen, Harvald & Hauge (1977) reported that the genetic component varied depending on the type of depression. Table 11.3.1 records this.

Type of depression	Percentage chance for MZ twins	Percentage chance for DZ twins
Bipolar disorder	80	16
Severe depression (three or more episodes of depression)	59	30
Depression (fewer than three episodes of depression)	36	17

▲ Table 11.3.1 Genetic component and type of depression

Therefore, the strongest evidence for a genetic component comes from bipolar disorder, then severe depression, followed by depression. Finally, Kendler et al (1993) estimated that the heritability rate for depression falls in the range of 41–46 per cent.

In terms of a neurochemical cause, there are two neurotransmitters that have been investigated: norepinephrine and serotonin. Low levels of both of these may well be a cause of depression. Davison & Neale (1998) highlighted how certain drugs block the re-uptake of these neurotransmitters so that more of them can be used in the postsynaptic neuron. This is shown in Figure 11.3.1.

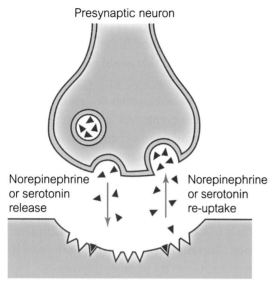

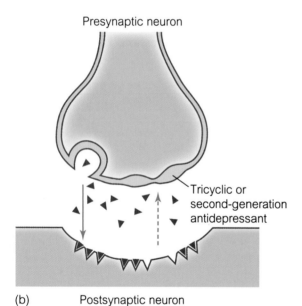

▲ **Figure 11.3.1 (a)** When a neuron releases norepinephrine or serotonin from its endings, a re-uptake mechanism begins to recapture some of the neurotransmitters before the postsynaptic neuron receives them.
(b) Antidepressant drugs called tricyclics block this re-uptake process allowing more norepinephrine or serotonin to reach the postsynaptic neuron

In addition, research has shown that depressed patients do have a lower level of serotonin metabolites in cerebrospinal fluid (suggesting lower levels of serotonin) compared to controls (McNeal & Cimbolic, 1986).

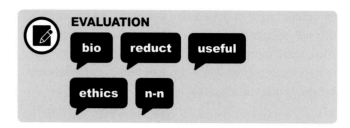

EVALUATION
bio · reduct · useful · ethics · n-n

Cognitive: Beck

Beck (1976) was interested in examining the irrational thought processes involved in depression. He believed that there were three factors which make people *cognitively vulnerable* to depression. These are called the cognitive triad and are:

▶ negative view of self

▶ negative view of the world

▶ negative view of the future.

These three factors can interact with each other to make a person depressed. They will also "change" the way information is processed as they become an "automatic" way of thinking. That is, when information is being processed it is affected by all three factors so the information will be processed in a "negative way". People may simply overestimate the negative aspects of a situation, meaning they will conclude that whatever happens, something bad will come of it. Depressives may also have negative self-schemas (packets of information about themselves) that have developed since childhood by having negative experiences and/or overly critical parents, peers or teachers. All new information that is processed will become negative as the mechanisms are all negative. As a result, depression develops.

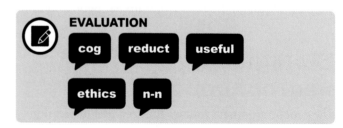

EVALUATION
cog · reduct · useful · ethics · n-n

Learned helplessness or attributional style

Learned helplessness is about individuals becoming passive because they feel they are not in control of their own life. This is caused by unpleasant experiences that they have tried to control in the past (unsuccessfully). This gives people a sense of helplessness which in turn leads to depression. The idea was based on Seligman's (1974) research on dogs. The dogs received electric shocks that they could not escape from (lack of control) and it did not take long for them to stop trying to escape. They all became passive and appeared to accept the painful situation they were in. When in future trials there was an opportunity to escape, the dogs still did not try to do this. This is the sense of helplessness that depressives will feel if they cannot escape situations that are negative and out of their control.

In addition, attribution theory could also explain depression. Weiner *et al* (1971) noted three levels of attribution that can affect people's views of their own behaviour:

1. internal (personal) or external (environmental)
2. stable or unstable
3. global or specific.

Table 11.3.2 gives an example of how the different attributional schemata can be used to explain why someone failed a psychology exam.

	Internal		External	
	Stable	Unstable	Stable	Unstable
Global	"I lack general intelligence for exams."	"I am really, really tired today."	"Exams are an unfair way to test my ability."	"It's an unlucky day."
Specific	"I lack the ability to pass psychology exams."	"I am fed up with studying psychology."	"The psychology exam was really unfair as it had 13 questions I did not know the answers to."	"My psychology exam had 13 questions, which is unlucky."

▲ **Table 11.3.2** Using attributional schemata to explain exam failure

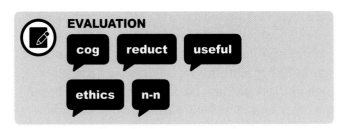

TEST YOURSELF
Describe and evaluate one explanation for the cause of depression.

Treatments for depression

Now we will look at the effectiveness of four different treatments for unipolar depression.

Biological: chemical or drugs

Two examples of antidepressants that are commonly used are as follows:

▸ Selective serotonergic re-uptake inhibitors (SSRIs) – see Figure 11.3.1 on page 218 to see how re-uptake inhibitors work. Possible side effects include fatigue, headaches and insomnia.

▸ Monoamine oxidase inhibitors (MAOIs) – these work by inhibiting monamine oxidase (this breaks down neurotransmitters such as norepineprhine and serotonin) which means more serotonin and norepinephrine is available in the synapse. Possible side effects include hypertension (which is potentially fatal), dizziness and nausea.

Rucci *et al* (2011) tested out the effectiveness of SSRIs versus interpersonal psychotherapy on suicidal thoughts in a group of 291 outpatients with major depression. Participants were randomly assigned to either treatment regime and suicidal ideation was measured using a questionnaire. The 231 patients who had shown no suicidal ideation pre-study were analysed and 32 of these did exhibit suicidal ideation during the treatment. For those on SSRIs, the time taken for these thoughts to emerge was much longer than in the psychotherapy group. Therefore SSRIs may reduce suicidal thoughts in people with major depression.

Nakagawa *et al* (2008) conducted a meta-analysis on the efficacy and effectiveness of a drug called milnacipran (a serotonin and norepinephrine re-uptake inhibitor) in comparison with other antidepressants. The studies selected for the analysis had to be randomised controlled trials with milnacipran compared to at least one other antidepressant. While there tended to be no differences in clinical improvement across all antidepressants, people taking antidepressants called tricyclics tended to withdraw from treatment sooner than any other drug group. There was also evidence that milnacipran may benefit patients who had adverse side effects from SSRIs and MAOIs.

Biological: electro-convulsive therapy (ECT)

See page 214 in section 11.2 for a description of the procedure for administering ECT.

Nordenskjold *et al* (2013) tested the effectiveness of ECT with drug therapy compared to drug therapy alone. A total of 56 patients were randomly assigned to either 29 treatments of ECT alongside drug therapy or just drug therapy. The researchers measured relapse of depression within one year of completing treatment. In the group of patients just on drug therapy 61 per cent relapsed within the year compared to just 32 per cent who had ECT and drug therapy.

There have been several meta-analyses testing the effectiveness of ECT. Dierckx *et al* (2012) reviewed the field in terms of whether response to ECT differs in bipolar disorder patients versus unipolar depressed patients. A total of six studies formed their analysis. The overall remission rate was nearly 51 per cent for unipolar and over 53 per cent for bipolar disorder. The data covered over 1 000 patients. Overall, the data were encouraging as they showed similar efficacy rates for the two types of depression.

Dunne & McLoughlin (2012) reviewed the effectiveness and side effects of three types of ECT: bifrontal (BF), bilateral (BL) and unilateral (UL). Eight studies were used in the analysis. It covered data on 617 patients. There was no difference in the effectiveness of the three types in terms of efficacy – all appeared to have some level of effectiveness. UL ECT impaired complex figure recall more than BF ECT. However, BF ECT impaired word recall more than UL ECT.

Finally, Jelovac, Kolshus and McLoughlin (2013) reviewed relapse rates following successful ECT for

major depression. Thirty-two studies were used in the analysis and all had at least a two-year follow up. Compared to relapse rates for drug therapy (51.1 per cent 12 months following successful initial treatment with 37.7 per cent relapsing in the first six months), ECT did not fare any better, with a 37.2 per cent relapse rate in the first six months. Those who took antidepressants post-ECT had a risk of relapse half of those who took a placebo.

Cognitive restructuring

The idea of this therapy follows Beck's cognitive triad approach to the potential causes of depression. It is a six-stage process as follows:

1. The therapist explains the rationale behind the therapy and what its purpose is.

2. Clients are taught how to monitor automatic negative thoughts and negative self-schemata.

3. Clients are taught to use behavioural techniques to challenge negative thoughts and information processing.

4. Therapist and client explore how negative thoughts are responded to by the client.

5. Dysfunctional beliefs are identified and challenged.

6. The therapy ends with clients having the necessary "cognitive tools" to repeat the process by themselves.

Hans & Hiller (2013) conducted a meta-analysis on the effectiveness of CBT on adults with unipolar depression. A total of 34 studies formed the analysis and they had to assess the effectiveness of individual or group CBT as well as drop-out rates. The studies also had to have at least a six-month follow up. It would appear that outpatient CBT was effective in reducing depressive symptoms and these were maintained at least six months after the CBT ended. The average drop-out rate was 24.63 per cent. This was reported as being quite high by the researchers but they also noted that better quality effectiveness studies are needed to assess how good CBT truly is with depressive patients.

Cuijpers *et al* (2013) also conducted a review examining CBT in relation to depression and comparing it to other treatments. A total of 115 studies were used and they had to be a CBT study that either had a control group or a comparison other treatment (e.g. psychotherapy or drug therapy). CBT was effective at reducing depression in adults but the effect size was lower when the study was classed as high quality. Therefore, the positive effects of CBT may well have been overestimated and more high-quality studies are needed.

Burns *et al* (2013) conducted a pilot study to assess the effectiveness of CBT for women with antenatal depression. Thirty-six women who met the diagnostic criteria for depression were randomly assigned to either a CBT treatment programme or usual care. Of those who completed nine or more sessions of CBT, or completed their usual care, 68.7 per cent of the CBT group had recovered from their depression 15 weeks after treatment compared to 38.5 per cent in the usual care group.

EVALUATION

cog reduct useful ethics

Rational emotive behaviour therapy (REBT)

Ellis (1962) stated that rationality consists of thinking in ways that allow us to reach our goals; irrationality consists of thinking in ways that prevent us from reaching our goals. The idea behind the therapy follows an ABC model:

▶ **A**ctivating event – this refers to a fact, behaviour, attitude or an event.

▶ **B**eliefs – the person holds beliefs about the activating event.

▶ **C**ognitive – this is the person's cognitive response to the activating event as well as emotions.

Using the example from Table 11.3.2 (page 219) failing a psychology exam would be the A. The B that

might follow could be "I am a failure" or "I hate it when I do not pass an exam" and then the C would be depression.

Szentagotai *et al* (2008) examined the effectiveness of REBT, CBT and drug therapy for the treatment of a major depressive episode. A range of outcome measures were taken based on a questionnaire that tested three main depressive thoughts: automatic negative thoughts, dysfunctional attitudes and irrational beliefs. A general measure of depression was also taken. There were 170 participants randomly assigned to either the REBT (n=57), CBT (n=56) or drug therapy (n=57) groups. In terms of depressive symptoms, there were no significant differences between the three groups but the REBT groups had an average score significantly lower than the drug therapy group. In terms of the three main depressive thoughts, all three treatments appeared to decrease these immediately post-treatment and then at follow up.

Sava *et al* (2008) compared REBT, CBT and the use of prozac in a sample of depressives. The participants were split into the three treatment groups and all had 14 weeks' therapy. All participants completed the Beck Depression Inventory (see Beck, page 218) prior to the therapy and then at 7 and 14 weeks post-therapy. There were no significant differences between the three groups in terms of scores on the inventory *but* REBT and CBT cost less for the same outcomes so are a preferred treatment.

EVALUATION

cog reduct useful ethics

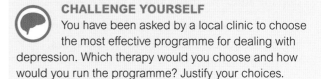

CHALLENGE YOURSELF
You have been asked by a local clinic to choose the most effective programme for dealing with depression. Which therapy would you choose and how would you run the programme? Justify your choices.

11.4 ADDICTION AND IMPULSE CONTROL DISORDERS

DEFINITIONS, TYPES AND CHARACTERISTICS

A range of addiction and impulse control disorders can be diagnosed by a psychologist.

ASK YOURSELF
What behaviours would you expect people to show if they had an impulse control disorder?

Definitions

According to Griffiths (2005), there are six components to any addiction disorder:

▷ Salience – when the addiction becomes the single most important activity in the person's life. It dominates the person's behaviour, thoughts and feelings.

▷ Euphoria – the subjective experience that is felt while engaging in the addictive behaviour, like a "rush" or a "buzz".

▷ Tolerance – when the person has to do *more* of the addictive behaviour to get the same effect.

▷ Withdrawal – this refers to the unpleasant thoughts and physical effects felt when the person tries to stop the addictive behaviour.

▷ Conflict – when the person with the addiction begins to have conflicts with work colleagues, friends and family.

▷ Relapse – the chances of the person "going back" to the addictive behaviour are high.

Types

Alongside alcoholism (abusing the use of alcohol) there are a range of impulse control disorders. They include these disorders:

▷ Pyromania – when people deliberately start a fire because they are attracted to fires or seeing the fire

service in action. They may feel a sense of arousal and satisfaction once the fire has started.

▷ Kleptomania – when people have the urge to collect and hoard items in their homes. They may go out and steal objects even if the items have little monetary value or they could afford to buy them. The more difficult the challenge of gaining the objects, the more thrilling and addictive it becomes.

▷ Compulsive gambling – when people feel the need to gamble to get a sense of euphoria especially if they win. They will continue to gamble whether they win or lose.

Physical and psychological dependence

Physical dependence refers to times when the body becomes used to functioning with the drug in its system and so "requires" the drug to maintain normal functioning. Psychological dependence is when the drug or activity becomes of great importance to the person's life to maintain a "stable" mental state.

CAUSES OF ADDICTION AND IMPULSE CONTROL DISORDERS

There are several ideas about the potential causes of addiction and impulse control disorders. Some of them are covered below. Examples of these are attempting to ingest more of a drug or gamble more as the person 'feels' they 'need' to engage in the activity to function. For example, a person may go to the casino as they 'feel' being on a roulette wheel 'calms them down'.

Genetic: alcohol

Could there be a genetic link to alcoholism? Edenberg & Foroud (2006) reported on findings from the *Collaborative Study on the Genetics of Alcoholism*. Early research suggested that there are three potential candidate genes that had been found in families with multiple alcoholic members: GABRA2 CHRM2 and ADH4. A further five genes were noted that needed further investigation. Edenberg (2013) also noted evidence relating to two variants in genes that encode two enzymes involved in the metabolism of alcohol: alcohol dehydrogenase (ADH1B) and aldehyde dehydrogenase (ALDH2). Agrawal & Bierut (2013) also noted that the same two genes (ADH1B and ALDH2) appear to play a key role in alcoholism. They added that GABRA2 could also play a role as it encodes information about receptor sites in neurons linked to alcohol-related processing. Biernacka *et al* (2013) analysed 43 single nucleotide polymorphisms in 808 alcoholics and 1 248 control participants. One in particular (rs1614972) in the ADH1C gene was found to be a key difference between the two groups. This was irrespective of the sex of the participant. Ducci & Goldman (2008) stated that more than 50 per cent of the variance for vulnerability to alcoholism could be accounted for by genetics but the exact pathways were still unknown.

Biochemical: dopamine

Dopamine has been linked to addiction and impulse control disorders as when it is released in the body it gives us the feelings of pleasure and satisfaction. Once these feelings become a desire, we then repeat behaviours that cause the release of dopamine and the cycle continues with repetitive behaviours. Voon *et al* (2010) reported that when participants were given a dopamine agonist (it activates dopamine receptors), impulsive choice increased, reaction times became faster and participants showed fewer decision conflicts compared to a control group. One drawback is that participants had Parkinson's disease so whether this can be related to people with impulse control disorder needs investigating.

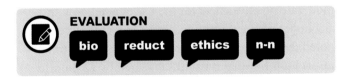

Behavioural: positive reinforcement

This follows the idea of rewards. When an action is followed by a pleasurable outcome, the person is more likely to engage in that behaviour again. For example, if an addictive behaviour or impulse control behaviour is followed by a positive outcome (e.g. feeling a sense of arousal when setting fire to a house or winning on a fruit machine), the person is likely to repeat the behaviour.

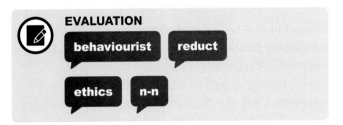

Cognitive or personality

There has been much research examining personality differences in pyromaniacs compared to controls. Gannon *et al* (2013) examined 68 pyromaniacs and 68 control participants. All were given a range of questionnaires to complete that measured a range of personality traits. The characteristics more common in the pyromaniacs were:

- higher anger-related cognitions
- interest in serious fires
- lower levels of perceived fire safety awareness
- lower general self-esteem
- external locus of control.

Therefore, there were differences in the personality and cognitive mechanisms of participants in the two groups.

Kennedy *et al* (2006) reviewed the literature (six studies) and reported the following about adolescent pyromaniacs who set fires again after being convicted (compared to those who did not go back to fire-setting). The adolescents repeating the behaviour:

- had a great interest in fire-setting and showed higher levels of covert antisocial behaviours
- were more more likely to be male and older
- had poorer social skills with a high level of family dysfunction.

Moore, Thompson-Pope & Whited (1996) examined the responses on the Minnesota Multiphasic Personality Assessment Questionnaire (MMPI) of 28 adolescent boys with a history of pyromania compared to 96 without a history. The following subscales differentiated the two groups: depression, feelings of alienation, anger, conduct problems, family problems and school problems.

Cunningham *et al* (2011) interviewed nine women who were pyromaniacs. The qualitative analysis revealed that they had distressing experiences and lack of support pre-pyromaniac behaviour and conducted the fire-setting to influence others, gain help and feel a sense of achievement and control.

Wedekind *et al* (2013) studied the personality and attachment profiles of 59 alcoholics (43 male and 16 female). Participants completed a battery of questionnaires as well as taking part in a structured interview. Only one-third of participants were securely attached. All had high levels of trait-anxiety and showed higher levels of cognitive avoidance as well as higher scores on a number of pathological measures.

EVALUATION
cog   reduct   ethics   useful

TEST YOURSELF
Describe and evaluate one cause of addiction and impulse control disorders.

COPING WITH AND REDUCING ADDICTION AND IMPULSE CONTROL DISORDERS

Behavioural

One technique that has been used with alcoholics is token economy (see page 214 for a description of token economy). Petry *et al* (2000) researched 42 alcohol-dependent older adults in an outpatient setting. They were randomly assigned to two groups: one to receive standard treatment only; the other to receive a standard treatment plus token economy (the TE group). The latter had the chance to earn tokens that could go towards prizes for submitting negative breathalyser tests and completing set steps towards desired behaviours. The treatment lasted eight weeks. The first measure was the percentage of participants who completed the full treatment: 84 per cent in the TE group and 22 per cent receiving standard treatment only. By the end of the treatment phase, 69 per cent of the TE group were still abstinent compared to just 29 per cent in the other group. Participants in the TE group earned, on average, about $200 worth of prizes.

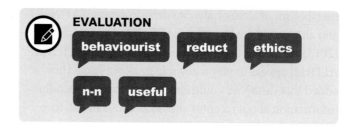

EVALUATION
behaviourist   reduct   ethics
n-n   useful

Aversion therapy

This is a therapy based on classical conditioning. The idea is that an undesirable behaviour (e.g. when an alcoholic drinks alcohol) is paired with an aversive stimulus (something unpleasant). This decreases the frequency of the behaviour as the two elements are associated and the undesirable behaviour is no longer enjoyable. For alcoholics this could be that whenever they smell or taste alcohol they are given an emetic drug (this will make them vomit). They should begin to associate being sick with drinking alcohol and avoid drinking or drink less alcohol, so their behaviour will be changed.

Howard (2001) examined the effectiveness of aversion therapy using 82 hospitalised patients. They all went through a pharmacological aversion treatment and these were the results:

▶ The strength of "positive outcomes for drinking alcohol" were significantly reduced.

▶ The confidence that they could avoid drinking alcohol in "high-risk situations" was significantly increased.

▶ Those who had a greater experience of alcohol-related nausea pre-treatment or were involved in antisocial conduct showed reduced effectiveness for the treatment.

Thurber (1985) reviewed the field and reported a moderate positive effect for the use of emetics with alcoholics whereas Cannon, Baker & Wehl (1981) noted that the same effect was seen at 6-month follow-up sessions but that it had disappeared by 12 months post-treatment. Finally, Smith, Frawley & Polissar (1997) assessed the effectiveness of aversion therapy compared to counselling with alcoholics. A total of 249 patients went through the aversion therapy and were matched with participants who had the counselling. The group who received aversion therapy had significantly higher rates of alcohol abstinence at 6 and 12 months post-treatment.

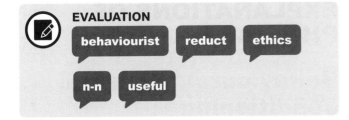

EVALUATION

behaviourist reduct ethics

n-n useful

CBT for kleptomania

See page 162 for a description of how CBT works. Hodgins & Peden (2008) reviewed the current field at the time in relation to CBT usage for kleptomania. The first thing they noted was that there was little systematic research in the area. The main CBT techniques used for kleptomania tended to be as follows:

▶ Covert sensitisation – this is when patients have to visualise a negative (aversive) image with the kleptomania behaviours. The idea is to make them associate the two so the behaviour decreases.

▶ Imaginal desensitisation – this is when patients are taught relaxation techniques. They have to visualise themselves engaging in the impulsive behaviour while also engaging in relaxation. Impulsion and relaxation cannot happen at the same time and the idea is that relaxation takes over when people have the urge to involve themselves in kleptomania.

The review concluded that CBT appears to be the most effective way of controlling kleptomania.

Kohn & Antonuccio (2002) noted that CBT is very successful with kleptomaniacs especially if kleptomania-related consequences are used (e.g. getting arrested and going to jail) instead of just general aversive imagery (e.g. nausea and vomiting). It is also effective when the kleptomaniac describes the scenarios out loud, in as much detail as possible, so that the anxiety continues to increase with the imaginings. This repeated pairing of aversive stimuli with kleptomania thoughts and ideas does decrease behaviour especially if patients are then reinforced for not engaging in kleptomania-related behaviours.

CBT has been used successfully with other impulse control disorders. As Jimenez-Murcia *et al* (2011) reported, it worked very well with male slot-machine addicts over a 16-week period and even an online CBT-based programme for alcoholics showed good levels of success (van Deursen *et al*, 2013).

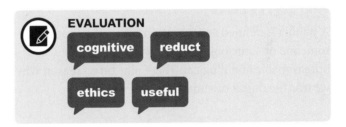

EVALUATION

cognitive reduct

ethics useful

CHALLENGE YOURSELF
You have been asked by a local mental health charity to choose the most effective programme for dealing with addiction and impulse control disorder. Which therapy would you choose and how would you run the programme? Justify your choices.

11.5 ANXIETY DISORDERS (PHOBIAS)

DEFINITION, TYPES AND EXAMPLES

 ASK YOURSELF
What types of behaviours would you expect people with a phobia to show when in the presence of their phobia or a situation relating to it?

Definition

A phobia is defined as an irrational fear of something, someone or some object. By irrational we mean unreasonable and illogical. There may be no reason why we fear the object or situation.

Types and examples

▷ Agoraphobia is the intense fear of open spaces and/or public areas. For example, a person may fear leaving the house.

▷ Social phobia is the intense fear of being in social situations. People with this phobia actively avoid social situations. They may also feel that other people are judging them and they dislike social interactions.

▷ Clinophobia is a fear of going to bed.

▷ Hippophobia is a fear of horses.

▷ Pteronophobia is a fear of being tickled by feathers!

CHALLENGE YOURSELF
Find the names of five more phobias that interest you. Also, find a real-life case study of someone with a phobia.

EXPLANATIONS OF PHOBIAS

Behavioural: classical conditioning

Classical conditioning is all about learning through association. It is a form of conditioning where the organism (be it human or animal) associates an **unconditional stimulus** with a **neutral stimulus**. After repeated associations, the organism then responds to the neutral stimulus (now called a **conditioned stimulus**) without having the **unconditional stimulus** present anymore. Figure 11.5.1 (on the next page) shows what happens in classical conditioning.

THE CASE OF LITTLE ALBERT

Watson & Rayner (1920) were interested in two aims. The following is taken directly from the paper they wrote about the case of Little Albert:

> "1. Can we condition fear in an animal (e.g. a white rat by visually presenting it and simultaneously striking a steel bar)?
>
> 2. If such a conditioned emotional response can be established, will there be a transfer to other animals or other objects?"
>
> (Watson & Rayner, 1920.)

At approximately nine months of age, Little Albert was presented with a range of stimuli (e.g. a white rat, a rabbit, a dog, a monkey). Albert showed no fear towards any of the objects.

When Albert reached 11 months and 3 days, the experimental procedure began to test out the first aim. Albert was presented with a white rat again and as before he showed no fear. However, as Albert reached out to touch the rat, Watson struck an iron bar immediately behind the Albert's head. Albert "jumped violently and fell forward, burying his face in the mattress." (1920: 4).

Albert tried to approach the rat again but as soon as he got close the iron bar was struck. After the two associations of the rat and loud noise the rat was taken away.

Seven days later, the researchers wanted to see whether his experience with the loud noise had made Alfred fearful of white rats. He was very wary around the rat and did not really want to play with it or touch it. When he did reach for it the loud noise was made, the same as in the previous week. This was done five times during the session. So, in total, Albert experienced the loud noise and white rat occurring together on seven occasions. Finally, the rat was presented by itself and Albert began to cry and crawled away rapidly. This was the first time he had cried during the study in response to the rat.

Over the next month Albert's reactions to a range of objects were observed. He was still fearful of the white rat. He showed negative reactions to a rabbit being placed in front of him and a fur coat (made from seal skin). He did not really like cotton wool but the shock was not the same as it was with the rabbit or fur coat. He even began to fear a Santa Claus mask.

His experiences can be explained via the mechanisms of classical conditioning, as shown in Figure 11.5.1.

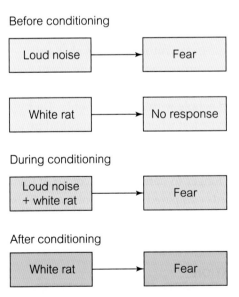

▲ **Figure 11.5.1** Classical conditioning of Little Albert

Classical conditioning may be able to explain why we form some of our phobias:

▶ *Generalisation* occurs when we produce a conditioned response to a stimulus that is *similar* but not the same as the conditioned stimulus. For example, we may produce a fear response to wasps. We could *generalise* this fear to other flying insects such as bees and hornets.

▶ *Extinction* occurs when the conditioned stimulus no longer produces the conditioned response. This could be because the conditioned stimulus has no longer been paired with the unconditional stimulus. So, for example with a person who fears wasps, over time the conditioned response of fear disappears in the presence of the conditioned stimulus of the wasp.

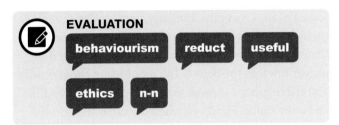

Psychoanalytic (Freud)

Refer back to Core study 5.2 for AS level (page 52) that investigated Little Hans.

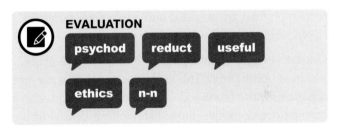

Biomedical or genetic

Could it be that we are pre-programmed to fear certain objects that may be potentially harmful? That is, are there certain objects or things that we are *expected* to be frightened of so we are *biologically prepared* to fear them? This theory could help us to explain fears that are not totally irrational (e.g. fear of snakes – they can be dangerous). Seligman (1971) had proposed the idea that we had evolved to be frightened of fear-relevant stimuli. So, we fear objects and things that might be of a survival threat in evolutionary terms (Mineka & Öhman, 2002). We have fear-relevant stimuli such as snakes that we may be "prepared" to fear. We also have fear-irrelevant stimuli such as flowers that we are *not* "prepared" to fear.

One study into this used rhesus monkeys as the participants not humans. Cook & Mineka (1989) wanted to see if the monkeys could become phobic of objects such as a crocodile, a flower, a snake or a rabbit even though they had never seen the object before. A group of rhesus monkeys was split into four groups and each group only saw one of the objects. The researchers controlled what the monkeys saw as they watched a video. Using the technique of splicing the video, each monkey saw the same rhesus monkey being scared of the object that its group had been assigned. For example, one monkey saw another monkey on the video being scared of the crocodile. The next monkey saw the same monkey on the video but this time the monkey was scared by the flower. Each monkey was then tested on its fear towards the object. The monkeys in the crocodile and snake groups showed fear towards a toy crocodile and a toy snake. However, when the other two groups were shown their "feared object" (e.g. the flower or the rabbit), they did *not* show any fear. The researchers took this as showing that the monkeys were already *prepared* to fear the dangerous objects but not the neutral objects.

Could it be that we are born fearful of certain objects? This takes the idea of *preparedness* further by saying that certain phobias are encoded into our genetic make-up (DNA) and passed down through generations.

Öst *et al* (1991) examined people who were needle-phobic within the same family. This study reported that 64 per cent of patients with a blood and/or injection phobia had at least one first-degree relative (immediate family member) with the same phobia. In the general population, 3–4 per cent of people are phobic of blood and/or needles.

Fredrikson, Annas & Wik (1997) examined 158 phobic females who were scared of snakes or spiders. The participants had to report on their family history of their phobia. The researchers discovered that 37 per cent of mothers and 7 per cent of fathers also had the same phobia. This seemed to support the idea that the phobic women had *inherited* their phobia.

However, the researchers asked participants another question about what had happened: they asked whether participants had experienced direct exposure to the phobic stimulus (they had been frightened by the phobic object directly) or had experienced indirect exposure to the phobic stimulus (they had seen someone else being phobic towards the object). Indirect exposure

was the most common for snakes – 45 per cent of participants – and for spiders it was 27 per cent. So, even though it looked as if the phobia was caused by genetics, nearly half of the snake-phobic participants could have their phobia explained via social learning.

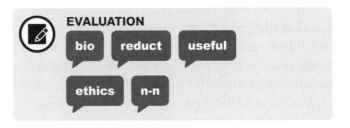

EVALUATION

bio   reduct   useful

ethics   n-n

Cognitive

The view of cognitive psychologists is that phobias being caused by the anxiety is linked to the phobic: being more likely to attend to negative stimuli; and to *believe* that negative events are much more likely to happen in the future. DiNardo *et al* (1988) reported that in a group of dog phobics, only 50 per cent could report having a previous traumatic experience. However, in a group of people with *no* phobia of dogs, 50 per cent could also report a previously traumatic experience involving a dog. The key difference was that those who developed a phobia of dogs tended to focus on and become anxious about the possibility of having a similar experience in the future and this obviously affected the way they processed information about dogs. Kindt & Brosschot (1997) conducted a study to test cognitive biases in people with arachnophobia. They created a Stroop-type test where participants had to read out the colour of the ink of spider-related words or pictures. Those who claimed to be arachnophobic took significantly longer to name the ink colour of the spider-related words compared to a control group. This hints at phobics having an automatic cognitive process of attending to phobias stimuli for longer than usual.

EVALUATION

cog   reduct   useful   ethics

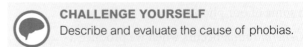

CHALLENGE YOURSELF
Describe and evaluate the cause of phobias.

TREATING PHOBIAS

Systematic desensitisation (Wolpe)

If we look at the case of Little Albert again (see page 226), it can be clearly seen that the conditioned stimulus of the white rat elicited the conditioned response of fear. The phobia had been *learned*. Systematic desensitisation works on the idea that the phobia can then be *unlearned*. The end point should recondition the patient so that the conditioned stimulus (which will be the phobic stimulus) produces a conditioned response of relaxation and not fear.

First, patients are taught relaxation skills so that they understand what it feels like to have relaxed muscles. This should enable patients to recreate this feeling in a variety of situations including when confronted with their phobic stimulus.

Second, the patient produces an anxiety or fear hierarchy to work through with the therapist. A simple hierarchy, for use by a person fearful of snakes, would be as follows:

1. This is the least anxious situation – looking at a cartoon snake in a children's book.

2. The person looks at a real snake in a book.

3. The person watches a snake on a wildlife programme.

4. The snake is in the same room as the person but in a cage.

5. The snake is in the same room as the person and out of the cage.

6. The person is within three feet of the snake.

7. The person touches the snake.

8. This is the most anxious situation – the person lets the snake go around his or her neck.

Patients can only move to a higher stage of the hierarchy once each stage has been successfully completed; that is, the patient is showing signs of relaxation in relation to a specific stage on the hierarchy (e.g. for stage 2 above it would be when looking at a book; for stage 7, when touching the snake).

Figure 11.5.2 shows the principles of classical conditioning linked to systematic desensitisation.

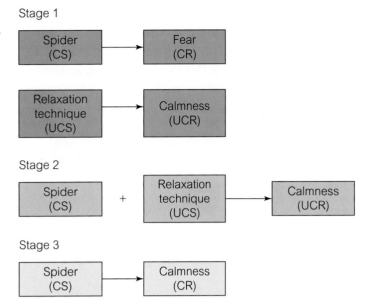

Figure 11.5.2 Principles of classical conditioning linked to systematic desensitisation.

You can see from Figure 11.5.2 that in the conditioning phase there are competing responses of fear and relaxation. This is called *reciprocal inhibition* whereby it is impossible to experience both emotions at the same time. The idea is to promote the relaxation response more than the fear response. If the patient is feeling more fear than relaxation then that stage of the hierarchy is stopped until the patient feels relaxed again and is willing to have another go.

There have been many studies that support the use of systematic desensitisation to treat phobias and fears. For example, Capafons, Sosa & Avero (1998) reported that for their 20 patients with a fear of flying who had several sessions progressing up their anxiety hierarchy became much less fearful of flying after the study ended. However, as with most studies in this area, there was no follow-up session to see whether the fear reduction had lasted.

Zettle (2003) showed that systematic desensitisation can be applied to people who fear maths. Twenty-four college students underwent treatment for six weeks (split between systematic desensitisation and a different therapy) and had to rate their anxieties towards maths before, during and after the treatment. Anxiety decreased markedly for those who completed their systematic desensitisation even though their maths ability never changed.

Finally, Ventis, Higbee & Murdock (2001) found that both relaxation techniques and simply laughing at the phobic stimulus were effective in reducing the fear in arachnophobics. All participants had been matched on fear: some progressed up their hierarchy with relaxation and others by laughing. However, no follow-up sessions were conducted by Zettle or by Ventis, Higbee & Murdock.

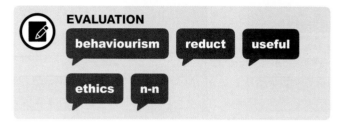

Flooding

This is another way to treat phobias using the idea behind classical conditioning. However, it does not take the "gentle" approach of systematic desensitisation. The patient is exposed to the largest anxiety-provoking stimuli straight away (usually direct contact with the stimuli – this is called *in vivo*). Obviously, the patient is going to feel extreme levels of fear and anxiety when confronted with the phobic stimulus. However, this dies off quite rapidly as the body cannot sustain such a high level of arousal for a long time. Therefore, the fear and anxiety will diminish. As a result of the phobic stimulus *not* causing any more fear or anxiety, the patient quickly learns that there is now nothing to be fearful of. The association between phobic stimulus and fear has been broken to form a new relationship of phobia stimulus producing calm.

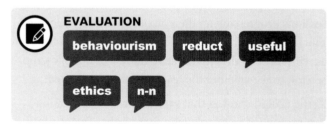

Applied tension (Öst)

Applied muscle tension is a technique developed by Öst in the 1980s. It was developed to help people with blood and injury phobias. They had to repeatedly contract the major muscle groups of the arms and legs to decrease vagovasal (fainting) reactions when highly anxious. It has been reported to increase cerebral blood flow.

Ditto *et al* (2003) tested out the effectiveness of applied tension with people who were phobic of giving blood (having fear of needles, etc.). A total of 605 donors were randomly assigned to one of three groups: applied tension, a no-treatment control or a placebo control. Participants in the applied tension group watched an instructional video that taught them how to contract and relax the main muscle groups in the arms and legs. Participants in the placebo control watched the video but they were not told to use the technique. Those in the applied tension group reported significantly fewer phobic symptoms about being blood donors and actually produced more full quotas of blood than the other two groups. They were also more likely to recommend blood donation to a friend as a result. However, there were no differences across the three groups on the probability that they would give blood again.

Holly, Balegh & Ditto (2011) examined the role of applied tension on anxiety in people giving blood. Participants were 70 people randomly assigned to either a control group or the experimental group who were taught applied tension before watching a video that showed someone giving blood. The females in the applied tension group showed significant reduction in vasovagal symptoms (especially in those who reported high fear of needles). This was backed up with physiological data that showed it was decreased anxiety that brought about the reduction in vasovagal reactions.

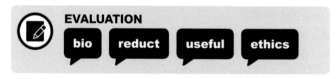

CBT

See page 162 for a description of how CBT works. There have been numerous studies assessing the effectiveness of CBT in relation to phobias. For example, Lilliecreutz, Josefsson & Sydsjö (2010) tested out the effectiveness of CBT for blood and injection phobia in pregnant women. A total of 30 women took part in the study and they had been diagnosed with the phobia. They took part in two sessions of CBT. The comparison groups were 46 pregnant women who received no CBT and 70 healthy pregnant women. The CBT group showed significant reductions in their anxiety levels (measured by the

Injection Phobia Scale-Anxiety) after each CBT session. This continued after the birth of their child. Therefore, CBT is effective in these situations and appears to be sustained up to three months after childbirth.

Melfsen *et al* (2011) examined the effectiveness of using CBT for socially phobic children. A total of 44 children who were diagnosed with social phobia were randomly assigned to a CBT condition or a "waiting-list" condition. The main outcome measure was clinical improvement but other aspects were measured (e.g. coping ability, dysfunctional cognitions and frequency of interactions). There were significant differences between the groups post-therapy, with those in the CBT group being more likely to be free from their previous diagnosis of social phobia. In addition, Andrews, Davies & Titov (2011) tested out the effectiveness of face-to-face versus Internet-based CBT for people with social phobias. The researchers randomly assigned 70 participants to either group. Both groups made "significant progress on symptoms and disability measures". However, the total amount of time that the therapist was required differed markedly: 18 minutes for the Internet-based CBT whereas it was 240 minutes for the usual CBT. Therefore, Internet-based CBT would be more cost-effective in areas where healthcare budgets are limited.

Finally, Galvao-de Almeida *et al* (2013) reviewed the impact that CBT had on people with phobias. However, all studies in the review had to have functional neuroimaging measures as part of them. A total of six studies met the inclusion criteria for the review. It would appear that people who underwent CBT had significant "deactivations" in the amygdale, thalamus and hippocampal regions of the brain. Therefore, CBT appears to directly affect brain functions linked to anxiety.

EVALUATION

cog   reduct   useful

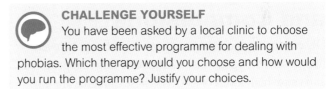

CHALLENGE YOURSELF
You have been asked by a local clinic to choose the most effective programme for dealing with phobias. Which therapy would you choose and how would you run the programme? Justify your choices.

11.6 ANXIETY DISORDERS (OBSESSIONS AND COMPULSIONS)

DEFINITIONS, MEASURES AND EXAMPLES

> **ASK YOURSELF**
> What behaviours would you expect to see from someone who has been diagnosed with obsessive-compulsive disorder (OCD)?

Defining obsessions and compulsions

Obsessions are recurring and persistent thoughts (even images and thoughts) that are intrusive and inappropriate and cause high levels of anxiety. These thoughts are not just excessive worries about life's problems. Compulsions are repetitive behaviours (e.g. hand washing or checking the order of something) or mental acts (e.g. counting or repeating words). The people affected feel driven to perform these behaviours in response to an obsession. They also perform the behaviours to reduce anxiety or prevent some devastating event or situation from occurring.

For a diagnosis of OCD, the person must recognise that the obsessions and/or compulsions are excessive and unreasonable. Also, they may consume time (more than one hour per day) and interfere with aspects of the person's life such as his or her job and relationships.

Case studies and examples

Rapoport (1989) reported on Charles in his book *The Boy who Couldn't Stop Washing*. At the age of 12 he began to wash obsessively. For some time he managed to keep it under control but then spent more and more of his school day washing. Eventually, he did it so often he had to leave school. The ritual was always the same: he would hold the soap in his right hand and place it under a running tap for exactly one minute. He would then transfer the soap to his left hand and keep it there for another one minute but *not* under the running tap. He would repeat that for about one

hour. He would then wash for a further two hours before getting dressed. His mother tried to discourage him to begin this ritual but as she saw how upset Charles became, she then cleaned all items in the house with alcohol. She then stopped people visiting their home as they would have 'germs' and this would upset Charles. Rapoport wanted Charles to undertake an EEG but he refused as he found stickiness to be 'terrible' like a 'disease'. Charles had drug therapy and his symptoms disappeared after about one year. However, he did develop a tolerance for the drug - he then only engaged in any OCD behaviours in the evening so it would not disrupt his day.

> **CHALLENGE YOURSELF**
> Find **at least two** real-life case studies of people with OCD. Write down what obsessions and compulsions they have plus what they think may have caused their OCD-related behaviours. If they are being treated, make a note of this too.

Measures

There are a few validated measures of OCD. This section covers three.

The Obsessive-Compulsive Inventory (OCI) (Foa *et al*, 1998) is a 42-item questionnaire that patients complete. They answer each statement from 0 (not at all) to 4 (extremely) based on the previous month in their lives. There are seven sub-scores that are added together to make a total OCI score:

▶ Washing: "I wash and clean obsessively" is a statement on the OCI that measures this. Further examples of statements on the OCI are given below.

▶ Checking: "I ask people to repeat things several times, even though I understood them the first time."

▶ Doubting: "Even when I do something very carefully I feel that it is not quite right."

▶ Ordering: "I feel obliged to follow a particular order in dressing, undressing and washing myself."

▶ Obsessions: "Unpleasant thoughts come into my mind against my will and I cannot get rid of them."

▶ Hoarding: "I collect things I don't need."

▶ Neutralising: "I feel that I must repeat certain words or phrases in my mind in order to wipe out bad thoughts, feelings and actions."

Using the patient's scores, a clinical psychologist can see if a particular component of OCD is strong or weak, then an appropriate treatment can be chosen. If the person scores 42 or more on the OCI it suggests the presence of OCD.

The Vancouver Obsessional Compulsive Inventory (VOCI) (Thordarson *et al*, 2004) is another validated measure of OCD. This scale has 55 items that patients complete and they rate each statement on a scale of 0 (not at all) to 4 (very much). There are six sub-scales that are added together to give a total score:

▶ Contamination: "I feel dirty after touching money" is a statement on the VOCI that measures this. Further examples of statements on the VOCI are given below.

▶ Checking: "One of my major problems is repeated checking."

▶ Obsessions: "I am often upset by my unwanted thoughts of using a sharp weapon."

▶ Hoarding: "I become very tense or upset when I think about throwing anything away."

▶ Just right: "I feel compelled to be absolutely perfect."

▶ Indecisiveness: "I find it difficult to make even trivial decisions."

The final scale, called the Yale-Brown Obsessive Compulsive Scale (Y-BOCS), is a very popular measure used in many studies. There are two parts to the measurement and it is used as a semi-structured interview technique:

▶ Symptom checklist – there is a list of 67 symptoms for OCD and the interviewer notes whether each symptom is current, past or absent (in the latter case it is not recorded). This helps the interviewer determine whether a group of clustered symptoms exists (the list is divided into groups such as aggressive obsessions, sexual obsessions, contamination obsessions, checking compulsions, ordering compulsions cleaning/washing compulsions.) An example is shown in Figure 11.6.1.

Symptom checklist

CLEANING/WASHING COMPULSIONS			
	Current	Past	Examples
43. Excessive or ritualised hand washing	☐	☐	Washing your hands many times a day or for long periods of time after touching, or thinking you have touched, a contaminated object. This may include washing the entire length of your arm.
44. Excessive or ritualised showering, bathing, tooth brushing, grooming or toilet routine	☐	☐	Taking showers or baths or performing other bathroom routines that may last for several hours. If the sequence is interrupted the entire process may have to be restarted.
45. Excessive or ritualised cleaning of household items or other animate objects	☐	☐	Excessive cleaning of faucets, toilets, floors, kitchen counters or kitchen utensils.

2. INTERFERENCE DUE TO OBSESSIVE THOUGHTS

0 = None.
1 = Mild, slight interference with social or occupational activities, but overall performance not impaired.
2 = Moderate, definite interference with social or occupational performance, but still manageable.
3 = Severe, causes substantial impairment in social or occupational performance.
4 = Extreme, incapacitating.

Q: How much do your obsessive thoughts interfere with your social or work (or role) functioning? Is there anything that you don't do because of them? [If not currently working, determine how much performance would be affected if the patient were employed.]	☐ 0
	☐ 1
	☐ 2
	☐ 3
	☐ 4

▲ **Figure 11.6.1** Excerpt from the Y-BOCS symptom checklist and an example question

▶ The Y-BOCS itself – there are 19 items here that the interviewee completes during the interview based on responses and observations. An example question is shown in Figure 11.6.1.

As you can see there is a part-script for the question outlining how to score it. The scores are transferred to a grid that measures obsessions, compulsions and other aspects of the condition. A person is given an obsessions score out of 20 and a compulsion score out of 20. Nine other items are noted on the 1–4 scale for severity. There is also a children's version of the scale.

EVALUATION
psychometrics interview quest

EXPLANATIONS OF OCD

There are various potential causes for OCD. This section looks at three.

Biomedical

There is some evidence to suggest that OCD could be genetic. Ozomaro *et al* (2013) noted that the SLITRK1 gene appears to be linked to some aspects of OCD. They examined 381 individuals with OCD and 356 control participants. They discovered three novel variants on this gene present in seven of the OCD individuals and concluded that the SLITRK1 and variants need more research but currently they appear linked to OCD. Taj *et al* (2013) researched another candidate gene called DRD4 (dopamine D4 receptor). A total of 173 individuals with OCD were compared to 201 healthy controls. They completed a range of questionnaires that measured OCD and mental health and all were genotyped for the DRD4 gene and variants. It was revealed that the 7R allele frequency was higher in the OCD group (especially so for females), suggesting another potential genetic cause for OCD.

Humble *et al* (2011) wanted to test whether the neuropeptide oxytocin was correlated with OCD symptoms as previous studies had hinted at this. Even though the researchers were testing whether SSRIs affect oxytocin, the main result they reported was that, at baseline, levels of oxytocin were positively correlated with OCD symptoms as measured by the Y-BOCS.

Those with early onset OCD had the highest levels of oxytocin. Finally, reduced levels of serotonin may be linked to OCD and the drugs used in the studies do affect serotonin levels (see the treatment section of OCD on page 235).

EVALUATION
bio reduct ethics n-n

Cognitive-behavioural aspect

The behavioural aspect is linked to the compulsions that people perform during OCD. Psychologists consider it to be a learned behaviour that is being reinforced by the consequences of performing the compulsions. For example, if a compulsive behaviour ends in a favourable outcome (e.g. reductions of anxiety or hands are now free of germs) then this is positive reinforcement. As we know, positive reinforcers increase the probability of repeating that behaviour again. For example, if the end goal of a compulsion is to have arranged clothes in some form of order and this reduces anxiety and also fulfils the compulsion to have things in order, then two reinforcement mechanisms are working here: negative (removal of anxiety) and positive (clothes are now arranged in order).

The cognitive aspect of this is linked to the obsessive thoughts that OCD individuals have. It would appear that these thoughts increase with levels of stress. In an everyday situation most people can learn to control these but people with OCD tend to have thoughts that are more vivid and elicit greater concern. Psychologists believe that this could be due to childhood experiences that have taught these people that some thoughts are dangerous and unacceptable and this has affected their information-processing networks. When new information is being processed, it is affected by these processing networks and generates anxiety and stress that can only be alleviated with compulsive behaviours.

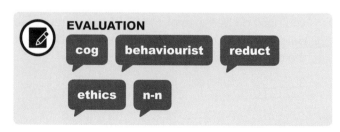

EVALUATION
cog behaviourist reduct
ethics n-n

Psychodynamic

OCD is caused by instinctual forces (driven by the id in the unconscious) that are not under full control due to traumatic experiences in the anal stage of psychosexual development. The person with OCD is therefore fixated in the anal stage. It is the battle between the id's desires and the superego's morals that can cause OCD as the ego (and its defence mechanisms) fail to control either. Obsessive thoughts may be generated by the id (e.g. to be messy and out of control) but the ego uses defence mechanisms to counteract this by making the person behave in a way that is completely opposite to that (e.g. being neat and tidy). This defence mechanism is called reaction formation. For example, if a child has a traumatic experience while potty training (e.g. if the child is harshly treated for being messy) then the obsessive thoughts of being neat and tidy re-emerge in adolescence and adulthood. The person develops OCD as a result because any thoughts of being messy cause great anxiety because of those early unresolved traumatic experiences.

EVALUATION

psychod   reduct   ethics   n-n

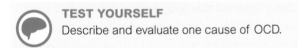

TEST YOURSELF
Describe and evaluate one cause of OCD.

TREATMENTS FOR OCD

There are a range of potential treatments for individuals diagnosed with OCD. This section looks at three.

Drug therapy

Selvi *et al* (2011) studied the effects that two "extra" drugs has on OCD patients who had not responded successfully to just taking SSRIs (see page 219 on how SSRIs work). The initial part of the study assessed 90 patients with OCD to assess that just taking SSRIs *did not* work on reducing symptoms. The researchers chose 41 patients from this part of the study and randomly assigned them to either the risperidone (n=21) or aripiprazole (n=20) group. They were then given these drugs too for eight further weeks. The researchers measured success by a patient having a 35 per cent or more reduction in scores on the Y-BOCS. In the aripiprazole group 50 per cent of participants did reduce their scores by at least this, as did 72.2 per cent of the risperidone group. Therefore, risperidone appears to be more effective at treating OCD when SSRIs fail by themselves.

Another study by Askari *et al* (2012) examined the effectiveness of using granisetron in conjunction with fluvoxamine (an SSRI). Participants were people aged 18–60 who were diagnosed with OCD via DSM-IV-TR. They were randomly assigned to either a granisetron or placebo group. They received 1 milligram of their "drug" every 12 hours for 8 weeks. All patients were assessed using the Y-BOCS at baseline then at weeks two, four, six and eight. Outcomes were measured in the following ways:

- A partial response was a minimum 25 per cent reduction in Y-BOCS scores.

- A complete response was a minimum 35 per cent reduction in Y-BOCS scores.

- Remission was scoring 16 or less on the Y-BOCS.

By week 8, 100 per cent of the granisetron group had scored a complete response and 90 per cent had met the remission criterion. Only 35 per cent of patients in the placebo group managed the same. There were no differences in the tolerance levels of both groups to the "drugs". Therefore, it would appear that the additional drug helped people with OCD reduce their symptoms.

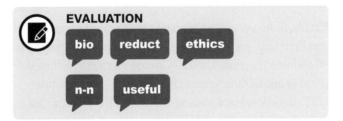

EVALUATION

bio   reduct   ethics

n-n   useful

CBT

Read about how CBT works on page 162 before studying this section. There has been much research into the potential effectiveness of CBT with people diagnosed with OCD.

Reynolds *et al* (2013) wanted to investigate if when parents got involved in their children's CBT for OCD it was more effective compared to children with OCD receiving

CBT by themselves. Participants were 50 patients aged 12–17 who had a diagnosis of OCD. They were randomly allocated to either a "parent-enhanced" CBT programme or regular CBT. Patients received up to 14 sessions of CBT in the trial. The main outcome was an analysis in the reduction of scores on the Y-BOCS. Both forms of the CBT were equally effective in reducing the severity of OCD so it would make sense to give young people with OCD the choice of having their parents involved.

Olatunji *et al* (2013) tested the effectiveness of CBT and BT with OCD patients. A total of 62 adults diagnosed with OCD were randomly allocated to the CBT or BT group. The main therapy lasted for 4 weeks (16 hours) with 12 weeks of maintenance therapy thereafter (4 hours). OCD symptoms were measured using the Y-BOCS and measures were taken at baseline, weeks 4, 16, 26 and 52. The participants in the BT had lower scores at the final assessment compared to the CBT group so it would appear that BT is superior to CBT for reducing OCD symptoms in this sample.

Storch *et al* (2013) examined whether CBT used in conjunction with a drug (sertraline) was more effective with OCD patients than CBT alone. Participants were 47 children and adolescents aged 7–17 with OCD. They were randomly assigned to one of three groups: CBT plus standard sertraline; CBT plus slow-release sertraline; or CBT plus placebo. The treatment lasted 18 weeks. Assessments of OCD severity were measured at baseline, at weeks 1–9, 13, 17 and then post-treatment using the Y-BOCS. All groups showed a significant decrease in OCD symptoms but not one group showed more improvement than the others, hinting that CBT is an effective tool for people with OCD.

Finally, Bolton *et al* (2011) examined the effectiveness of full and brief CBT for children with OCD. The researchers took 96 children diagnosed with OCD and randomly assigned them to one of three groups: full CBT (12 sessions), brief CBT (5 sessions) or a waiting-list group. The measure for OCD severity was the child version of the Y-BOCS. For both types of CBT there was a significant improvement in OCD symptoms compared to the waiting-list group, showing that brief CBT is useful and cost-effective.

Psychoanalytic therapy

Psychoanalysis follows the psychodynamic model of abnormality. A psychoanalyst can use a range of techniques to help patients deal with their unconscious thoughts and feelings:

▸ Free association – the patient lies back on a couch and is allowed to talk at length and the therapist then has to interpret the monologue to see what could be troubling the patient. The idea is that at some point the core problem will be exposed by the patient, especially if it is linked to the anal stage of psychosexual development.

▸ Dream analysis – the patient tells the therapist about a dream (manifest content) and then the therapist has to analyse it for symbols to uncover the underlying meaning (latent content).

▸ Hypnosis – this can be used to help access the unconscious mind too.

Chlebowski & Gregory (2009) noted that psychoanalysis can be particularly effective with OCD that is labelled as "late onset that coincides with stressors in the patient's lives" or with patients who have a borderline personality disorder too. This allows the therapist to delve into the unconscious mechanisms causing the OCD. Leichsenring *et al* (2008) examined the long-term effectiveness of using psychoanalytic therapy with OCD patients. The researchers reported that long-term psychoanalysis was associated with a significant reduction in the OCD symptoms reported by patients and this was still seen one year after treatment had ended.

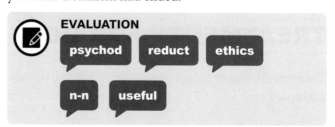

CHALLENGE YOURSELF
You have been asked by a local mental health charity to choose the most effective programme for dealing with OCD. Which therapy would you choose and how would you run the programme? Justify your choices.

CHALLENGE YOURSELF
Now that you have completed this chapter, prepare a table listing all of the disorders that you need to know. Then list each therapy and make a note of how effective it is. Finally, for each disorder, decide which therapies are appropriate and which are not.

EXAMPLES OF HOW TO EVALUATE

For the 12 mark question in Paper 3, you will be asked to evaluate one of the topics covered in this section. You will have noticed that after each topic in this chapter there are the icons for the different issues, debates, approaches, perspectives and research methods that *could* be used to help you answer the 12 mark question in the examination. Below are three examples of the types of things you *could* write in the examination.

You should aim to make *at least* four different evaluation points for the 12 mark question. Our accompanying Revision Guide has a series of student answers with marks and examiner comments attached to them.

Treatment of schizophrenia (biological)

Research into the treatment of schizophrenia has some *ethical* issues. For example, the use of ECT involves fitting elctrodes to specific areas of the head and a small electrical current is passed through them for no longer than one second. The seizure may last up to one minute and the patient regains consciousness in around 15 minutes. The argument is whether a person truly understands what the procedure involves if they have a serious mental health issue that affects thought processes like schizophrenia. With any long term memory problems unknown after using ECT, is it fair to give it to patients who may not understand this? However, research has shown that it is a *useful* treatment for schizophrenia. Thirthalli *et al* (2009) reported that in a sample of schizophrenics (split into catatonic and non-catatonic), those who were catatonic required fewer ECT sessions to help control their symptoms. As a result of this study it may be more useful for those with catatonic schizophrenia than other types. However, biological treatments for schizophrenia are *reductionist*. They are based on the idea that we need to treat the biology of the condition (e.g. excess dopamine) without tacking the psychological elements of the disorder. It ignores aspects like schizophrenia being caused by faulty information processing. Frith (1992) noted that schizophrenics might have a deficient 'metarepresentation' system. This would deal with being able to reflect on thoughts, emotions and behaviours. Therefore, a different treatment might be more appropriate.

Explanations for anxiety disorders (phobias) – behavioural

There is *evidence* that supports the behavioural explanation for anxiety disorders that took place under controlled conditions. Watson & Rayner successfully created a phobia into little Albert by banging a loud metal bar behind him every time he was in the presence of a white rat. After a few trials just showing him the rat caused him to cry and be fearful of it. As this was a study conducted under controlled conditions it means it can be replicated and tested for reliability. However, this would not happen due to *ethical* reasons as it would cause immense stress to the child. The behavioural explanation can be said to be *reductionist* as it ignores other factors that could be causing a phobia like could it be that we are pre-programmed to fear certain objects that may be potentially harmful? That is, there are certain objects or things that we are *expected* to be frightened of so we are *biologically prepared* to fear them! This can explain why we fear certain objects we have never even seen as it is encoded in our genetic history – for classical conditioning to explain a fear we have to have direct contact with the phobic stimulus.

Treatment for anxiety disorders (obsessions and compulsions) – cognitive

There is some evidence that it is a *useful* therapy for OCD. For example, Reynolds *et al* (2013) wanted to investigate if when parents got involved in their child's CBT for OCD it was more effective compared to the child receiving OCD by themselves. Patients received up to 14 sessions of CBT in the trial. The main outcome was an analysis in the reduction of scores on the Y-BOCS. Both forms of the CBT were equally effective in reducing the severity of OCD. This is useful to know as it gives a child a choice of CBT – with or without their parent being present. Also, this can be linked to the *nature-nurture debate*. If treatments are based on what causes OCD, then if a psychological treatment is effective it shows that OCD may be based more on nurture rather than nature. It could be ways in which people process information that needs treating to help with OCD rather than the nature approach of affecting the biology of a person by getting them to take drugs for their OCD.

Exam centre

Try the following exam-style questions.

Section A

(a) Explain, in your own words, what is meant by the term 'deviation from statistical norm'. (2 marks)

(b) Explain, in your own words, what is meant by the term 'abnormal affect'. (2 marks)

(c) Describe **two** explanations of anxiety disorders (phobias). (4 marks)

(d) Outline **one** biological treatment for schizophrenia. (4 marks)

Section B

(a) Describe what psychologists have discovered about treatments for addiction and impulse behaviour disorders. (8 marks)

(b) Describe what psychologists have discovered about explanations for anxiety disorders (obsessions and compulsions). (8 marks)

(c) Evaluate what psychologists have discovered about the treatments for abnormal affect and include a discussion on the nature-nurture debate. (12 marks)

(d) Evaluate what psychologists have discovered about defining abnormality and include a discussion on ethics. (12 marks)

Section C

(a) Describe the characteristics of addiction. (6 marks)

(b) Suggest how you would treat someone with an addiction to alcohol. What psychology is your suggestion based upon? (8 marks)

(c) Describe one biological treatment for schizophrenia. (6 marks)

(d) Suggest how you would diagnose someone with schizophrenia. What psychology is your suggestion based upon? (8 marks)

PSYCHOLOGY AND ORGANISATIONS

12.1 THE SELECTION OF PEOPLE FOR WORK

For virtually all jobs on the market there has to be a selection process by law. There are many different ways in which an organisation can collect information about prospective employees to draw up a shortlist of preferred candidates. This section looks at the different types of procedures and decision making that an organisation can go through.

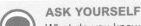

ASK YOURSELF
What do you know about how organisations select their workforce? Have you known anyone who has been through a selection process?

SELECTION OF PEOPLE FOR WORK

Selection procedures: applications

Many organisations use "in house" **application forms** to collect all of the relevant demographic, occupational and biographical data needed to be able to select employees "fit for the job". A standard application form may ask for personal details, employment records, educational records, any skills or employment training and referees. Personnel staff can look at all of the application forms and, from the information provided, produce a shortlist of the best candidates.

A company may also choose to use a **weighted application form (WAB)**. This is a standard application form but certain aspects of the form have been "pre-scored". This means that certain areas of, say, education or previous experience carry more weight in the application. Therefore, each application can be given a score depending on the weightings and the candidates with the highest scores go through to the next selection stage.

Sometimes companies ask for biographical inventories. The most widespread example of these is the curriculum vitae (CV). This contains a brief overview of the applicant's biographical and employment history and some companies prefer to receive a CV if there are a lot of applicants as CVs can be easy to read, sort through and even score like a WAB. The information provided can be "built upon" by candidates if they are interviewed so any gaps in employment or education can be explained face to face.

Selection interviews

As we have covered in AS level, **structured** and **unstructured interviews** can be used. In terms of the psychology of organisations, they can be used in the following ways:

In structured interviews, members of the interview panel will have a pre-determined list of questions that *must* be asked at each interview. Each candidate gets the same questions in the same order for the sake of consistency.

In unstructured interviews members of the interview panel will have certain "bits of information" that they need to get the candidate to talk about and therefore can use any question they think of to get it. Therefore, each candidate has a different interview "pathway". However, all relevant material is covered in terms of the information that the panel need from the interview.

It would appear from research that the structured interview is preferred and has more validity as all the necessary information is covered and there is a set time for the interviews so the selection day can run smoothly. There appear to be other issues with any type of interview, including the prejudices of the panel, the gender ratio of the panel and any other bias an interviewer may have. These can affect the validity of the interview as a selection tool for a job. Also, reliability may be questioned – if at the end all of the panel do not agree on who is the best candidate then the interview will have low reliability. Another issue that organisational psychologists point out is that people can be chosen on erroneous first impressions based on limited information. This can obviously have a huge impact on post-recruitment working if the selected candidates do not live up to what they presented at interview.

Decision making in selecting personnel

An additional method of making decisions during the selection process is for the interview panel to score the candidate on certain dimensions that were agreed pre-interview. All panel members can have a record sheet of the interview so they can write down comments and then generate a score for each criterion that they want to assess the candidate on. They can then simply sum up the values and the highest score is the strongest candidate.

Interview Record Sheet	
Date:	Interviewers: KT, PL, AC
Job title of vacancy: Project Coordinator, UK (Grade 3)	Interviewee's name:

Score for evidence on the criteria listed below. Use a scale of 1–10 where 1 = weak or no evidence and 10 = very strong evidence.

Criteria	Score
Verbal communication skills	7
Teamwork skills	7
Relevant experience in project planning and management	5
Accurate data input and record keeping	6
Willingness to undertake part-time college training	8
Experience in managing external contractors	3
Ability to coordinate projects with other departments	5
Ability to work in an environment of change	5
Familiarity with relevant software	9

▲ Figure 12.1.1 Example interview record sheet

Use of psychometric tests

Companies can choose from a wide range of psychometric tests, depending on the skills they want to assess. Here are some examples:

Cognitive ability tests – for example, the Comprehensive Ability Battery (CAB) Test. This comprises 20 tests with each designed to test a very specific cognitive ability. This gives companies an overall assessment of individuals but also how well they perform on all 20 tests.

Mechanical ability tests – for example, the Bennett Mechanical Comprehension Test. This is a 68-item questionnaire that assesses the person's ability to understand physical and mechanical principles across a range of situations.

Motor and sensory ability tests – for example, the O'Connor Finger Dexterity Test. This measures the ability to use fine motor skills with small objects. It is timed to see how the candidate copes with pressure.

- Job skills and knowledge tests – for example the Minnesota Clerical Assessment Battery. This is a computer-administered test that assesses abilities such as proofreading, filing and clerical knowledge.

- Personality test – for example the Sixteen Personality Factor Questionnaire. This measures 16 basic personality elements and is used quite extensively in personnel selection procedures.

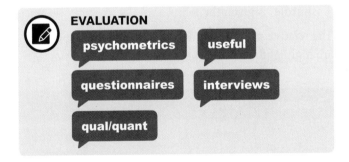

	Strongly disagree	Disagree	Neither agree nor disagree	Agree	Strongly agree
I let other people make the decisions					
I am quite hard to get to know					
I enjoy being part of a big crowd					
I like to take control of things					
I trust others					
I enjoy my privacy					

Chose the word that most describes you, and the word that least describes you, in a work setting.

	Most	Least	
			creative
			decisive
			modest
			persuasive

▲ **Figure 12.1.2** Example questions from different psychometric tests

One issue some people have about these types of psychometric testing is whether they have **predictive validity**. That is, does performance on a paper and pen task predict how well people will cope with the actual job or whether they perform well at the tasks that had been measured? Riggio (1999) noted that some standardised tests for managerial jobs have been quite successful in predicting who is then the best manager or who then performs well in the managerial role. Also, companies have to look at test utility. Riggio (1999) noted an example of this whereby a company can assess how much it will *gain* from performing such tests on applicants. A computer programming company reportedly tested a lot of people to find "the best people for the job" and it cost the company $10 per applicant. The estimated monetary gain for finding which programmers performed the best on a psychometric test was nearly $100 million. Therefore, psychometric testing can improve productivity as well as finding the perfect employees.

CHALLENGE YOURSELF
Devise a system that an organisation could use to recruit someone to a new job at that organisation. What would you devise and on what psychology is it based?

EVALUATION

psychometrics   useful

questionnaires   interviews

qual/quant

PERSONNEL SELECTION DECISIONS AND JOB ANALYSIS

Selection of personnel: decision making

There are a number of different main techniques that companies can use to make decisions on selecting employees. Below are three that are used:

- Multiple regression model – this takes scores from a variety of tests or interviews that the applicants have completed and combines them into one final score. Various predictors of potential job performance are "added together" to generate a final score. A high final score means that candidate correlates well with the job on offer. Beforehand, different criteria can be "weighted" based on previous appointments (e.g. better predictors have more weighting).

▶ Multiple cutoff model – this is when there are still many different predictors of the job that the applicants are trying to obtain, but there is a minimum score set for each of the predictors or tasks. As soon as an applicant fails to reach the minimum score *on any one predictor or task* the individual is eliminated from the recruitment process. Therefore, those who remain have at least the minimum amount of ability required for the position.

▶ Multiple hurdle model – this is when there is an ordered sequence of tasks that an applicant has to go through. At each stage (called a "hurdle" here), there is a decision whether the applicant has passed or failed. If applicants pass they continue with the next task but if they fail then they have "fallen at that hurdle" and they are eliminated from the process. The applicant who is left after the "final hurdle" is given the job.

The relative strengths and weaknesses of each approach are highlighted below.

Biases in selection decisions and equal opportunities

A number of biases can occur during the selection process for any job. They include the following:

▶ Stereotyping – for example, Hayward (1996) noted that females can still be stereotyped as "not management material" and are therefore overlooked as they do not have the "masculine traits" needed to take on such roles. Therefore, many female applicants may never be called for interview.

▶ Previous similar candidates – for example, Hayward (1996) also notes that some interviewers may see applicants as being "similar" to other workers (this can be positive or negative) and therefore make instant judgments based on this rather than the applicants themselves.

▶ Decision-making models (which are noted above) – there could be bias introduced when weighting the tasks or setting the standard for the multiple cutoff and multiple hurdles methods, for instance. Who is to say the person setting them is correct?

▶ Subjectivity in interviews – Riggio (1999) notes that there will always be people questioning the accuracy of interviews. This is because a lot of information is qualitative rather than quantitative and therefore subject to interviewer interpretation bias.

Technique	Strength	Weakness
Multiple regression	This method may give a more "rounded" overview of a candidate. For example, a lack of previous experience of a similar job can easily be compensated for by a strong skill needed for the job.	If a score is very low on one criterion it could prevent a person being employed who scores well on other criteria that are also relevant to the job.
Multiple cutoff	This method does ensure that all eligible applicants have the minimum amount of ability across the different criteria for the job.	Some of the cutoff points may be subjective and discriminate against certain applicants unfairly. How do we calculate what the cutoff points are?
Multiple hurdle	This method allows for the elimination of candidates early on in the process who are unqualified – this means fewer resources are wasted on unsuitable applicants.	This technique can be very time consuming and expensive for businesses as many hurdle criteria could be in place and each applicant needs to be assessed on them (and the information may not simply be in their application)

▲ **Table 12.1.1** Strengths and weaknesses of the multiple regression, multiple cutoff and multiple hurdle methods

Also, if an unstructured method is chosen then there is reduced reliability as not all candidates will have the same experience.

▶ Snap judgments – Riggio (1999) also notes that the idea of a snap judgment (similar issue to snapshot studies) can happen in interviews. Interviewers can make a very quick instant decision on someone (e.g. based on what the person is wearing or the person's answer to the first question) that may bear no resemblance to who the person actually is or the individual's competencies for the job.

▶ Use of psychometrics – the general idea of whether a psychometric test really is measuring the skill it is supposed to be measuring can invalidate people's scores on them (which is not good if you are recruiting people based on the results of these tests.)

 TEST YOURSELF
Explain three biases that can happen during the selection process for workers in an organisation.

Job descriptions and specifications

An organisation will produce documents that will have all of the necessary information on them for potential applicants to read and decide if they want to (or can) apply for the job. When a person specification is produced, the organisation *must* have details that are *directly relevant* to the job – organisations can list *personal preferences* in terms of the characteristics of the "ideal candidate" for the job. Many UK organisations have "essential" and "desirable" aspects to person specifications. Essential aspects are those that applicants *must have* whereas desirable aspects are those that applicants *may have* and if they do it will make their application stronger. These are generated after a job analysis has taken place.

Job analysis techniques

Job analysis is a fundamental part of any personnel role. Personnel staff need to assess a job and then list all of the qualities, skills and personal characteristics an employee would need to do it. Therefore, they need to assess what the job entails and who would be best suited

for it. There are two main techniques that personnel departments can use:

▶ Functional job analysis (FJA) – this is a technique developed in the United States to help create the *Dictionary of Occupational Titles* (*DOT*). This is a reference guide to over 40,000 job titles. It has general descriptions of these jobs as a starting point for personnel staff to tailor them to a specific job. The *DOT* classifies all the jobs using a nine-digit code which represents the sector of work, type of work and how much interaction with people needed in that job. Once the nine-digit code has been established for a job, personnel staff can use the description as part of their recruitment process. Table 12.1.2 shows the categories for the fourth, fifth and sixth digits.

Data (4th digit)	People (5th digit)	Things (6th digit)
0 Synthesising	0 Mentoring	0 Setting up
1 Coordinating	1 Negotiating	1 Precision working
2 Analysing	2 Instructing	2 Operating-controlling
3 Compiling	3 Supervising	3 Driving, operating
4 Computing	4 Diverting	4 Manipulating
5 Copying	5 Persuading	5 Tending
6 Comparing	6 Speaking, signalling	6 Feeding, Off-bearing
	7 Serving	7 Handling
	8 Taking instruction, helping	

▲ Table 12.1.2 Examples of functions used in FJA
Source: Adapted from: US Department of Labor. 1991. *Dictionary of Occupational Titles*. Rev. 4th ed. Washington DC, Government Printing Office.

▶ Position analysis questionnaire (PAQ) – this is a structured questionnaire that can be used to analyse a job in terms of 187 "elements" that are split into six different categories:

● information input: what the applicant needs in terms of skills

- mental processes: the cognitive skills needed for the job

- work output: what tasks need to be performed as part of the job

- relationships with other people: what interactions will be necessary in the job and with whom

- job context: physical and social contexts that are part of the job

- other job characteristics: anything else that is necessary to the specific job being analysed.

A series of statements are rated either with an N (does not apply) or from 1 to 5 with 1 being very infrequent and 5 being very substantial. The completed questionnaire can then be used to create the job specification or job description to ensure that the applicants are people that the organisation will want to recruit.

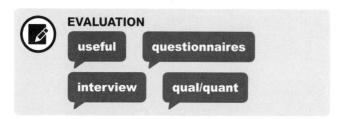

EVALUATION

useful   questionnaires

interview   qual/quant

CHALLENGE YOURSELF
Advise a personnel department on what you think is the best job analysis technique. Why do you think it is the best one?

PERFORMANCE APPRAISAL

All jobs require a "review" of progress and these are called performance appraisals. Usually, a worker is assessed against predetermined standards that the organisation has, to see how well the worker is progressing in his or her job.

Performance appraisal: reasons for it and techniques

There are many reasons for performance appraisals. For example, performance appraisals:

- allow both the company and worker to see, in a supportive environment, how well the worker is doing his or her job

- can be linked to pay increases and potential promotion opportunities

- can provide feedback on strengths and areas of improvement

- can allow communication between workers and managers which sometimes is logistically not possible on a day-to-day basis.

The range of techniques that an organisation can use to collect information necessary for a complete performance appraisal of an employee include the following:

- Objective performance criteria – these are aspects of the job that can be quantified and measured objectively (based on factual data). They could include number of sales, number of days off sick, etc.

- Subjective performance criteria – these are aspects of the job that *cannot* be accurately measured quantitatively. These include elements such as how a manager *feels* workers have been progressing in their job or asking workers how happy they are in their current role.

- 360-degree feedback – information about the worker is gathered from managers, peers, customers (if applicable) etc. to get an overall feel of the worker. Workers are also allowed to give feedback about the performance of their managers in supporting them in their job.

- Rankings – a manager can rank everyone who works for him or her on different criteria. Then when an individual is appraised the manager can compare the individual to other workers who have a similar or the same job to see how well the person is progressing.

- Self-rating – workers can assess themselves on progress by completing a questionnaire where they assign values to how well they think they are doing on a range of criteria pre-selected by the organisation as those that require assessing.

- Behaviour observation scale (BOS) – the person who is conducting the appraisal needs to complete a document highlighting how often certain elements of the job have been observed in that worker.

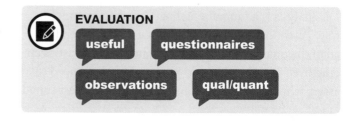

EVALUATION

useful   questionnaires

observations   qual/quant

APPRAISERS, PROBLEMS WITH APPRAISAL AND IMPROVING APPRAISALS

When conducting and analysing an appraisal a number of problems and biases can occur:

▶ Errors – these can be leniency errors in which the appraiser always assesses workers positively or severity errors where the appraiser always assesses workers negatively. In between these is the central tendency error where an appraiser always rates workers near the mid-point of any rating scale.

▶ Halo effect – this is a psychological phenomenon that can be applied here. It is when an overall appraisal is very positive based on the worker doing an outstanding job on *one* task. The idea is that if the worker did so well on that task then he or she *must be doing well* on all other tasks so any negative issues with the worker are overlooked.

▶ Recency effect – another psychological phenomenon that can be applied here. It is when the appraiser only uses *recent* performance indicators to judge the work on in the appraisal. Therefore, the whole procedure is weighted towards recent successes and failures rather than looking at the whole picture.

▶ Attribution errors – these can take the form of an appraiser giving more "extreme appraisals" to workers who are perceived to be working well (or not) due to effort rather than actual ability at the job.

TEST YOURSELF
Outline three potential problems with appraisals.

So, how can appraisals be improved, given the above issues? Riggio (1999) noted several ways:

▶ The appraiser can use online systems to record performance "instantly" rather than waiting 12 months to remember how the worker has performed in the job. Therefore, the appraisal will accurately reflect what has happened during the period. This makes it more valid.

▶ The appraiser can be descriptive rather than evaluative while being specific about performance.

▶ The appraiser can give "constructive feedback" based on things that a worker can actually do something about and change.

▶ Feedback given should always be clear and honest and understood by everyone.

▶ Getting both the appraiser and worker actively involved in performance target setting is important. This will make it easier to agree on final performance targets for the next appraisal.

12.2 MOTIVATION TO WORK

Why do people work? This question has been tackled by organisational psychologists from a variety of angles, but one of the main areas is motivation. This section looks at factors that affect motivation in workers.

ASK YOURSELF
What motivates people to work? Make a list of as many possible factors as you can.

NEED THEORIES OF MOTIVATION

This section looks at psychological theories about motivation that can be linked to the workplace. Recent research as highlighted by Greenberg & Baron (2008) showed that challenging projects, a feeling of team spirit and getting paid well were the three main motivators to work.

Hierarchy of needs (Maslow, 1970)

One idea from humanism that attempts to explain motivation was proposed by Maslow (1970, but based on his earlier research). He created a *hierarchy of needs* that starts at basic needs and moves up to higher-level "meta needs". The hierarchy progresses from physiological needs to safety needs, to social needs, to esteem needs and finally to self-actualisation needs. The model is illustrated in Figure 8.4.1 on page 128.

A human being must work up the hierarchy of needs to achieve self-actualisation – this is realising and reaching one's full potential. The basic (physiological) needs always have to be met (even if partially) before a person can consider working up the hierarchy towards self-actualisation. Therefore, a worker has to be motivated and fulfilled at a physiological and safety level before attempting anything higher.

Greenberg & Baron (2008) set out how this can be applied to the workplace in the following ways:

▶ To satisfy physiological needs, organisations can make sure that workers take breaks (e.g. for refreshments). Some companies, especially those where the workforce is quite sedentary in an office environment, provide exercise facilities for free. This can improve the health of workers and make them more productive.

▶ With regard to safety needs, organisations can ensure that workers have protective clothing if necessary and use specifically designed products, for example to reduce the strain of using computers and keyboards all day as part of a worker's job.

▶ To meet social needs, organisations can organise events that can build a "team spirit" into the workforce. A company may have a "family day" for everyone to get together out of the pressures of work. There is a company called The Picnic People which coordinates events to get the workforce together, for example.

▶ Esteem needs might be met through incentives organisations create such as "employee of the month" or annual awards ceremonies for the workforce. They can also award bonuses for suggestions for improvements within the organisation.

▶ Self-actualisation needs are met when organisations nurture their workforce to allow people to reach their full potential (via things such as career progression and appraisals).

ERG theory (Aldefer, 1972)

Aldefer (1972) built on the model proposed by Maslow and reduced the five main motivation levels to just three as follows:

▶ **E**xistence needs – these are similar to what Maslow called physiological needs.

▶ **R**elatedness needs – these are similar to what Maslow called social needs.

▶ **G**rowth needs – these are similar to what Maslow called self-actualisation needs.

The main difference between Maslow's idea and the ERG model is that for the latter there is no strict hierarchy. All of the needs have to be addressed at work in some form or another. The greatest motivator is when all *three* are being fulfilled at work. However, when one is not totally fulfilled, the worker may still feel a good sense of motivation if the other two are. An example would be gaining a pay rise when there is no current chance of being promoted; this fulfils the ER but not the G. However, the worker will still feel motivated to work.

Achievement motivation (McClelland, 1965)

This theory is based around the idea that people (and workers) are motivated by different needs and motives in different situations. There are three key needs and motives that people are driven by and they differ from individual to individual:

▶ People have a need for achievement. This is about having the drive to succeed in a situation. Therefore, workers driven by this will love the challenge of their job. They want to get ahead in their job and be excellent performers. They like to solve immediate problems swiftly and will go for challenges that offer a moderate level of difficulty (so that they feel challenged but know the goal is achievable). They also desire feedback about their efforts so will thrive on appraisals.

▶ People have a need for power. This is about having the drive to direct others and be influential at work. Workers in this category are status driven and are more likely to be motivated by the chance to gain prestige. They will want to solve problems individually and reach appraisal goals. The drive for power can be for personal gains or organisational gains.

▶ People have a need for affiliation. This is about having the drive to be liked and accepted by fellow workers in the organisation. People driven by this prefer to work with others and get motivated by the need for friendship and interpersonal relationships. Therefore, their main motivator is on cooperative tasks.

Workers can be assessed on these three key needs and motives by taking a thematic apperception test (TAT). To do this, workers have to look at a series of ambiguous pictures that tell a story. They have to tell whatever story they feel is behind the picture and their stories are then scored on a standardised scale that represents the three key needs and motives. From these, it can be seen if a worker is driven by achievement, power or affiliation.

▲ **Figure 12.2.1** Example picture used during a TAT

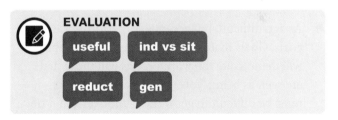

EVALUATION

useful   ind vs sit

reduct   gen

TEST YOURSELF

Outline one psychological theory of motivation and relate it to a worker in an organisation of your choice.

MOTIVATION AND GOAL SETTING

Goals can be important in everyday life as motivators. However, in the workplace they can be used as powerful motivators for an organisation to get the best out of its workforce. This section will examine the relationship between goal setting and motivation in workers.

Goal-setting theory (Latham) & Locke, 1984)

This idea appears relatively straightforward. Performance at work is affected by the goals that a workforce is set. The setting of these goals affects people's beliefs about whether they can perform a task or not. However, goals need to be specific to an individual or group. Simply saying "work harder" has very little effect on people as they may already feel that they are working hard. Setting specific and achievable goals allows workers to direct their attention towards achieving them while assessing how well they are doing. If workers feel that they may not reach a specified goal, they will be motivated to work harder to try to attain it.

An organisation must set challenging but attainable goals, give workers the necessary equipment and support to attain the goals and give them feedback throughout the process as this will motivate them to attain each goal.

Greenberg & Baron (2008) noted three main guidelines for setting effective goals:

▶ Assign specific goals. Goals have to have clarity, be measurable and achievable. An organisation cannot say "do your best" and then hope the workforce gets motivated. Research has shown that workers may find the goal challenging but this motivates them to want to achieve it.

▶ Assign difficult, but acceptable, performance goals. Goals that are perceived as unachievable will demotivate the workforce as will those that are seen as being "too easy". Therefore, a goal must be difficult to get workers motivated but not impossible. There can be vertical stretch goals which challenge workers to achieve higher success in activities that they are currently involved with (e.g. sales). There are also horizontal stretch goals which challenge workers to perform certain tasks that are new to them.

▶ Provide effective feedback on goal attainment. Feedback throughout the process allows workers to know how far they are progressing and what is left to attain a goal. This keeps motivation at an optimal level. If feedback is used wisely, workers will believe *even more* that they can attain the goal and will be *more motivated* to achieve it.

VIE (expectancy) cognitive theory (Vroom, 1964)

This theory attempts to explain motivation more from a cognitive angle. Motivation is based on three factors that are multiplicative:

▶ **V**alence – this refers to the value that workers place on any reward they believe they will receive from the organisation. The overall reward must be one that reflects the efforts put into attaining a goal and therefore be *desired*.

▶ **I**nstrumentality – this refers to any perceived relationship between effort and outcome that may affect motivation. This can be based around rewards as well. If any performance or motivation is not perceived as being instrumental in bringing about a suitable reward, then it is less likely to happen – motivation will be low.

▶ **E**xpectancy – this refers to any perceived relationship between effort and performance that may affect motivation. If workers do not expect their efforts to make any difference to attaining a goal then their motivation will be low. If they do feel effort brings about reward then their performance will increase as they will be motivated.

This can be expressed as an equation:

$$M = V \times I \times E$$

Therefore, motivation is determined by how the three factors interact, so if one of them is low then motivation as a whole will be low as a result. All have to be reasonably high for motivation to be high too.

Managerial applications of expectancy theory

How can the above be used by managers in an organisation to improve motivation of its workforce? Riggio (1999) and Greenberg & Baron (2008) highlight the following practical ways:

▶ Managers need to define any goal-based work outcome very clearly to all workers. Clarity is the key to success. All rewards and costs of performance based around these rewards must be known and be transparent.

- Managers should get workers involved in the setting of any goals and listen to their suggestions about ways to change jobs and roles to help attain them. This should help to increase VIE levels.

- For the valence element, managers should ensure that the rewards are ones that employees desire and see in a positive light. These may need to be individually specific as not all workers are motivated by the same things. Greenberg & Baron (2008) highlight how many companies now use a "cafeteria-style benefit plan" where employees can choose their own personalised incentives from items such as pay, additional days off and lower day-care costs for their children. The valence element for workers is very high if they are striving for something *they have chosen.*

- Progression from performance to rewards has to be achievable. Any performance-related goal (especially if workers have some performance-related pay) has to be attainable for all. Workers whose portion of their wage is based on performance need goals that are attainable but where motivation is the key to reaching them. Greenberg & Baron (2008) state that if there is a pay-for-performance method in the company then this should increase the instrumental motivation element of expectancy theory and motivation increases.

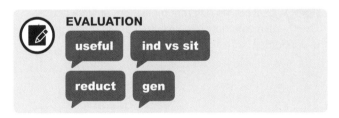

EVALUATION

useful   ind vs sit

reduct   gen

CHALLENGE YOURSELF
You need to help out a company that has recently discovered that its workforce is not motivated. You need to devise a strategy that the company can use and tell managers on what psychology it is based.

MOTIVATORS AT WORK

We have discussed the use of incentives and rewards for workers, but which ones are useful and motivate workers to achieve goals set? The next section covers this.

Intrinsic and extrinsic motivation

Extrinsic motivation is a desire to perform a task or behaviour because it gives positive reinforcement (e.g. a reward) or it avoids some kind of punishment happening. In terms of the workplace, this might mean workers gain extra pay or a day off for their efforts. Intrinsic motivation is a desire to perform a task or behaviour because it gives internal pleasure or helps to develop a skill. In terms of the workplace, people will attribute success to their own desires (autonomy) and may be interested in simply mastering a task rather than focusing on something such as extra pay.

Types of reward system

There are many reward systems that organisations can use with their workforce. They tend to be based around both extrinsic and intrinsic motivators. They can include the following:

- Pay – having some pay linked to a certain task or goal can increase the motivation of workers as they want to have more money.

- Bonus – offering a bonus is are quite widespread in organisations linked to sales and finance. At the end of each year (maybe after an appraisal), workers will be given a bonus payment based on the performance of themselves and the company as a whole.

- Profit-sharing – a certain percentage of any profit a company makes can be "ring fenced" to be shared by all workers. Therefore, everyone may be more motivated to attain goals and reach performance criteria so that there is a monetary reward.

Performance-related pay

When we covered the VIE (expectancy) theory of motivation we covered performance-related pay (see page 248). In addition, sales organisations may set minimum targets which give workers basic pay and anything achieved above the target earns them commission. This should motivate workers to exceed minimum targets as they will gain a reward in the process.

Non-monetary rewards

As we have seen, not all motivators have to be extrinsic. There are important intrinsic motivators in the workplace such as the following:

▶ Praise – simply gaining praise from a superior at work can motivate a worker to continue to work hard and meet targets and goals. It is a form of positive reinforcement.

▶ Respect – gaining respect from superiors and fellow colleagues is also important in an organisation. This internal feeling of "good" can motivate workers to continue to try hard at a task.

▶ Recognition – simply being recognised for any "over and above" effort can motivate a worker to continue to work hard. For example, an "employee of the month" scheme or being mentioned in a work newsletter can motivate people greatly.

▶ Empowerment – when workers succeed at a difficult task or achieve a difficult goal they may have a sense of empowerment. This may make them believe that the next task is attainable even if it looks difficult. It equips them to continually try hard at a task.

▶ Sense of belonging – making workers feel "part of the team" and that their individual efforts are appreciated can motivate them to keep trying hard and reaching even difficult goals.

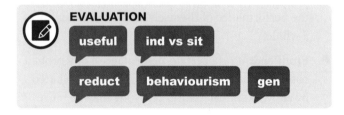

EVALUATION

useful   ind vs sit

reduct   behaviourism   gen

Career structure and promotion prospects

These can also be motivators for workers in the following ways:

▶ Career structure – having a set career structure when a worker begins employment can keep workers motivated. If a worker's career is "mapped out" showing a career development within the company then the worker can be motivated by both extrinsic and intrinsic motivators. These will include assistance with career decisions, enriching the current job with job satisfaction, improving communication with the worker's manager, setting more realistic goals that fit in with the career structure and giving the worker a great sense of personal responsibility about helping to manage his or her own career. All of these would certainly keep a worker motivated.

▶ Promotion prospects – as part of the career structure, a manager could also map out potential promotion prospects with workers. This could be within their own company or a sister company. The workers would then have clearer ideas about what they need to achieve to be promoted which is both an extrinsic motivator (more money) and an intrinsic motivator (the satisfaction of being promoted).

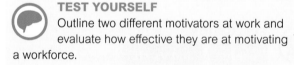

TEST YOURSELF
Outline two different motivators at work and evaluate how effective they are at motivating a workforce.

Other noted aspects included having a drive for success, being trustworthy, having a solid knowledge of business practices, being creative and being open about ideas.

Riggio (1999) added learning to delegate and giving constructive feedback as other vital leader qualities.

CHALLENGE YOURSELF
You have been asked by a local company to give training to its leaders. What would you do and on what psychology is it based?

EVALUATION
useful   qual/quant   reduct

LEADERS AND FOLLOWERS

Leader–member exchange model

It would appear that the theories we have presented so far are based on the ideas that every leader treats every member of his of her workforce equally and in the same way every time. This is clearly not the case in reality! The leader–member exchange (LMX) model looks into this.

Leaders form different relationships with their workforce early on in any process and, based on very limited information, classify workers into two distinct groups. The favoured ones (be it because they follow the same ideals as the leader or are seen as hard workers, etc.) form part of the "in group". There is then, by default, an "out group" which consists of workers that do not "fit in" with what the leader wants (be it because of a personality clash or that they are perceived to not be hard workers, etc.). Obviously, the in group will get more attention and praise and recognition compared to the out group. This can demotivate the latter group considerably while those in the in group get bolstered. Riggio (1999) noted that an LMX can be of low quality where the leader has a very negative view of the out group and the out group does not see the leader as effective. An LMX can also be of high quality where the leader has a very positive view of his or her in group

and that in group sees the leader as being encouraging and motivated.

Normative decision theory (Vroom & Yetton, 1973)

This theory has a focus on strategies for choosing the most effective way to make important decisions in an organisation. There appear to be five potential strategies for decision making by leaders:

- AI (autocratic) – leaders will solve a problem or make a decision by themselves using whatever information they can find.

- AII (autocratic) – leaders will solve a problem or make a decision by themselves but only after they have obtained the necessary information from their workforce.

- CI (consultative) – leaders will solve a problem or make a decision by themselves but only after they have shared it with the workforce individually.

- CII (consultative) – leaders will solve a problem or make a decision by themselves but only after they have shared it with the workforce as a group.

- GII (group decision) – leaders will share the problem or potential decision with the workforce in a group meeting. A decision is reached by consensus.

Originally, a leader being assessed in terms of this theory would have to answer 7 questions with a yes or no (now expanded to 12). Example questions are "Is the problem structured?" and "If I make the decision alone, is it likely to be accepted by my workforce? Once all of the questions have been put into a decision tree, the most effective strategy from the five above is recommended.

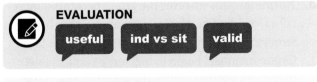

EVALUATION
useful   ind vs sit   valid

TEST YOURSELF
Outline either the LMX model or the normative decision theory in your own words.

12.4 GROUP BEHAVIOUR IN ORGANISATIONS

Riggio (1999) defines a group as two or more individuals, engaged in social interaction, for the purposes of achieving some goal.

 ASK YOURSELF
What do you think the advantages and disadvantages are of working in a group?

GROUP DYNAMICS, COHESIVENESS AND TEAMWORK

Group development

The dynamics of a group can be assessed when we look at how groups form in organisations. Tuckman & Jensen (1977) noted a five-stage formation process:

1. Forming – members of a group get to know each other and ground rules are established in terms of conversations and appropriate behaviours. These are based around the job (the reason) that they are working on but also the social skills side (e.g. hierarchy).

2. Storming – this stage is characterised by group conflict. Members may want to resist any authority from whoever becomes the "group leader" and there may be conflict between equals too (e.g. personality clash). If nothing can be resolved then the group dissipates. If the conflict can be overcome then the leadership stage is accepted and the group can move on.

3. Norming – this involves the group becoming more cohesive. Identification as a group member becomes stronger and the unit begins to work well on tasks. Group members begin to feel more comfortable in sharing feelings and responsibilities plus ways in which goals can be met. This stage is complete when all group members accept a common set of expectations of group behaviour.

4. Performing – the group is now set to work as a cohesive unit on tasks and to attain any goal or goals set. The group energy is diverted towards completing tasks to a high standard. The leader is now fully accepted.

5. Adjourning – once the goals have been attained, there may be no longer any need for the group so the group dissipates. This can happen abruptly (e.g. as a charity event ends) or take longer (e.g. new goals are formed that only some members of the group want to attain).

Some psychologists disagree about the nature of group formation and cohesiveness and that the order may differ between groups. This is tackled in a theory called punctuated-equilibrium model. There are just two phases that any group in an organisation goes through:

1. Phase 1. This is when group members define who they are and what they want to achieve (e.g. goals). This phase usually lasts around 50 per cent of the group's entire lifetime so new ideas tend not to be acted upon and the group is in a state of "equilibrium" moving slowly towards its target.

2. Phase 2. Then, suddenly, the group has a "midlife crisis" and members realise that they will not achieve their goal. They recognise that they must change their outlook and pathway towards a target so they can take on new ideas and work harder to attain any goals. They move into a state of "punctuating" to cope with these changes.

Group cohesiveness, team building and team performance

Cohesiveness, according to Riggio (1999), is the amount or degree of attraction among group members. This can be used to explain "team spirit" in organisations and groups experiencing this tend to be more satisfied at work. However, it does not seem to increase productivity. It seems that smaller groups, where everyone is of an equal status, show the most cohesiveness. The two ideas above link to cohesiveness as the group members have to work well and be as a unit to succeed in an organisation.

Greenberg & Baron (2008) note that there are some factors that can greatly increase group cohesiveness:

- Severity – if the initiation to the group is severe then the group becomes more cohesive (i.e. the more difficulties people have to overcome to be part of a group, the more they will want to stick with that group.

- Competition – groups tend to be more cohesive if they are competing against other groups (especially from other competitor organisations).

- Time – the more time its members have to spend together on a task, the more cohesive the group should become.

- Group size – smaller groups tend to be more cohesive.

- History – if the group has succeeded many times in the past then cohesiveness tends to be higher.

Team building is about making an effort to make teams more effective in what they do. It can be used on new teams that have not reached a level of cohesiveness or for an established team that is not being as effective as previously. According to Greenberg and Baron (2008) there are two areas that have to be covered in any team-building intervention:

- Being a team member matters. There has to be harmony and cohesiveness in a team with group decisions being the norm. Members have to be able to advocate ideas, enquire about ideas, share responsibilities and value the diversity of the group.

- Self-management is important. Members have to be able to manage themselves for a team to work. Various skills such as observing, setting difficult goals, practising new skills and being constructively critical are key behaviours.

In terms of exercises that can be used, these are the most common:

- Exercises to define roles – members of the group talk about what they think their roles are and the roles of others to see where disagreement lies. This can then be resolved.

- Exercises to set goals – clarification may be needed on what goals the group are trying to attain.

- Exercises in problem solving – these can be set up in such a way that all team members have to work together to succeed.

- Exercises about interpersonal processes. Tasks that can re-establish trust and cooperation can be used.

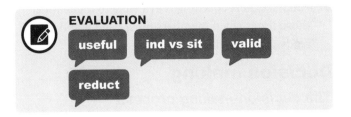

TEST YOURSELF
Explain how groups may develop at work.

Characteristics of successful teams

Hackman (2000) noted six main mistakes that happen to make teams *not* successful

- Use a team for work that is better done by individuals

- Call the performing unit a team but really manage members as individuals

- Fall off the authority 'Balance Beam' by being too authoritative too often

- Dismantle existing organizational structures so that teams will be fully "empowered" to accomplish the work

- Specify challenging team objectives, but skimp on organizational supports

- Assume that members already have all the skills they need to work well as a team

Therefore, the main characteristics of a successful team would be, according to Hackman:

1. The task is one that is fully appropriate for performance by a team.

2. The team is an intact performing unit whose members perceive themselves as a team

3. The team has a clear, authoritative, and engaging direction for its work.

4. The structure of the team—its task, composition, and core norms of conduct—promotes rather than impedes competent teamwork.

5. The organizational context provides support and reinforcement for excellence through policies and

257

systems that are specifically tuned to the needs of work teams.

6. Ample, expert coaching is available to the team at those times when members most need it and are ready to receive it.

Decision making

The decision-making process

We have covered aspects of this in the section 12.3 on leadership and management regarding autocratic and permissive styles (see page 253). These affect decision making, so reread section 12.3. One thing to add is that consensus ought to be made, which means that all group members have agreed on the chosen action plan.

Decision style and individual differences in decision making

Decision style has also been covered in section 12.3 (see page 255). As there are so many decision-making styles, they inevitably lead to individual differences in approaches to decision making.

Individual versus group decisions

In an organisation there will be decisions made by individuals and ones made by groups. Is one method more effective than the other? Are there times when a group decision is the best option? Are there situations where it is best for an individual to make the decision?

Riggio (1999) highlights the advantages and disadvantages of group decisions:

▶ The advantages are that different parts of the decisions can be delegated to different members of the group who have different specialities. There is more of a knowledge base to draw on and the final decision will be accepted by group members as they have all helped out. The final decision will be well critiqued already.

▶ The disadvantages are that the process can be very slow as everyone is involved. Also, conflict can be generated if not everyone agrees, so there is potential for the group simply to break down. In addition, leaders may dominate and make the decision their own.

In addition, Greenberg & Baron (2008) noted that group decisions are superior to individual ones when the overall decision is complex. They use an example of deciding whether two companies should merge.

A group decision would cover a lot more "bases" than an individual pondering the issue as the group will have a wide range of viewpoints to discuss and consider before making the very important decision. As long as the group is cohesive and respecting then a group decision here would be much more favourable than a decision made by an individual.

When a task requires creativity and it is poorly structured, individuals work better and come up with more productive ideas than a group would. Greenberg & Baron (2008) noted a study conducted to see if this was truly the case. People were given poorly structured ideas that needed creativity such as "What if everybody grew an extra thumb?" and were asked to consider the consequences of each situation given to them. Individuals came up with many more creative ideas compared to groups of between four and seven people.

Groupthink and group polarisation

There may be other situations when a group decision may appear to be a good idea but it truly is not. There are two things that can happen to make the decision-making process go wrong: groupthink and group polarisation.

Groupthink is what happens when a highly cohesive group where all members respect each other's viewpoints comes to consensus on a decision too quickly without any critical evaluation. The group then makes a very poor decision as a result. Riggio (1999) notes eight symptoms of groupthink:

▶ Illusion of invulnerability – as the group is so cohesive the members sees themselves as powerful and invincible. They then miss poorly made decisions.

▶ Illusion of morality – all group members see themselves as the "good guys" and can doing nothing wrong.

▶ Shared negative stereotypes – group members hold common beliefs.

▶ Collective rationalisations – group members easily dismiss any negative information that goes against their decision with no thought.

▶ Self-censorship – group members suppress any desire to be critical.

- Illusion of unanimity – group members can easily (and mistakenly) believe that the decision was a consensus.

- Direct conformity pressure – all those showing doubts have pressure applied to them to join the majority view.

- Mindguards – some of the group members buffer any negativity away from the group's decision.

Another factor that can adversely affect group decision making is group polarisation. This refers to when groups make "riskier" decisions compared to those made by individuals. Group polarisation follows the idea that, after discussion, people begin to hold even stronger views about a decision. For example, imagine certain members of the group really want to sell off part of a company and after discussing the issue they feel even more strongly about wanting to sell. However, there may be some people who do not want to sell. After discussion, they feel even more strongly about not selling. They "polarise" towards a stronger position than before discussion. This shift towards the polar end of a decision is called a "risky shift" as the group will then attempt to take the riskier option if a consensus can be reached (or just a majority one). Therefore, the majority may win but then take a more extreme view of the decision. However, some psychologists state that group polarisation can still happen even with a "cautious risk" – the group may still polarise after discussion but not in an extreme way.

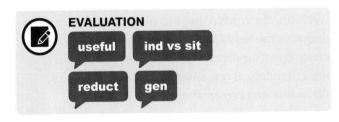

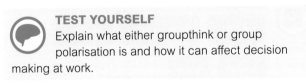

TEST YOURSELF

Explain what either groupthink or group polarisation is and how it can affect decision making at work.

Strategies to overcome groupthink and training to avoid poor decisions

Greenberg & Baron (2008) noted four different ways in which groupthink can be avoided:

- Promote open enquiry. A group leader could question all decisions made in order to get the

group to think again and not go for the first, easy option. Leaders should also encourage members to question and be sceptical so that all decisions are thoroughly assessed.

- Use subgroups. Split the members of the main group up and set them exactly the same decision-making tasks. Get them to present their findings; differences between the subgroups can be discussed to form an overall group decision. If the subgroups agree then you can safely say that groupthink has not generated that decision.

- Admit shortcomings. You need to get members of the group to be critical and point out any *potential* flaws or limitations of the decisions being made. This should allow the group as a whole to discuss these to ensure that group members have not simply decided on the easiest option.

- Hold second-chance meetings. Allow group members to digest the original decision then get them back for a second meeting so they can discuss anything that is worrying them about the decision. This allows "freshness" to be resumed; if a decision task is tiring group members they will go for the easy option. Having two "fresh" attempts at the decision should reduce the probability of groupthink.

GROUP CONFLICT

There may be times in any organisations where there is group conflict. There are different types:

- Intra-group conflict is when people within the same group conflict and this interferes with the pathway towards a goal.

- Inter-group conflict is when there is conflict *between* different groups within an organisation.

- Inter-individual conflict is when two individuals within a group or organisation have a dispute.

Major causes of group conflict: organisational and interpersonal

There can be any number of reasons why group conflict can happen within an organisation. There appear to be two broad categories according to Riggio (1999), as follows:

- Organisational factors form one broad category. For example, status differences within an organisation might cause friction. There could be conflict between people about the best pathway towards a goal. There may be a lack of resources such as money, supplies or staff which can cause conflict too. Also, when there are groups that form a "chain of events" for a task to be completed, there are many opportunities for things to go wrong and hence conflict occurs.

- Interpersonal reasons make up the other broad category. These are things such as the personal qualities of two workers "clashing", meaning they do not cooperate on tasks. It may be that individuals simply cannot get along with each other or due to a failed task may never want to work with each other again. Sometimes, if the conflict is between two heads of different departments this can escalate into conflict between those departments as a result.

Positive and negative effects of conflict

Conflict that occurs within an organisation can have both negative and positive effects:

- There could be the following negative effects. Group cohesiveness may diminish as people do not get on. Communication can be inhibited as a result of people not talking. Workers may no longer trust each other due to conflict. Constant "bickering" can reduce productivity and goal attainment.

- Here are some examples of positive effects. Conflict may get group members to rethink what they are doing. This improves creativity and innovation (and reduces the problems of groupthink). Workers may become less complacent with their work if conflict is occurring. If it means that the whole workforce is listened to and consulted then productivity may increase as all workers feel "part of the organisation".

Managing group conflict

Thomas (quoted in Riggio, 1992) identified five different strategies that can be used to manage group conflict in

an organisation:

- Competition – individuals may persist in conflict until someone wins and someone loses and then the conflict, apparently, diminishes within the groups these individuals are from.

- Accommodation – this involves making a "sacrifice" in order to reduce conflict. This can help to cut losses and save the relationship between the two groups in conflict.

- Compromise – each group under conflict must give up something to help resolve the conflict. This can only be achieved if both sides can lose things that are comparable.

- Collaboration – the groups need to work together to overcome the conflict as long as resources are not scarce.

- Avoidance – this involves suppressing the conflict or withdrawing from the conflict completely. Neither side can truly resolve the conflict; the differences are still there and have not been worked through. This strategy can be used if the conflict is so aggressive that both sides need to "cool off".

Another technique might be for managers to create a superordinate goal. This is a goal that the conflicting groups are willing to work for together. This will focus them away from the original conflict. Also, managers can use their authority to call a vote on the conflict situation. As a result, the majority of workers will "win" the conflict and managers then have to deal with the losing workers. Managers could also create opportunities for both groups to get a better understanding of one another through workshops, discussion and presentations.

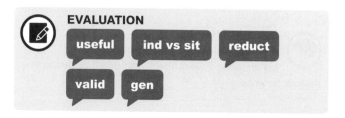

EVALUATION

useful · ind vs sit · reduct · valid · gen

CHALLENGE YOURSELF
An organisation wants you to deliver a presentation on why groups conflict at work. They also want some hints and tips on how to manage group conflict. What would you say to them and on what psychology is it based?

12.5 ORGANISATIONAL WORK CONDITIONS

Some organisational psychologists examine how the surroundings at work and people's "work stations" affect their productivity and attitude to work. This section will take a look at factors that are important for workers, including shift patterns and potential errors that could cause accidents.

ASK YOURSELF
How do you feel your surroundings affect how you work? What things make you want to work and what things put you off?

PHYSICAL AND PSYCHOLOGICAL WORK CONDITIONS

Below we look at the role of physical and psychological work conditions and how they may affect workers in an organisation.

Physical work conditions

This category includes illumination, temperature, noise, motion, pollution and aesthetic factors. We will look at each in turn.

In terms of lighting (illumination), workers require adequate levels in order to perform any given task. Artificial lighting must be provided if natural daylight is not enough to complete a task at work. Obviously, different jobs require different amounts and types of light. A worker who is performing a fine motor skill may need much more illumination compared to someone on a production line. Illumination is necessary for night workers and many companies provide light that mimics sunlight so that the workers' biological mechanisms are tricked into believing it is actually daytime. However, too much illumination from devices can be detrimental. For example, the issue of glare from computer screens has to be dealt with and workers should be able to control the contrast and brightness on their screens.

In terms of temperature, there must be an optimal level set depending on the job being undertaken. There are rules about minimum temperature although no rules about maximum temperature. Air conditioning can obviously keep temperature at a set level in offices. People who work in refrigerated areas need protective clothing to stop them from getting too cold. When people become too hot or too cold they begin to slow down in terms of cognitive functioning and motor skill coordination so an optimal temperature needs to be set.

Noise can be very distracting in the workplace especially if it is loud and uncontrollable. There are legislations that state workers should not be exposed to more than 90 decibels in a "normal" working environment. Anything above this and workers will lose concentration and their task efficiency will suffer. However, there are jobs where the noise will be over 90 decibels constantly (e.g. a pneumatic drill is nearly 130 decibels), so workers will need ear protectors to stop any permanent damage occurring to their' hearing.

Motion can be an issue for certain types of jobs too. Workers who use pneumatic equipment where the whole body vibrates when it is used may have longer-term issues. These can include decreasing ability to perform fine motor skills and developing a repetitive strain injury affecting joints or tendons.

Pollution and aesthetic factors are covered in chapter 10. More information about noise is given in section 10.1. (see page 177).

TEST YOURSELF
Outline how two physical factors affect workers in an organisation.

Psychological work conditions

Psychological work conditions include feelings of privacy or crowding, excess or absence of social interactions, sense of status or importance as opposed to anonymity or unimportance.

Density and crowding are covered in section 10.2 (see page 183).

In terms of social interactions, there can be two extremes that workers have to contend with: excess or absence. Excess social interactions can obviously reduce productivity in workers and even though some of it can be blamed on people simply chatting and not paying attention to their work or the time, there may be other factors that contribute to it. The layout of an office can promote or inhibit communication. If desks face each other and have an opportunity for face-to-face communication then there will be an excess of social interaction. Solitary booths will reduce social interaction. However, there are some jobs where there is an absence of social interaction with other workers. For example, people working in laboratories where only one person is needed to handle trials will have very limited social interactions; although sales and call centre staff interact over the telephone, their worker-to-worker social interactions may be limited.

A sense of status or importance can enhance productivity in a workforce. If people are given job titles which show they have some status within the organisation (e.g. supervisor) then they are more likely to be motivated to work. This psychological sense of being important can boost self-esteem and self-efficacy and has a very positive knock-on effect on productivity and goal attainment. However, the opposite can happen if people are not given status for their job (especially if they feel they play a vital role in the organisation). This can quickly demotivate people who will then fail to attain goals or care about the quality of their work.

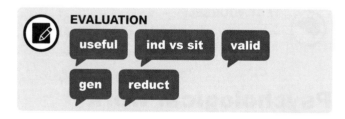

EVALUATION

useful · ind vs sit · valid · gen · reduct

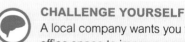

CHALLENGE YOURSELF
A local company wants you to help it redesign an office space to improve conditions for workers. It wants one physical change and one psychological change. What would you design and on what psychology is it based?

TEMPORAL CONDITIONS OF WORK ENVIRONMENTS

Temporal conditions refer to the time conditions in which people work. There are many different work patterns that people follow around the world, from the 9 a.m. to 5 p.m. work pattern, to shift-workers' hours, to those "on call". Below we look at some of the options organisations have when choosing the temporal conditions for its workers.

Shift work

Rapid rotation theory and slow rotation theory

Shift work refers to when a worker does not do the same work pattern each week. Workers need to alternate the times they work so that an organisation can, say, operate on a 24-hour basis. Workers alternating between day and night shifts is a good example. However, more organisations run a rotation of three shifts per day: day shift (typically 6 a.m. to 2 p.m.), afternoon or twilight shift (2 p.m. to 10 p.m.) and night shift (10 p.m. to 6 a.m.). Therefore, workers need to change their "working day". There are different options that an organisation can use for this:

▶ Rapid rotation – these are frequent shift changes that workers have to follow. There are two types:

– A metropolitan rota is where workers complete two day shifts, then two twilight shifts, then two night shifts. This is then followed by two days off work.

– A continental rota is where workers complete two day shifts, two twilight shifts, three night shifts, two days off work, two day shifts, three twilight shifts, two night shifts, then three days off work. After this, the rotation begins again.

▶ Slow rotation – these are infrequent changes of shift that workers have to follow. For example, they may work day shifts for three weeks or more, have a few days off then work night shifts for three weeks or more, etc. This type of shift pattern allows workers' circadian rhythm (their daily rhythm of sleep and wake) to adapt to a particular shift rather then it being "out of sync" with work patterns, which can happen on a rapid rotation. Circadian rhythms need time to adapt to a change in shift pattern. If they do not there can be long-term health implications and some studies have even suggested that people who work shifts have higher rates of mortality. Also, when working at night, workers are attempting to go against their biological clock. During the night, humans are expected to sleep so our cognitive functioning decreases. This means we are more prone to accidents and making errors on tasks at night.

Compressed work weeks and flexitime

There are other options that organisations can use to help workers strike a good work–life balance. Here are two examples:

▶ They might adopt a compressed working week. Workers can work three 12-hour shifts per week leaving them with four days off. They have still worked a standard 36 hours. However, Riggio (1999) notes that completing a series of longer shifts is tiring and there has to be concern about the quality of work being finished and levels of productivity. However, research has pointed towards workers feeling more satisfied with their jobs if they follow this method.

▶ They might offer flexitime. Workers still have a contracted amount of hours that they have to be engaged in work for the organisation. However, they can help to choose their daily working hours as long as the total time spent at work is their agreed contracted hours. A worker may decide to work 9 a.m. to 5 p.m. on Monday but only work 2 p.m. to 6 p.m. on Tuesday and work extra hours on days later in the week. This can allow workers to have the flexibility of fitting work into their lives rather than fitting their lives into work. However, it is unlikely that total flexibility will be possible. For example, organisations may require regular team meetings.

EVALUATION

useful gen reduct ind vs sit

TEST YOURSELF
Explain how temporal conditions at work can affect a worker.

ERGONOMICS

Ergonomics refers to the study of attempting to match (or improve on) the design of tools, gadgets, machines, work stations and work systems for the workers who will have to use them. Engineers and psychologists will work together to design, for example, work stations and some machines and gadgets, with 90 per cent of any given population's dimensions covered (e.g. height, weight, knee height when sitting down, etc.).

Operator–machine systems

Operator–machine systems are those where human workers have to interact with machinery to do their job. We will look at visual and auditory displays and controls. With technological advances still happening at a rapid pace, organisational psychologists need to help companies with the design of machinery to make the job more efficient but also to stop errors and accidents from occurring.

Visual displays and controls

There are three types of visual displays that can be used in organisational machinery:

▶ Quantitative – these are displays that project numbers giving data – temperature, time, speed, etc. Digital displays have taken over from, for example, "clock-like" displays as they are much easier to read and fewer errors occur.

▶ Qualitative – these are displays that allow for a judgment using words as the tool. For example, a piece of machinery may not project temperature as a number but have sections simply labelled "cold", "normal" and "hot" – workers can then judge what to do based on this information.

▶ Check-reading – these are simpler displays where the information is limited but highly useful For example, there may be a simple on-off button, or a light that comes on when something is not working correctly (or is working correctly).

Auditory displays and controls

In addition to a variety of visual displays noted above, auditory displays can be used. Buzzers, bells or a constant pitched sound can alert workers to a potential problem or that a job is completed in a production line. Workers no longer have to be looking at a display to know what is happening; the sound tells them. The type of noise needs to be what Riggio (1999) called "psychologically effective". That is, a really loud blaring horn or repetitive short beeps are usually perceived as danger so a worker will be alerted to something that is occurring.

Riggio (1999) noted when it was better to use either visual displays or auditory displays:

▶ It is better to use visual displays when a message is complex, a permanent message is needed, the work area is too noisy, the workers' jobs involve reading information from displays, etc.

▶ It is better to use auditory displays when a message is simple, the work area is too dark to see a visual readout, workers need to move about as part of their job, the message is urgent, information is continually changing, etc.

Errors and accidents in operator–machine systems

When a worker and machine are interacting, it is inevitable that at some point an error will be made. According to Riggio (1999), this can happen in four different ways:

▶ An error of omission is made. This refers to a failure to do something (e.g. a worker may fail to switch something on or off).

▶ An error of commission is made. This refers to performing a task incorrectly (e.g. a worker may simply not follow an instruction).

▶ An error of sequence is made. This refers to not following a set procedure for a task (e.g. a worker may work out of sequence, causing an error).

▶ An error of timing is made. This refers to performing a task too slowly or too quickly (e.g. a worker may press a button too quickly on a machine or not quickly enough to turn it off).

There are other factors which may well affect workers and cause them to perform a task incorrectly:

▶ There may be lack of training on using a piece of equipment or the manual may be too complicated to understand.

▶ Some workers have a personality trait called accident proneness – the way they coordinate themselves both physically and psychologically makes them more likely to have an accident or make an error.

▶ Fatigue may be a factor. Workers who are having to cover a night shift are more likely to have accidents or make an error as they are working against their natural circadian rhythm – between 1 a.m. and 4 a.m. the human body is in a "cognitive dip" as the body is primed for sleep not, for example, working machinery.

EVALUATION
useful | ind vs sit | gen | reduct

Reducing errors: theory A and theory B

Reason (2000) differentiated between two main types of errors in the workplace that can cause accidents:

▶ Theory A is when the individual may be to blame.

▶ Theory B is when work systems may be to blame.

See section 9.6 for more details of theory A and theory B.

12.6 SATISFACTION AT WORK

In many cases, a job takes up a large proportion of a worker's waking life. Therefore, it would be good to think that the worker is satisfied with the job. This is not always the case though. Organisational psychologists are interested in designing jobs that workers will find satisfying. This next section looks at these attempts.

ASK YOURSELF
What do you feel makes workers satisfied with their job? List as many reasons as possible. Keep the list with you as you read this section and tick off all of the ones that psychologists believe are important too.

JOB DESIGN

Greenberg & Baron (2008) noted that job design is about making workers more motivated by making their job or work more appealing. If a job involves repetitive and boring work then a worker will get demotivated very quickly. Therefore, there have to be ways to create jobs and maintain jobs so workers enjoy their time at work and are continually motivated.

Job characteristics

Hackman & Oldham (quoted in Greenberg, 1980) introduced us to the job characteristics model. Personnel, managers, leaders, etc. can use it to devise and create jobs that will appeal to workers and keep them motivated. There are five critical decisions that have to be incorporated into any job design:

▶ Skill variety – does the job require different activities that utilise a range of the worker's skills and talents? It should.

▶ Task identity – does the job require the completion of a whole piece of work from its inception to its completion? It should.

▶ Task significance – does the job have a real impact on the organisation or even beyond that? It should.

▶ Autonomy – does the job allow the worker some freedom in terms of planning, scheduling, carry out tasks and organising teams? It should.

▶ Feedback – does the job allow for easily measurable feedback to assess the effectiveness of the worker? It should.

All of these added together bring about three critical psychological states according to Hackman & Oldman (1980). Workers:

▶ experience meaningfulness at work

▶ experience responsibility in terms of the outcome of work

▶ have knowledge of the actual outcome of the job which can help employee growth.

All of this then makes workers much more motivated, their quality of work improves drastically, they become more satisfied and there is less absenteeism and fewer people leaving their job.

TEST YOURSELF
Outline three of the crucial decisions that should go into a job design.

Job design: enrichment, rotation and enlargement

In addition to the job characteristics model, there are other ways once a job has started which can allow for increased satisfaction and motivation in workers. Three of these are as follows:

▶ Job enrichment – this gives workers more jobs to do that involve more tasks to perform that are of a higher level of skill and responsibility. Workers can then have greater control over their job and it makes the job more interesting. Both of these increase satisfaction and motivation. One drawback is that this may be difficult to implement across many jobs within one organisation.

▶ Job rotation – this gives workers regular changes to tasks within their role at work. There may be daily, weekly or monthly changes to the tasks that they are required to perform and this should keep them "fresh" and highly motivated throughout their working day. This increases the workers' skills base too.

▶ Job enlargement – this gives workers more tasks to do but at the same level and usually as part of a team effort. There is no more responsibility or they are not required to learn new skills, rather they perform a wider variety of differing tasks during their working day.

Designing jobs that motivate

Taking all of the above on board, Greenberg & Baron (2008) examined four different ways in which a manager could follow to design a job or jobs that motivate the workforce:

- Combine tasks – have workers performing a variety of different tasks rather than just one task that is part of a "bigger picture".

- Open feedback channels – ensure that workers get a lot of feedback about each and every task that is assigned to them. This will improve task efficiency, productivity and motivation.

- Establish client relationships – try to make the job so workers have to meet the clients who will be buying the finished product. This allows them all to engage in feedback discussions.

- Load jobs vertically – give workers more responsibility for elements of their job. This gives workers some degree of autonomy which has been shown to be a core element of job satisfaction.

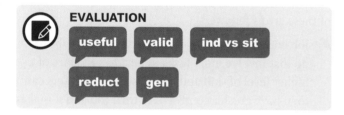

EVALUATION

| useful | valid | ind vs sit |
| reduct | gen |

CHALLENGE YOURSELF
You have been approached by a local company that needs your help in designing jobs that make workers satisfied. What would you recommend to the company and on what psychology is it based?

MEASURING JOB SATISFACTION

There are numerous ways in which workers' job satisfaction can be measured by an organisation. This allows them to assess how much they are allowing people to enjoy their work and be motivated.

Rating scales and questionnaires

There are some standardised rating scales and questionnaires that an organisation can use to measure the degree of satisfaction individual workers feel with their job. Here are two examples:

- Job descriptive index – this is a self-report questionnaire for workers. It measures satisfaction on five dimensions: the job, supervision, pay, promotions and co-workers, as shown in Table 12.6.1. Phrases are read and the worker has to answer "Yes", "No", or "?" if undecided. Each answer to each phrase is already assigned a numerical value based on standardisation scoring. Therefore, the worker's satisfaction can be summed for the five different dimensions to see whether all or just one or two dimensions are bringing about satisfaction or dissatisfaction.

Think of your present work. What is it like most of the time? In the blank space beside each word write:		Think of the pay you get. How well does each of the following words describe your present pay? In the blank space beside each word or phrase write:		Think of the opportunities for promotion that you have now. How well does each of the following words describe them? In the blank space beside each phrase write:	
Y	for "Yes" if it describes your work	Y	for "Yes" if it describes your pay	Y	for "Yes" if it describes your opportunities for promotion
N	for "No" if it does not describe it	N	for "No" if it does not describe it	N	for "No" if it does not describe them
?	if you cannot decide	?	if you cannot decide	?	if you cannot decide

Work on present job	**Present pay**	**Opportunities for promotion**
---- Routine ---- Satisfying ---- Good	---- Income inadequate for normal expenses ---- Insecure ---- Less than I deserve	---- Dead-end job ---- Unfair promotion policy ---- Regular promotions

Think of the kind of supervision you get on your job. How well does each of the following words describe this supervision? In the blank space beside each word or phrase write:		Think of the majority of people that you work with now or the people you meet in connection with your work. How well does each of the following words describe these people? In the blank space beside each word write:		Think of your job in general. All in all, what is it like most of the time? In the blank space beside each word or phrase write:	
Y	for "Yes" if it describes the supervision you get on your job	Y	for "Yes" if it describes the people you work with	Y	for "Yes" if it describes your job
N	for "No" if it does not describe it	N	for "No" if it does not describe them	N	for "No" if it does not describe it
?	if you cannot decide	?	if you cannot decide	?	if you cannot decide

Supervisor on present job	**People on present job**	**Job in general**
---- Impolite ---- Praises good work ---- Doesn't supervise enough	---- Boring ---- Responsible ---- Intelligent	---- Undesirable ---- Better than most ---- Rotten

▲ **Table 12.6.1** Job descriptive index – the five dimensions
Source: Smith, Kendall & Hulin quoted in Riggio (1999)

▶ Minnesota Satisfaction Questionnaire – this is also a self-report questionnaire for workers. It measures satisfaction on 20 dimensions (e.g. supervisors, task variety, responsibility, promotion, potential). Each item is read and the worker has to rate how much he or she agrees with the statement on a five-point scale from very dissatisfied to very satisfied. Again, each worker generates a score overall and for each of the 20 dimensions so satisfaction and dissatisfaction can easily be identified. Examples of the 20 dimensions are given in Table 12.6.2.

On my present job, this is how I feel about ...	Very dissatisfied	Dissatisfied	Neutral	Satisfied	Very satisfied
1 Being able to keep busy all the time	1	2	3	4	5
2 The chance to work alone on the job	1	2	3	4	5
3 The chance to do different things from time to time	1	2	3	4	5
4 The chance to be "somebody" in the community	1	2	3	4	5
5 The way my boss handles his/her workers	1	2	3	4	5
6 The competence of my supervisor in making decisions	1	2	3	4	5
7 The way my job provides for steady employment	1	2	3	4	5
8 My pay and the amount of work I do	1	2	3	4	5
9 The chances for advancement on this job	1	2	3	4	5
10 The working conditions	1	2	3	4	5
11 The way my co-workers get along with each other	1	2	3	4	5
12 The feeling of accomplishment I get from the job	1	2	3	4	5

▲ Table 12.6.2 Excerpt from the Minnesota satisfaction questionnaire
Source: Weiss et al: 'Vocational Psychology Research', University of Minnesota, copyright 1977. Reproduced by permission.

Critical incidents

Critical incidents technique is a way of collecting information about workers on their job performance. Workers can fill in questionnaires about their progress and be interviewed about it. Their fellow workers and managers can do the same. The interviews or questionnaires will ask people about any incidents at work, both positive and negative, which have contributed to successful or unsuccessful tasks happening. There will be hundreds of these. A job analyst can then analyse all of them to see which incidents make for a satisfying job for the worker. This is good as the qualitative data can give a "whole feel" for the job, knowing exactly what satisfies a worker across a range of tasks and jobs.

Interviews

These can take the form of structured or unstructured and usually follow one of the above. Reread about these types of interview on page 3 from AS level and apply them to organisations.

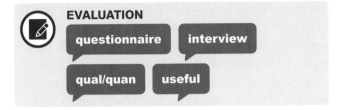

ATTITUDES TO WORK

Another area of interest for organisational psychologists
is researching people's attitudes to work. By uncovering
the reasons why people work an organisation gets a
clearer picture on motivational needs, productivity and
how people see their jobs.

Theories of job satisfaction and dissatisfaction

We have already looked at motivation to work
and these theories can easily apply here when
it comes to job satisfaction and dissatisfaction.
However, another theory that can be applied here
is Herzberg's (1966) two-factor theory. He believed
that job satisfaction and job dissatisfaction are two
independent things when it comes to the workplace.
Prior to this, many psychologists believed there was a
continuum from being satisfied to being dissatisfied
at work. Herzberg surveyed many workers and
asked them what made them feel especially bad or
good about their job. He analysed the contents of
these surveys and concluded that there are two main
factors at work here:

▶ Motivators – these are related to the content of the
actual job and include:

- level of responsibility within the job

- how much workers had already achieved in the
job

- what recognition workers had received while
doing the job

- the content of work within the job, how much
they had advanced (or could advance) within
the job

- how much they felt they had grown with the job.

These have to be *present* to achieve job satisfaction.

▶ Hygienes – these are related to the context of the job
and include:

- how company policies and administration affect
the job

- what level of supervision workers have in the job

- what interpersonal relations are like within
the job

- what the working conditions are like within
the job

- salary.

These have to be *absent/negative* for job dissatisfaction
to occur.

Therefore, workers need a range of motivators to be
present to be satisfied with their job but when hygiene
factors are absent this leads to dissatisfaction. Riggio
(1999) does note that other organisational psychologists
have tried to replicate Herzberg's findings but they keep
failing to find these two distinct factors.

Job withdrawal, absenteeism and sabotage

A variety of things can happen once a person becomes
dissatisfied with his or her job. These include job
withdrawal (leaving the job), job absenteeism and job
sabotage. We will look at each in turn.

Job withdrawal (or employee turnover) can come in
two forms: voluntary and involuntary. Involuntary
withdrawal is when an organisation has to fire people
for various reasons (e.g. the company is not making
enough profit or the worker is not performing his or
her job properly or up to the standards expected).
Voluntary withdrawal is when the worker decides
to leave and the main reason is that the worker has
found other employment (this could be linked to job
dissatisfaction but not always). This does "damage" an
organisation as it may have lost a very valued member
of its team and is now faced with the cost of advertising

and interviewing the people who could take over the position. Research has been rare in this area as it can be very difficult to dissect what is voluntary and involuntary withdrawal and even within each category there may be subgroups of different reasons why people may leave their job. Therefore, it is a low valid method of measuring job dissatisfaction.

Job absenteeism can also be categorised as voluntary and involuntary. Voluntary absenteeism refers to instances where the worker has chosen to take the time off (e.g. the worker may choose to have an extra day for a long weekend or may have errands to run such as going to the vet). Involuntary absenteeism refers to times when the worker does not choose to be off work but is absent.

The main reason for this is illness. Organisations have to be prepared for a certain number of instances occurring *per worker* and have policies in place to deal with it (e.g. use temporary workers or use an agency to find cover workers). Voluntary absenteeism may well be a measure of job dissatisfaction but, as with withdrawal above, the reasons vary so widely that it is another low validity attempt (people may just take the odd day off to do other things but really love their job). Therefore, as Riggio (1999) points out, there are problems with using this as any measure due to the complexity of reasons that people give for voluntary absenteeism. Greenberg & Baron (2008), however, noted a study that had found the relationship. This is shown in Figure 12.6.1.

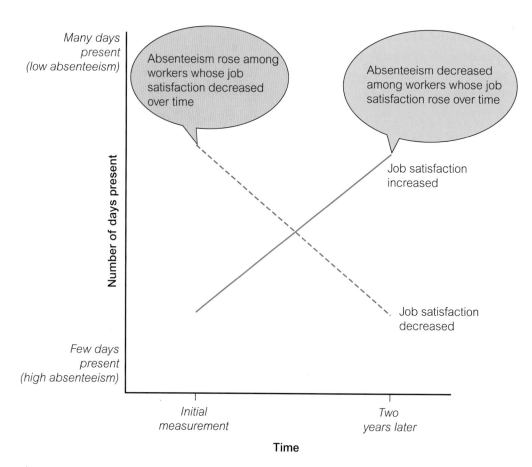

▲ Figure 12.6.1 Relationship between job satisfaction and absenteeism

Job sabotage is about rule breaking and workers making a conscious effort to stop themselves and others from working for an organisation. This can be caused by frustration as workers begin to feel powerless in their job. It can also be brought about as an attempt to make working conditions better, for instance to gain better

wages or physical conditions in a factory. Finally, it can be an attempt to challenge authority as workers feel that their managers or leaders are not performing in *their* job. This is an extreme form of dissatisfaction so cannot be used to discover job dissatisfaction on a daily basis and in the majority of workers.

TEST YOURSELF
Outline what psychologists have told us about attitudes to work.

Organisational commitment

Organisational commitment refers to the attitudes that workers have towards the organisation that they work for. It looks at how much they get involved with the organisation they work for and why they choose to stay in employment there. Greenberg & Baron (2008) note that there are three types of organisational commitment:

▶ Continuance commitment – workers stay in the job as it is probably too costly for them to leave it financially. The longer workers have been in the same organisation, the more difficult it is to leave when they reflect on all that they have given to the organisation and what it has given them. Therefore, workers are not willing to risk leaving the organisation.

▶ Affective commitment – workers stay in the job because they strongly agree with the organisation's goals and overall beliefs and views. They fully support what the organisation does and *how* it does it. As long as the goals and beliefs of the workers match those of the organisation, the workers feel committed to the job.

▶ Normative commitment – workers stay in the job because of pressure from other people. They may not want to leave a company because they fear "what people might say" about them doing so. They do not want to disappoint their organisation by leaving and even though they may feel a bit dissatisfied, they remain committed to the job.

So, why would an organisation be concerned about commitment? According to Greenberg & Baron

(2008), committed workers are much less likely to withdraw from the organisation and work tasks, they are willing to make some life sacrifices for the good of the organisation and their productivity will be higher. Organisations have to enrich jobs, match the values of their current employees with their own values, and when recruiting choose employees whose values are the closest match to theirs.

Promoting job satisfaction

All of the sections in this chapter have ideas about promoting job satisfaction:

▶ through the selection process

▶ by exploring why people are motivated to work

▶ by identifying what leaders are present in the organisation

▶ by identifying how groups work in the organisation

▶ when considering the physical surroundings of the workplace

▶ through assessing job satisfaction.

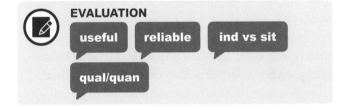

EVALUATION

useful   reliable   ind vs sit

qual/quan

CHALLENGE YOURSELF
Using all of the sections in this chapter, how do you think an organisation can promote job satisfaction in its employees? On what psychology is your idea based?

EXAMPLES OF HOW TO EVALUATE

For the 12 mark question in Paper 3, you will be asked to evaluate one of the topics covered in this section. You will have noticed that after each topic in this chapter there are the icons for the different issues, debates, approaches, perspectives and research methods that *could* be used to help you answer the 12 mark question in the examination. Below are three examples of the types of things you *could* write in the examination.

You should aim to make *at least* four different evaluation points for the 12 mark question. Our accompanying Revision Guide has a series of student answers with marks and examiner comments attached to them.

Personnel selection

Some of the selection procedures may be *subjective*. For example, Hayward (1996) noted that females can still be stereotyped as 'not management material' and are therefore overlooked as they do not have the 'masculine traits' needed to take on such roles. Therefore, many female applicants may never be called for interview. This may not be based on any truth or objective reasoning. Also, there may be *bias* in some methods. For example, a lot of information is qualitative rather than quantitative and therefore subject to interviewer interpretation bias. Also, if an unstructured method is chosen then there is reduced reliability as not all interviewee's will have the same experience. Also, someone has to decide the different 'hurdles' in the multiple hurdles approach to selection but this might be based on one person's idea and is therefore not objective and more likely to be biased. However, selection procedures can be *useful* in reducing the candidate pool down to those who are best suited to the job. With the multiple cutoff method, as soon as an applicant fails to reach the minimum score *on any one predictor or task* they are eliminated from the recruitment process. Therefore, those who remain have at least the minimum

amount of ability that is required for the position. This can make the whole selection procedure more valid as a result as you are interviewing people who have the qualities you need for the job.

Need theories of motivation

One problem with these theories is that they *generalise* without taking into account *individual differences*. For example, Maslow's Hierarch of Needs suggest we all progress up the pyramid in the same way. We could all progress up the pyramid in different ways with different motivations and needs – some people may never want to self-actualise in the workplace, instead choosing to do it with leisure activities outside of work therefore any attempt to 'involve all in the same way' may not work very well. The measuring of the needs as predicted by some theories like the Need for Achievement can be *subjective*. Workers can be assessed on these three key needs and motives by taking as Thematic Apperception Test (TAT). To do this, the worker has to look at a series of ambiguous pictures that tell a story. They have to tell whatever story they feel is behind the picture and these are then scored. One personnel member may score the response in a different way to someone else working in personnel.

Measuring job satisfaction

Many of these methods are based on questionnaires so they may be more *valid* than an interview because workers may be more likely to reveal truthful answers in a questionnaire as it does not involve talking face-to-face with someone. Therefore, information from the Job Descriptive index may be more valid compared to an interview using some of the same questions. However, some workers may give *socially desirable* answers as they want to look good rather than giving truthful answers – this lowers the validity of measuring satisfaction. A worker may want to look more satisfied about their job if a stern manager is going to read the responses so that they appear to be enjoying their work and so they look good, especially if it is linked to a potential promotion at work.

Exam centre

Try the following exam-style questions.

Section A

(a) Explain, in your own words, what is meant by the term "selection interviews". (2 marks)

(b) Explain, in your own words, what is meant by the term "intrinsic motivation". (2 marks)

(c) Describe two ways in which you could improve motivation in workers. (4 marks)

(d) Outline one theory of leadership. (4 marks)

Section B

(a) Describe what psychologists have discovered about organisational working conditions. (8 marks)

(b) Describe what psychologists have discovered about performance appraisals. (8 marks)

(c) Evaluate what psychologists have discovered about leadership style and effectiveness and include a discussion about how useful the findings have been. (12 marks)

(d) Evaluate what psychologists have discovered about personnel selection decisions and include a discussion about questionnaires. (12 marks)

Section C

(a) Describe **one** way we can measure job satisfaction. (6 marks)

(b) Suggest how you would improve job satisfaction and motivation in a workforce. On what psychology is your suggestion based? (8 marks)

(c) Describe two ways in which physical work conditions can affect people in their place of work. (6 marks)

(d) Suggest how you might redesign an office to reduce any negative psychological effects it may have on a worker. (8 marks)

EXAM CENTRE (A LEVEL)

The questions, example answers, marks awarded and/or comments that appear in this book/CD were written by the author. In examination, the way marks would be awarded to answers like these may be different.

This unit constitutes 50 per cent of the A level qualification. Students need to have studied **two options** from the five on offer. For this unit, the focus is on knowledge and understanding of *each option* with methodological assessments, issues and debates, and approaches and perspectives added too. Also, students have to "think on their feet" during the exam via a methods question. The exam lasts for 3 hours and is marked out of 80.

The structure of the exam is as follows:

▶ Section A – there are usually two short-answer questions that are expected to directly test knowledge and understanding of some aspect of one option. There is a 2-mark question and a 4-mark question so this section carries 6 marks in total.

▶ Section B – this is usually a structured essay broken into two parts. Part (a) would allow students to write about what psychologists have found out about a certain topic within the option (it is specified in the question). Part (b) would ask students to evaluate what psychologists have found. Part (a) is marked out of 8 and part (b) is marked out of 12 so this section carries 20 marks in total.

▶ Section C – this is normally a smaller structured essay split into two parts. Part (a) usually asks students to write about how something could be measured or how a named topic is useful in the real world. Part (b) usually asks students to suggest ways to improve a measure or improve something in real life based on the psychology they have studied. Part (a) is marked out of 6 and part (b) is marked out of 8 so this section carries 14 marks in total.

Students then repeat this with their second option.

Section A

Example questions could be as follows:

1. (a) Explain, in your own words, what is meant by the term "intrinsic motivation". (2 marks)

(b) Describe **one** cause of anxiety disorders (phobias). (4 marks)

(c) Describe **two** ways in which we can control pain. (4 marks)

Section (a). For the 2 mark question, you must write out a definition of whatever the key term is, in your own words (you can base it on an actual definition). The answer would have to be clear and accurate. For the 4 mark question, if it asks for a study then briefly cover the aim, method, results and conclusion. The answer would have to show a clear understanding of the study or area being tackled. If the question asks for two things then ensure that you supply two brief outlines of what is being asked.

Section B

Example questions could be as follows:

2. (a) Describe what psychologists have discovered about the misusing of health services. (8 marks)

(b) Evaluate what psychologists have discovered about the misusing of health services and include a discussion on case studies. (12 marks)

Section B. For the 8 mark question, you need to demonstrate everything you know about the area in the question. This can include studies, theories and research methods. Try to outline them in as much detail as possible, but remember it is only marked out of 8 so you need to select four or five things that you can write about. The answer would have to show excellent use of terminology and be accurate and detailed to show understanding. It should be structured and organised well.

For the 12 mark question, it is based on how many different points you make, based on what the question is asking (similar to what you would do in part (c) of section B in Paper 2). You *must* tackle the issues/debate/research method that is specifically asked for in the question. Evaluation points can be taken from supporting or conflicting evidence, issues and debates and methodology.

Section C

Example questions could be as follows:

3. (a) Describe the cause of one disruptive behaviour seen in the classroom. (6 marks)

(b) Suggest how you would correct and prevent disruptive behaviour in the classroom. On what psychology are your suggestions based? (8 marks)

For (a), to be likely to get into the top band the description **would have to be** appropriate with relevant evidence and show a clear understanding. For (b), to be likely to get into the top band the suggestion will be likely to have explicit links to psychological knowledge and be accurate, coherent and detailed.

When evaluating, use the general tables that appear in Chapters 1 and 2 (methods, issues and debates, approaches and perspectives) and apply them to the topic area of the question. If you have completed the evaluation tasks in the book then you will already have many of these.

Index

Page numbers in *italics* refer to question
sections.

A

abnormal affect 216–21, *238*
abnormality 207, *238*
  behavioural model of abnormality 209
  cognitive behavioural approaches 210
  cognitive model of abnormality 209
  deviation from ideal mental health 208
  deviation from social norms 207
  deviation from statistical norms 207, *238*
  effectiveness and appropriateness of
    treatments 210
  failure to function adequately 208
  medical or biological model of
    abnormality 208
  problems with defining and diagnosing
    abnormality 208
  psychodynamic model of abnormality
    209
  psychotherapies 209
absenteeism 270
accidents 172, *176*
  accident reduction 173–4
  causes: theory A and theory B 172, *264*
  cognitive overload 173
  individual and systems errors 172
  personality factors in accident proneness
    173
  shift work 173, 174
achievement 129, 247
addiction disorders 222, *238*
  behavioural explanation (positive
    reinforcement) 223
  biochemical explanation (dopamine) 223
  cognitive or personality explanation
    223–4
  coping with and reducing 224–5
  definitions 222
  genetic explanation 222–3
  physical and psychological disorders 222
aggressive behaviour study 47, *50*
  aim 47
  conclusion 49
  design 47–8
  evaluation 49–50
  participants 47
  procedure 48
  results 48–9
alcoholism 222, 224, *238*
  aversion therapy 224
  behavioural techniques 224
  genetic explanation 224–5
Alderfer, Clayton P. 246
alpha space 193
animals 11
  cognitive maps 202–3
  crowding and social density studies
    183–4

perceptual development study 25–8, *28*
anxiety disorders (obsessions and
  compulsions) 232–6, *238*
anxiety disorders (phobias) 226–31, *238*
application forms 239
  weighted application forms (WABs) 239
applied tension 230
approaches to study inventory (ASI) 124–5
attention deficit hyperactivity disorder
  (ADHD) 132–3
attractiveness and smells study 82, *86*
  aim 82
  conclusion 84
  design 82
  evaluation 84–5
  participants 82
  procedure 83
  results 83–4
attractiveness study 55, *59*
  aim 55
  conclusion 57
  design 55, 56
  evaluation 58
  participants 55, 56, 57
  procedure 55–6, 56, 57
  results 57
attribution theory 130
Ausubel, David 116
autism spectrum disorders 119
autocratic leadership styles 253
aversion therapy 224

B

backward searching 144
  lily pad problem 144–5
Bandura, Albert 130
Beck, Aaron 218, 220
  Beck Depression Inventory 221
bees 202–3
behaviour modification 135
  behaviour-modification techniques
    113–14
  cognitive behaviour modification 135–6
behaviourist perspective
  abnormality 209
  alcoholism 224
  learning 112–13
  phobias 226–7
  programmed learning 113
Bennett Mechanical Comprehension Test
  240
Bennett, Milton 124
beta space 193
Binet, Alfred 137
biofeedback 167–8
bipolar disorder 216
Blanchard, Ken 253
body dysmorphic disorder (BDD) study
  101, *106*
  aim 101

conclusion 105
design 101–2
evaluation 105
participants 102
procedure 102
results 103–4
British Ability Scale (BAS) 138, 140, 141
Brophy, Jere 129
Bruner, Jerome 115–16
bullying 132
  causes 133–4
  effects 134
bystander behaviour study 38, *42*
  aim 39
  conclusions 40
  design and procedure 39
  diffusion of responsibility 39
  evaluation 41
  participants 39
  results 40

C

career structure 250
case studies 3
  Münchausen syndrome 151
  schizophrenia 211
casinos 200
catastrophes *see* disasters; emergency
  situations, technological catastrophe
Cattell, Raymond 142
Chernobyl 172
children 10–11
  aggressive behaviour study 47–50, *50*
  attractiveness study 55–8, *59*
  child development 115
  educational performance and exposure to
    noise 179–80
  moral behaviour study 60–3, *64*
  Pediatric Pain Questionnaire 160–1
Chu Attention Test 182
classical conditioning 226
  Little Albert 226–7
cognitive approaches to learning 115–17,
  146
  cognitive behaviour modification 135–6
  motivation 128–9
cognitive behavioural therapy 210
  depression 220–1
  kleptomania 225
  obsessive-compulsive disorder (OCD)
    235–6
  pain management strategies 162
  phobias 230–1
  schizophrenia 215
cognitive maps 201, *206*
  animals 202–3
  errors 201–2
  individual differences 202
  map design 203–4
  multidimensional scaling 201

sketch maps 201
virtual way-finding 204
way-finding 204
cognitive psychology
    abnormality 209
    alcoholism 224
    eyes test study 21–3, *24*
    false memory study 17–20, *20*
    lying behaviour study 13–15, *16*
    perceptual development study 25–8, *28*
    phobias 228
    pyromania 223–4
community environmental design 199–200, *206*
Comprehensive Ability Battery (CAB) Test 240
compressed work weeks 263
compulsions 232–6
compulsive gambling 222
conditioning 111–12
    classical conditioning 226–7
    higher-order conditioning 112
    operant conditioning 112–13
consumer behaviour 180–1
contingency theory 252–3
control 164
    noise 178
controlled observations 4
creativity 143
    unusual uses test 143–4
crowding 183, *206*
    animal studies 183–4
    coping with crowding 186–7
    effect on health 185
    effect on performance 185
    modifying architecture 185–6
    pro-social behaviour 184–5
    visual escape 186
Curry, Lynn 123

D

decision making 258
    decision style and individual differences in decision making 258
    individual versus group decisions 258
defensible space 195–6
    urban renewal and housing design 198–9
density *see* crowding; social density; spatial density
dependent variables (DVs) 1, 2
depression 216
    biological (chemical or drugs) treatment 219–20
    biological (genetic and neurochemical) explanation 217–18
    cognitive explanation 217–18
    cognitive restructuring 220–1
    electro-convulsive therapy (ECT) 220
    learned helplessness or attributional style 218–19
    manic depression 216

rational emotive behaviour therapy (REBT) 221
    sex differences in depression 216–17
    types 216
developmental psychology
    aggressive behaviour study 47–50, *50*
    attractiveness study 55–8, *59*
    moral behaviour study 60–3, *64*
    Oedipus complex study 51–3, *54*
diffusion of responsibility 39
disasters 188, *206*
    evacuation plans 189–90
    Herald of Free Enterprise 172, 191
    tornado and hurricane preparation 189
    treating post-traumatic stress disorder (PTSD) 190–1
discovery learning 115–16
discrimination study 43, *45*
    aim 43
    conclusion 45
    design 43, 44
    evaluation 45–6
    participants 43, 44
    procedure 43–4
    results 44, 45
disruptive behaviour in school 132, *146*
    attention deficit hyperactivity disorder (ADHD) 132–3
    behaviour modification 135
    bullying 132
    cognitive behaviour modification 135–6
    conduct 132
    effective classroom management 135
    effective discipline 134–5
    poor teaching style 133
dopamine 212, 223
dreams and REM sleep study 71, *78*
    aim 72
    conclusion 75
    design 72
    evaluation 76
    method 72
    participants 72
    procedure 72–3
    results 73–5
dyslexia 118–9, *146*
    causes and effects 120
    educational strategies 121–2

E

ecological validity 7
educational performance 141
emergency situations 188, *206*
    contagion behaviour 188
    evacuation plans 189–90
    July bombings, London 2005 191
    preparedness 189
    scripts 188
    treating post-traumatic stress disorder (PTSD) 190–1
emotional intelligence 143

emotions study 65, *70*
    aim 65
    conclusion 68
    design 65–7
    evaluation 69
    participants 67
    procedure 67
    results 67–8
Entwistle, N.J. 124–5
equal opportunities 242–3
ERG (existence, relatedness and growth) model of needs 246–7
ergonomics 263
    operator-machine systems 263–4
ethics 7–8
ethnocentric bias 8
exam centre (A Level) 275
    Section A 275
    Section B 275–6
    Section C 276
exam centre (AS Level) 107
    Unit 1 Section A 107
    Unit 1 Section B 107
    Unit 2 Section A 108
    Unit 2 Section B 108–9
expectancy theory 248–9
expository teaching 116
eyes test study 21, *24*
    aim 21
    conclusion 23
    design 21–2
    evaluation 23
    participants 22
    procedure 22
    results 22

F

factor-analytic approach to intelligence 142
false memory study 17, *20*
    aim 17
    conclusion 19
    design 17
    evaluation 19–20
    participants 17
    procedure 17–18
    results 18–19
fear arousal 169
Fiedler, Fred 252
field experiments 2
flexitime 263
flooding 210, 230
Fontana, D. 124
formal teaching styles 124
four stage learning system 126–7
Freud, Sigmund 51, 229
    Little Hans 51–2, 229

G

Gardner, Howard 142
GAS (general adaptation syndrome) model of stress 163–4

alarm reaction 163
 exhaustion stage 165
 resistance stage 163
gender-based subject selection study 96, *100*
 aim 96
 conclusion 98
 design 96–7
 evaluation 98–9
 participants 97
 procedure 97
 results 97–8
generalisations 10
giftedness 119–20
 educational strategies 121, *146*
goal-setting 247
 goal-setting theory 248
Grasha, Tony 123–4
group behaviour in organisations 256
 characteristics of successful teams 257–8
 decision making 258
 group cohesiveness, team building and team performance 256–7
 group conflict 259–60
 group development 256
 groupthink and group polarisation 258–9
group conflict 259
 managing group conflict 260
 organisational and interpersonal causes 259–60
 positive and negative effects of conflict 260
group polarisation 259
groupthink 258–9
 strategies to overcome groupthink and training to avoid poor decisions 259

H
Hassles Scale 166
health and safety 172
 accident proneness 173
 accidents 172
 human error and the illusion of invulnerability 173
 individual and system errors 172
 reducing accidents at work 173–4
 reorganizing shift work 174
health promotion 169, *176*
 communities 170–1
 fear arousal 169
 providing information 169–70
 schools 170
 specific problems 171, *176*
 worksites 170
 Yale model of communication 169
Herald of Free Enterprise 172, 191
Hersey, Paul 253
high initiative teaching styles 124
higher-order conditioning 112
House, Robert 253
housing estates 198–9

humanistic applications to learning 114–15
hypochondriasis 150

I
imagery 168
impulse control disorders 222, *238*
 causes 222–3
 coping with and reducing 224–5
 types 222
independent variables (IVs) 1, 2
individual explanations 8
informal teaching styles 124
intelligence 137, *146*
 British Ability Scale (BAS) 138, 140, 141
 concept of intelligence and IQ 137
 creativity and unusual uses test 143–4
 emotional intelligence 143
 factor-analytic approach 142
 intelligence and educational performance 141
 multiple intelligences 142
 problem-solving 144–5
 reliability, validity and predictive validity of tests 141
 Stanford-Binet test 137
 triarchic theory 142
 Weschler tests 137–8
interpersonal skills 147–8
interviews 3
 structured and unstructured interviews 239–40, 268

J
job analysis techniques 243–4
job applications 239
job descriptions and specifications 243
job design 265
 designing jobs that motivate 266
 enrichment, rotation and enlargement 265–6
 job characteristics 265
job satisfaction 266, *273*
 critical incidents 268
 interviews 268
 job withdrawal, absenteeism and sabotage 269–71
 organisational commitment 271
 promoting job satisfaction 271
 rating scales and questionnaires 266–8
 theories of job satisfaction and dissatisfaction 269
Johnson & Johnson Live for Life Program 170

July bombings, London 2005 191

K
kleptomania 222
 cognitive behavioural therapy (CBT) 225
Kolb, David 126
Kyriacou, Chris 125–6

L
laboratory experiments 1–2
 emergency situations 188
Latham, Edwin 248
leadership 251, *273*
 charismatic and transformational leaders 251
 great person theory 251
 leader-member exchange (LMX) model 255
 normative decision theory 255
 Ohio State studies 251–2
 University of Michigan studies 252
leadership style and effectiveness 252, *273*
 contingency theory 252–3
 leadership training and characteristics of effective leaders 254–5
 path-goal theory 253
 permissive versus autocratic 253
 situational leadership 253
learned helplessness 130–1, 218–19
learning 112
 behaviour-modification techniques 113–14
 conditioning 111–13
 cooperative learning 114
 discovery learning 115–16
 expository teaching or reception learning 116
 learning circles and the open classroom 114–15
 programmed learning 113
 Summerhill School 115
 underlying theory of cognitive development 115
 underlying theory of humanism 114
 zone of proximal development (ZPD) 116–17
learning effectiveness 126
 4-mat system 126–7
 PQRST method 127
 SPELT method 127
learning styles 123, *146*
 approaches to study inventory (ASI) 124–5
 formal and informal styles 124
 high initiative and low initiative 124
 Kolb's learning styles 126
 onion model 123
 six styles of learning 123–4
 teacher-centred and student-centred styles 125–6
life events 164–5
Locke, Gary 248
longitudinal studies 10
low initiative teaching styles 124
lying behaviour study 13, *16*
 aim 13
 conclusion 15
 design 13–14
 evaluation 16

participants 14
procedure 14
results 14–15

M

magnetite 203
manic depression 216
mans-end analysis 144
map design 203–4
Maslow, Abraham 128, 246
McCarthy, Bernice 126–7
McClelland, David 129, 247
McGill Pain Questionnaire (MPQ) 158–9
memory and brain function study 78, *81*
   aim 78
   conclusion 80
   design 78–9
   evaluation 80
   participants 79
   procedure 79
   results 79
mental health 208–9
   addiction and impulse control disorders
      223–5
   anxiety disorders (obsessions and
      compulsions) 232–6
   anxiety disorders (phobias) 226–31
   depression 216–21
   schizophrenia 211–17
   treatments 209–10
mental health diagnosis study 87, *91*
   aim 87
   conclusion 89
   design and procedure 88, 89
   evaluation 90
   participants 87–8, 89
   results 88–9, 89
Milgram, Stanley 29–32
Minnesota Clerical Assessment Battery 241
moral behaviour study 60, *64*
   aim 60
   conclusion 62
   design 60–1, 62
   evaluation 63
   participants 61, 62
   procedure 61
   results 61–2, 62
motivation 128, *146*, 246, *273*
   attributing causes to behaviours 130
   behaviourist theory 128
   changing attributions 131
   cognitive approach 128–9
   designing jobs that motivate 266
   effective praise 129
   ERG theory 246–7
   extrinsic and intrinsic motivation 128,
      249, *273*
   goal-setting 247–8
   humanistic theory 128, 129
   learned helplessness 130–1

Maslow's hierarchy of needs 128, 246
   motivators at work 249–50
   need for achievement 129, 247
   self-efficacy 130
   VIE cognitive theory 248–9
Muczyk, Jan P. 253
Mulcahy, Bob 127
multiple intelligences 142
multiple personality disorder (MPD) study
   92, *95*
   aim 92
   conclusions 94
   design and procedure 92
   evaluation 94–5
   participant 92
   results 93–4
Münchausen syndrome 150–1
   case studies 151
   Münchausen syndrome by proxy 151
music 180, *206*
   consumer behaviour 180–1
   performance 181–2
   stress reduction 181

N

natural disasters *see* disasters; emergency
   situations
naturalistic observations 3
nature and nurture 9
   perceptual development study 25–8, *28*
Newman, Oscar 195–6, 199
noise 177
   anti-social behaviour 179
   educational performance in children
      179–80
   factors that make noise annoying 178,
      206
   music 180–2
   pro-social behaviour 179
   transportation noise and occupational
      noise 178
non-verbal communications 147, *176*
   appearance 148
   facial expressions 147
   gestures 147–8
   paralanguage 147
   personal space invasion 148
normative decision theory 255

O

O'Connor Finger Dexterity Test 240
obedience study 29, *32*
   aim 29
   conclusion 31
   design 29
   evaluation 31–2
   participants 30
   procedure 30
   results 30–1
observations 3–4

obsessive-compulsive disorder (OCD) 232
   biomedical explanation 233
   case studies and examples 232
   cognitive behavioural therapy 235–6
   cognitive-behavioural aspect 234
   drug therapy 235
   measures 232–3
   psychoanalytic therapy 236
   psychodynamic explanation 235
Obsessive-Compulsive Inventory (OCI)
   232–3
occupational noise 178
Oedipus complex study 51, *54*
   aim 51
   case history 51–2
   conclusion 52
   design 51
   evaluation 53
   participant 51
   results 52
Ohio State University studies 251–2
open classrooms 114–15
operant conditioning 112–13
operator-machine systems 263
   auditory displays and controls 264
   errors and accidents 264
   reducing errors 264
   visual displays and controls 263–4
opportunity sampling 4
Öst, Lars-Göran 230

P

Pacific Western Airline 172
pain 156, *176*
   acute and chronic organ pain 156
   definitions of pain 156
   gate control theory of pain 156–7
   psychogenic pain 156
   specificity theory of pain 156
pain management 161
   alternative techniques 162
   cognitive strategies 162
   medical techniques 161–2
pain measurement 157, *176*
   children 160–1
   McGill Pain Questionnaire (MPQ) 158–9
   Pain Behavior Scale (UAB) 160
   self-report measures 157–8
   visual rating scales 160
paralanguage 147
participant observations 4
participant variables 1
participants 4–5
   aggressive behaviour study 47
   attractiveness and smells study 82
   attractiveness study 55, 56, 57
   body dysmorphic disorder (BDD) study
      102
   bystander behaviour study 39
   discrimination study 43, 44

dreams and REM sleep study 72
emotions study 67
eyes test study 22
false memory study 17
gender-based subject selection study 97
independent groups 5
lying behaviour study 14
matched pairs 6
memory and brain function study 79
mental health diagnosis study 87–8, 89
moral behaviour study 61, 62
multiple personality disorder (MPD)
    study 92
obedience study 30
Oedipus complex study 51
perceptual development study 26
prisoners study
repeated measures 5–6
path-goal theory 253
patient adherence to medical advice 152,
    176
improving adherence 153–4
letters 154–5
measuring adherence and non-adherence
    153
memory intervention 155
rational non-adherence 152–3
text messaging 154
types and extent of non-adherence 152
patient misuse of health services 149, *176*
delay in seeking treatment 149–50
hypochondriasis 150
Münchausen syndrome 150–1
patient-practitioner relationship 147
disclosure of information 149
doctor-centred and patient-centred styles
    148–9
non-verbal communications 147–8
type I and type II errors in diagnosis 149
verbal communications 148
Pavlov, Ivan 111–12
Pediatric Pain Questionnaire 160–1
perceptual development study 25, *28*
aim 25
conclusion 26
design 25
evaluation 27–8
participants 26
procedure 26
results 26
performance appraisal 244, *273*
problems and biases 245
performance-related pay 249
permissive leadership styles 253
personal space 192–3, *206*
alpha space and beta space 193
measuring space simulation 193
space invasions 193, 194–5, *206*
stop-distance 193
personnel selection 240
biases in selection decisions and equal

opportunities 242–3
decision making 241–2, *273*
use of psychometric tests 240–1
phobias 226
applied tension 230
behavioural explanation (classical
    conditioning) 226–7
biomedical or genetic explanation
    229–30
cognitive behavioural therapy (CBT)
    230–1
cognitive explanation 228
extinction 229
flooding 230
generalisation 229
psychoanalytic explanation 229
systematic desensitisation 229–30
types and examples 226
physiological psychology
attractiveness and smells study 82–5, *86*
dreams and REM sleep study 71–6, *77*
emotions study 65–9, *70*
memory and brain function study 78–80,
    81
Piaget, Jean 115
pigeons 203
planning strategies 144
positive reinforcement 223
post-traumatic stress disorder (PTSD) 181
treating post-traumatic stress disorder
    (PTSD) 190–1
PQRST method of learning 127
praise 129
predictive validity 241
Preschool Head Start Program 171
prisoners study 33, *37*
aim 33
conclusion 36–7
design 33
evaluation 37
participants 33–4
procedure 34
results 34–6
problem-solving 144–5
programmed learning 113
promotion prospects 250
psychodynamic perspective
abnormality 209
obsessive-compulsive disorder (OCD)
    235
psychology of individual differences
body dysmorphic disorder (BDD) study
    101–5, *106*
gender-based subject selection study
    96–9, *100*
mental health diagnosis study 87–90, *91*
multiple personality disorder (MPD)
    study 92–5, *95*
psychometrics 9
intelligence tests 137–41, *146*
pain measurement 158–61

use of psychometric tests 240–1
public building design 200, *206*
casinos 200
housing estates 198–9
shopping malls 199–200
pyromania 222, 223–4

Q
quantitative and qualitative data 9–10
questionnaires 2

R
random sampling 4
rational emotive behaviour therapy (REBT)
    210, 221
reception learning 116
reductionism 11
Reimann, B.C. 253
reliability 8
intelligence tests 141
research 1
animals 11
case studies 3
children 10–11
design of study 5–6
ecological validity 7
ethics 7–8
ethnocentric bias 8
field experiments 2
generalisations 10
individual versus situational explanations
    8
interviews 3
laboratory experiments 1–2
nature and nurture 9
observations 3–4
participants and sampling 4–5
psychometrics 9
quantitative and qualitative data 9–10
questionnaires 2
reductionism 11
reliability and validity 8
snapshot and longitudinal studies 10
usefulness 7
reward systems 249
career structure and promotion prospects
    250
non-monetary rewards 250
Rogers, Carl 114
Rosenhan, David 87–9

S
sampling 4–5
schizophrenia 211, *238*
biochemical explanation (dopamine
    hypothesis) 212
biochemical treatments 213
case studies 211
characteristics 211
cognitive behavioural therapy (CBT) 215
cognitive explanation 212–13

electro-convulsive therapy 214
genetic explanation 211–12
token economies 214–15
types 211
self-efficacy 130
self-instructional training 135–6
self-selected sampling 4
Seligman, Martin 130–1, 219
shift work 262
compressed work weeks and flexitime 263
rapid rotation theory and slow rotation theory 262–3
shopping malls 199–200
situational explanations 8
situational leadership 253
situational variables 2
Sixteen Personality Factor Questionnaire 241
snapshot studies 10
social density 183, 184–5, *206*
animal studies 183–4
social psychology
bystander behaviour study 38–41, *42*
discrimination study 43–6, *46*
obedience study 29–32, *32*
prisoners study 33–7, *37*
Social Readjustment Rating Scale (SRRS) 164–5
space *see* personal space
spatial density 183, 185
special educational needs 118, *146*
autism spectrum disorders 119
dyslexia 118–9, 120
giftedness 119–20
integration versus separation 120–1
SPELT method of learning 127
squirrels 202
SSRIs (selective serotonergic re-uptake inhibitors) 219, 220, 233, 235
Stanford University, USA 137
Sternberg, Robert 142
stop-distance 193
stratified sampling 4
stress 163
daily hassles 166
environmental stress 197
GAS (general adaptation syndrome) model 163–4
life events 164–5
locus of control 164
music and stress reduction 181
personality 166
stress management 167, *176*
medical techniques 167
preventing stress 168
psychological techniques 167–8
physiological measures 167
physiology of stress and effects on health 163
self-report questionnaires 167

stress inoculation therapy 168
work 164
student-centred learning styles 125–6
Summerhill School 115
systematic desensitisation 210, 229–30

T
teacher-centred learning styles 125–6
teaching styles 116, 124, 133
teams 256–7
characteristics of successful teams 257–8
technological catastrophe 188, *206*
territory 192–3, *206*
defending primary territory 195–6
defending public territory 196
theory A 172, 264
individual errors 172
theory B 172, 264
system errors 172
Three Mile Island 172
Titanic 172
token economies 173–4, 214–15, 224
topic evaluation 145, 175, 205, 237, 272
transportation noise 178
triarchic theory of intelligence 142
Type A behaviour 166
Type B behaviour 166

U
University of Alabama at Birmingham (UAB) Pain Behavior Scale 160
University of Michigan studies 252
Uplifts Scale 166
urban living 197
adaptation level 197
behaviour constraint 197
casino environments 200
effects on health 197–8
effects on social behaviour 198
environmental stress 197
overload 197
shopping mall atmospherics 199–200
urban renewal and housing design 198–9, *206*
usefulness 7

V
validity 7, 8
intelligence tests 141
psychometric tests 241
Vancouver Obsessional Compulsive Inventory (VOCI) 233
variables 1–2
verbal communications 148, *176*
VIE (valence, instrumentality and expectancy) cognitive theory 248
managerial applications 248–9
volunteer sampling 4
Vroom, Victor 248, 255
Vygotsky, Lev 116–17

W
Weiner, Bernard 130, 219
Weschler Adult Intelligence Scale (WAIS) 137–8, 139, 141
Weschler Intelligence Scale for Children (WISC) 137–8, 141
Wilkins, M. 125–6
Wolpe, Joseph 229
work 164, 239
attitudes to work 269–71
biases in selection decisions and equal opportunities 242–3
career structure and promotion prospects 250
decision making in selecting personnel 240, 241–2
group behaviour in organisations 256–60
health and safety at work 172–4
health promotion at work 170
job analysis techniques 243–4
job applications 239
job descriptions and specifications 243
leadership and management 251–5
motivation 246–7
motivation and goal-setting 247–8
motivators at work 249–50
non-monetary rewards 250
performance appraisal 244–5
performance-related pay 249
selection interviews 239–40, *273*
types of reward system 249
use of psychometric tests 240–1
work conditions 261, *273*
ergonomics 263–4
physical work conditions 261
psychological work conditions 261–2
temporal conditions 262–3
work satisfaction 265
job design 265–6
job withdrawal, absenteeism and sabotage 269–71
measuring job satisfaction 266–8
organisational commitment 271
promoting job satisfaction 271
theories of job satisfaction and dissatisfaction 269

Y
Yale model of communication 169
Yale-Brown Obsessive Compulsive Scale (Y-BOCS) 233, 234
Yetton, Phillip 255

Z
zone of proximal development (ZPD) 116–17